Homer's
ODYSSEY
A Critical Handbook

WADSWORTH GUIDES TO LITERARY STUDY

Maurice Beebe, General Editor

ALICE'S ADVENTURES IN WONDERLAND: A Critical Handbook
edited by Donald Rackin, Temple University

APPROACHES TO MACBETH
edited by Jay L. Halio, University of California, Davis

APPROACHES TO WALDEN
edited by Lauriat Lane, Jr., University of New Brunswick

A BENITO CERENO HANDBOOK
edited by Seymour L. Gross, University of Notre Dame

THE BROTHERS KARAMAZOV AND THE CRITICS
edited by Edward Wasiolek, University of Chicago

TRUMAN CAPOTE'S IN COLD BLOOD: A Critical Handbook
edited by Irving Malin, City College of New York

CONRAD'S HEART OF DARKNESS AND THE CRITICS
edited by Bruce Harkness, Kent State University

CONRAD'S SECRET SHARER AND THE CRITICS
edited by Bruce Harkness, Kent State University

STEPHEN CRANE'S MAGGIE: Text and Context
edited by Maurice Bassan, San Francisco State College

CRIME AND PUNISHMENT AND THE CRITICS
edited by Edward Wasiolek, University of Chicago

GOETHE'S FAUST PART I. Essays in Criticism
edited by John B. Vickery and J'nan Sellery, University of California at Riverside

HOMER'S ODYSSEY: A Critical Handbook
edited by Conny Nelson, Washington State University

JAMES JOYCE'S DUBLINERS: A Critical Handbook
edited by James R. Baker, San Diego State College, and Thomas F. Staley, University of Tulsa

THE KING LEAR PERPLEX
edited by Helmut Bonheim

LITERARY CENSORSHIP: Principles, Cases, Problems
edited by Kingsley Widmer, San Diego State College, and Eleanor Widmer

LITERARY SYMBOLISM: An Introduction to the Interpretation of Literature
edited by Maurice Beebe, Purdue University

MELVILLE'S BILLY BUDD AND THE CRITICS, Second Edition
edited by William T. Stafford, Purdue University

OEDIPUS REX: A Mirror for Greek Drama
edited by Albert Cook, State University of New York

THE RIME OF THE ANCIENT MARINER: A Handbook
edited by Royal A. Gettmann, University of Illinois

J. D. SALINGER AND THE CRITICS
edited by William F. Belcher and James W. Lee, North Texas State University

SATIRE: Theory and Pratice
edited by Charles A. Allen and George D. Stephens, California State College at Long Beach

A SCARLET LETTER HANDBOOK
edited by Seymour L. Gross, University of Notre Dame

SUCCESS IN AMERICA
edited by James J. Clark and Robert H. Woodward, San Jose State College

MARK TWAIN'S THE MYSTERIOUS STRANGER AND THE CRITICS
edited by John S. Tuckey, Purdue University

VOLTAIRE'S CANDIDE AND THE CRITICS
edited by Milton P. Foster, Eastern Michigan University

ROBERT PENN WARREN'S ALL THE KING'S MEN: A Critical Handbook
edited by Maurice Beebe and Leslie Field, Purdue University

WHITMAN THE POET: Materials for Study
edited by John C. Broderick, Wake Forest College

Homer's
ODYSSEY
A Critical Handbook

Edited by Conny Nelson
Washington State University

Wadsworth Publishing Company, Inc.
Belmont, California

L. C. Cat. Card No.: 69–18084
Printed in the United States of America

CONTENTS

Introduction   vii

Homer's Characters

W. B. Stanford: Athene's Odysseus, the Man of Action   1
Charles H. Taylor, Jr.: Odysseus, the Inner Man   18
Howard W. Clarke: Telemachus   28
J. W. Mackail: Penelope   41

Homer's Universe

M. I. Finley: The Human World of the *Odyssey*   55
G. M. A. Grube: The Divine World of the *Odyssey*   72

The *Odyssey*: Epic Style and Epic Form

Erich Auerbach: Homer's Realism, the Individual Voice   89
Denys Page: Homeric Epic, the Traditional Voice   107

The *Odyssey*: Theme and Structure

Frank W. Jones: Revenge   115
Edward F. D'Arms and Karl K. Hulley: Guilt and Free Will   121
Walter Morris Hart: The *Odyssey* as Comedy   127

The *Odyssey*: Three Contemporary Interpretations

L. A. Post: The Epic of Success   145
George E. Dimock, Jr.: The Epic of Suffering and Fulfillment   157
George de F. Lord: The Epic of Moral Regeneration   172

Suggestions for Study   187

Further Reading: A Selected Bibliography   193

Translations of the Odyssey: A Selected Bibliography   196

Names in the Odyssey: Pronunciation Guide   198

INTRODUCTION

WHETHER HOMER WAS ONE POET OR (AS SOME SCHOLARS INSIST) A GROUP of poets whose identities were lost even in antiquity, the literary greatness of the *Iliad* and the *Odyssey* is beyond question. Indeed, it has been argued that these epics, the earliest extant works of Western literature, are also the greatest—an argument that might startle the modern student, raised in a culture which always looks to next year's model as an "improvement" and which has unquestioned faith in the principle of obsolescence. In any event, only Dante and Shakespeare have places of honor in Western literature which are equivalent to Homer's. His high place has not always been wholly secure, however, and it is important for us to understand some of the reasons for this as we approach his work. To do so is to avoid falling into an error of expectation, and thus an error of judgment.

For a thousand years, from the dawn of Greek civilization to the twilight of the Roman empire, Homer was considered The Poet, the supreme master and model of serious poetry. Only the Roman epic poet Virgil, who wrote about seven hundred years after Homer and who sought inspiration for his *Aeneid* from the Homeric poems, achieved anywhere near as much respect as Homer during the classical period. But with the collapse of classical culture and the rise of the Middle Ages, all knowledge of Greek and Greek literature was lost in Western Europe for hundreds of years. Thus, the actual works of Homer were unknown. His reputation remained alive, and his name became proverbial, but to the Middle Ages Homer was like a figure from a legend about a legend, vague and mysterious. This is why the medieval poet Dante, even though he could not read the *Iliad* and the *Odyssey*, felt it necessary to seat Homer, "who hath surpassed all other poets," in a place of honor in the *Divine Comedy*. Dante's poem is the literary high point of the Middle Ages, and reflects the feeling and opinion of that era more completely than any other single document we possess.

While medieval culture gave lip service to Homer, it gave its real allegiance to Virgil. Despite his respectful bow to Homer, in Dante's mind it is Virgil who is The Poet. It is Virgil to whom he looks for inspiration, and it is Virgil who appears before Dante in the dramatic context of the *Divine Comedy* to lead him safely through the regions of Hell. This should not surprise us. The Latin language survived the collapse of the Roman world. Latin literature, with Virgil its supreme poet, became the foundation on which medieval literature was built. Homer was a legend, but Virgil was real and alive; and his epic poem, the *Aeneid*, shaped the medieval idea of what the classical epic should be. This fact had repercussions that can be felt to this day.

While Virgil drew much from the *Iliad* and, particularly, the
Odyssey, his *Aeneid* is a fundamentally different kind of poem. Virgil's
hero, Aeneas, was according to legend one of the Trojan heroes who
survived the fall of Troy. But the Roman poet set out to write a Roman,
not a Homeric, epic; he therefore developed his hero from a Roman,
not a Homeric, point of view. Virgil's Aeneas is a man with a mission.
His glory is that he has given himself to an ideal greater than himself
and to history and destiny. Personal satisfactions, personal relationships, personal desires are not for him. He lives for only one thing: to
found the city and empire of Rome, which will one day dominate and
order the entire world for the good and peace of all mankind. Aeneas
is a type of pagan-political Christ. He must sacrifice himself for the
good of others. He brings the world salvation, on the level of society
and politics. The analogy between Aeneas and Christ did not escape
the thinkers and writers of the Middle Ages. Virgil came to be thought
of as a kind of pre-Christian Christian; this, of course, tremendously
enhanced his reputation and influence.

As the Middle Ages drew to their close and the scholars of the
Renaissance recovered and renewed the study of Greek, Homer's
poems emerged from oblivion. As was to be expected, they were read
at first from the point of view of the Virgilian and the Christian idea
of what good men and good poetry should be; that is, in both Virgilian
epic and Christian doctrine, the good man is one who puts aside the
goods of this world for the sake of a better world to come. Man has a
mission greater than his personal satisfaction in this world. These
standards, when applied to Homer, caused difficulties which still
trouble readers of Homeric epic. That is, the Homeric poems (and
particularly the *Odyssey*, on which we shall concentrate from this
point) do not easily lend themselves to the Virgilian and traditional
Christian styles of interpretation. The Homeric hero thinks and acts in
terms of his own individuality. His glory is in his personal worth,
action, achievement, survival, and reputation. He lives, essentially, in a
Shame Culture, a culture in which the greatest evil is to lose face,
honor, reputation—to feel humiliated and shamed. When a Homeric
hero gives himself to something outside his ego, it is to an extension of
his ego, to something that is *his*: *his* love for *his* friend, *his* desire to
reach *his* home, *his* revenge on those who would take *his* goods. The
Virgilian and traditional Christian hero lives in a Guilt Culture, a
culture in which his glory and standards of good are outside his individuality: in an ideal, in a society, or in God's law. For him, the
greatest evil is to break the law, to proudly exalt ego, to betray the
revolution, to sin against the precepts of dogma or commandment—to
feel criminal and guilty.

During the Renaissance and up through the eighteenth century,
when men read both Homer and Virgil they tended to give Virgil the
crown. Homer, while recognized as a very great poet, seemed too

primitive, barbaric, and unchristian. For example, the *Odyssey* was interpreted as a Virgilian-Christian "mission," but the many moral lapses in the work—the brutalities and heroic pride in self—were difficult to rationalize. Slowly, however, critics began to realize that the defect was in the critical approach; and today many (but not all) critics read the *Odyssey* in ways which do justice to the Homeric in Homer. Homer once again sits enthroned as the greatest of classic poets, and Virgil occupies his proper place a little lower and to the left of the throne.

As he sets out to read the *Odyssey*, the student should keep the following idea in mind: The epic story of man the individual in tenuous possession of or in desperate search for his own being is no less real and dramatic than the epic story of man the social animal in firm possession of or in determined search for a "larger truth." The *Odyssey* is concerned with the first of these two kinds of story. It is an epic of an individual's will and ability to survive and shape the world in some measure as he wishes it to be shaped. Odysseus knows that "man is the frailest of all creatures on earth," and he knows that man must perish at last. But as long as life lasts, he will meet and strive for his own sake to overcome its obstacles and its sometimes hostile, sometimes only neutral reality. Such a story, treated honestly, may be grand, but it will not always be pretty. And Homer treated it honestly. We see Odysseus despair as well as exult, steal as well as give, sacrifice friends as well as strive to save them, cheat as well as deal honestly, brutally kill as well as tenderly love—he sometimes feels regret, but never remorse. The *Odyssey* is, on several levels, the epic of what man is capable of.

The *Odyssey* is a complex narrative. It is composed of four separate but related story lines: the story of Telemachus, the story of Penelope and the suitors, the story of Odysseus' wanderings, and the story of Odysseus' revenge. The poem is most famous for the story of the wanderings, but this is probably the least important part of the epic. From one point of view, Odysseus' account to King Alcinous of his wanderings (four books—only one sixth of the poem) can be considered a digression from the main action. Thus, any interpretation of the *Odyssey* which is wholly concerned with the wanderings is liable to distort the poem's structure. Also, while Odysseus is clearly the central character of the piece, his story is contingent to the stories of Penelope and the suitors, and of Telemachus. Again, any interpretation which focuses on Odysseus alone is liable to distort the complex structure of the *Odyssey*. Finally, Odysseus and other characters in the poem experience a great variety of conflicts and situations. As one reads the epic, he should interpret it in a way that does not minimize this variety and complexity. A "single central theme" type of analysis will probably not do justice to the poem. Moreover, one should attempt to see not only all the various themes of the action, but the system of connections that unites and combines these several themes.

This book has been set up with an eye to encouraging and facilitating the above kind of analysis. In the first section will be found essays which isolate the main characters, yet comment on them in such a way as to show their connection to the overall pattern of the narrative. The second section presents two essays which explain the human and divine contexts in which the characters operate. Section three contains two essays which discuss the unique style of the *Odyssey*, and the nature of the traditional epic form with which Homer had to work. This section has a special importance to the modern reader. Homer composed oral epic poems, not modern realistic novels. It is very tempting but only partially valid to approach the *Odyssey* as a novel. Techniques of characterization, motivation, style, and structure that we take for granted in reading modern novels are often irrelevant to a consideration of heroic poetry. On the other hand, certain techniques which inform the *Odyssey* and contribute mightily to its power are impossible in the novel. Section four complements section three. It contains three essays which consider specific stylistic devices, general motifs, structural devices, and matters of epic tone. Finally, section five contains three general interpretations of the *Odyssey* from different points of view. These three essays raise most of the important problems of the *Odyssey*. No one of these essays is likely to completely satisfy the student of the poem; a comprehensive, satisfying critique of the *Odyssey*, which takes into account both the insights of scholarship and literary criticism, remains to be written. However, these general interpretations, plus the other materials in this book and the student's own observations, should lead to a good insight into the literary greatness of the poem.

Since the major purpose of this volume is to serve as a basis for independent research and writing on the *Odyssey*, a set of leading questions and an annotated bibliography of additional studies of the *Odyssey*—as well as an annotated bibliography of translations of the poem, and a guide to the pronunciation of Homeric names—are included in the appendices. So that the student may document his writing as if he had read the materials included here in their original form of publication, exact bibliographical references for each selection are provided, and the original pagination is indicated by means of small raised numerals in the text. Although several of the selections originally appeared as parts of longer studies, none has been internally abridged, with the following exceptions: Since this book is intended for those who read the *Odyssey* in translation, a number of passages of Greek have been excised—though for various reasons many such passages have been retained. Also, since a number of the essays appeared originally in scholarly journals aimed at professional classicists, the editor has carefully edited the footnotes and has removed some which could be of interest only to the professional scholar and philologist. Footnote numbers in the affected essays have been changed accordingly. The editor has also taken the liberty of adding descriptive titles to the selections in order to point up their place in the overall plan of the book. In every case, however, the original title has been included in the bibliographical reference on the first page of each selection. Certain printer's errors in the original texts have been silently corrected. Lastly, the editor has followed the *MLA Style Sheet* in most matters of form, and he encourages the student to do so in his own writing.

Homer's
ODYSSEY
A Critical Handbook

HOMER'S CHARACTERS

Athene's Odysseus, the Man of Action

W. B. STANFORD

IN ESTIMATING THE AUTOLYCAN ELEMENT IN ODYSSEUS'S CAREER IT WAS necessary to rely mainly on innuendoes and hints, as one would have expected in a rather disreputable matter of that kind. In contrast, Athene's influence is presented quite differently. Except when she has to take precautions to avoid Poseidon's anger, she always intervenes in Odysseus's affairs openly and unambiguously. Further, Homer arranged that she should decisively intervene in Odysseus's fortunes at the beginning, middle, and end of both his poems. By this, too, Homer may have intended to indicate a contrast with the influence of Autolycus, which is only casually mentioned towards the end of the *Odyssey.*

But when one considers Athene's relations with Odysseus in the *Iliad* and the *Odyssey* separately, once more a significant difference of attitude would appear to arise. Her frequent, almost continuous, interventions in the plot of the *Odyssey* are devoted exclusively to Odysseus's personal welfare. In the *Iliad* only five[1] of her personal interventions concern Odysseus, and only one of the five concerns his private interests. To judge simply from the number of her approaches to the heroes in general, Achilles and Diomedes would seem to have been more her favourites in the *Iliad.*[2]

---

[1] Besides the three main interventions by Athene in Odysseus's career in the *Iliad,* which are to be described in detail in this chapter, she also prevents him from pursuing Sarpedon in *Il.* 5, 676, thereby saving him from Zeus's anger, and in *Il.* 11, 437–8, she prevents the spear of Sokos from inflicting a mortal wound. Neither of these interventions is emphasized.

[2] For an analysis of personal interventions of deities in the affairs of individuals in the *Iliad* see L. A. MacKay, *The Wrath of Homer* (Toronto, 1948), pp. 68–71. Athene makes more use of Achilles and Diomedes than of Ulysses to check the Trojans, but Homer makes it clear that she favours Achilles mainly as an instrument for slaughter and Diomedes less for his own sake than because he is the son of her former protégé Tydeus (see *Il.* 5, 124 ff., 406 ff., 800 ff.), though there

W. B. Stanford, "The Favourite of Athene." From *The Ulysses Theme, A Study in the Adaptability of a Traditional Hero,* 2nd ed. (Oxford: Basil Blackwell and Mott, 1963), pp. 25–42. Reprinted by permission of the author and the publisher.

This apparent difference can be accounted for without any assumption of different authorship for the two poems. The *Iliad* is primarily a saga of warriors, a poem of physical and psychological violence. Odysseus is never considered pre-eminent as a fighter in formal battles. Achilles, Ajax, Diomedes, and Hector, surpass him in this. Correspondingly, Athene's main purpose in the *Iliad* is a military one, to cause the destruction of Troy. She still hopes, apparently, that this can be achieved by main force. As a result, when Achilles sulks in his tent she employs the valiant Diomedes as her chief champion, not the resourceful Odysseus. His turn will come after the *Iliad's* story is done, when Achilles and Ajax are dead. Physical violence must first prove a failure before Odysseus's ruse of the Wooden Horse wins victory for the Greeks.

In the *Odyssey* the circumstances are entirely different. Athene has seen Troy destroyed with enough slaughter to satisfy even the [25/26] most bloodthirsty warrior-goddess—and Odysseus has been its main vanquisher. Also by the time the poem begins Odysseus is the only champion of the Greeks who has not reached home. Thus physically and psychologically the way has been cleared for Athene to show special favour towards Odysseus throughout his homeward journey from Calypso's island.

Besides this a closer examination of her interventions in Odysseus's career in the *Iliad* suggests that before the end of the poem she had come to take a more than military interest in his personal qualities. This preparation, as it were, for their closer relationship in the *Odyssey* is not emphasized. Even if Homer had wished to emphasize it, he could hardly have done so without distracting attention from the poem's main theme—the wrath of Achilles and its disastrous consequences. It would be characteristic of his masterly economy that he should both postpone exploration of the subtler aspects of Athene's favour towards Odysseus until well into the *Odyssey*, and at the same time give some indication of its widening potentialities in the earlier poem. This he seems to have done. If the analysis that follows here is correct, Athene's three main approaches to Odysseus in the *Iliad* are not merely random manifestations of her anti-Trojan zeal, but carefully graduated stages in a planned development of their relationship. This, of course, assumes that, whoever their author, the two Homeric poems were, sooner or later, composed as complementary poems.

Before Athene intervened in Odysseus's Iliadic career he had

is a touch of personal affection in her phrase 'thou who hast found favour in my heart' in *Il.* 8, 826. In general Athene uses Achilles and Diomedes when physical valour is needed and Odysseus in matters demanding prudence and tact. Athene's special regard for Odysseus is emphasized by Nestor in *Od.* 3, 218–24. Diomedes (as Davaux notes, p. 5) actually intervenes more often in the council of elders than Odysseus, but this may indicate boldness rather than wisdom. See further in n. 2 to chapter five.

played only a minor rôle. A few references had established him as an honoured but not a pre-eminent hero. He had been sent on the unenviable task of restoring Chryseis to her indignant father. The episode is passed over without *réclame:* everyone doubtless knew that Odysseus was good at this kind of negotiation. Some of the prouder heroes might have regarded it as little better than huckstering. But later, in Book Two, at Athene's prompting Odysseus takes the centre of the stage with a spectacular coup. Homer introduces it in a curious way. When Agamemnon's foolish ruse has precipitated the Greeks into a disorderly rush for the ships, Hera, always zealous for the Greek cause, orders Athene to go and restrain each warrior with her 'gentle (or acceptable) words'. Athene, instead of doing this herself, seeks out Odysseus, 'equal to Zeus in counsel', and tells him to restrain each warrior with *his* 'gentle words'. Odysseus obeys and with his gentle words (Homer repeats the phrase again) succeeds in checking the leaders from their flight (but [26/27] he uses his staff and some most ungentle words on the common soldiers). How he then quelled the mutinous Thersites and won the army's good-humoured support, is one of the most celebrated incidents in European literature. His prompt actions and apt words became a model for later statesmen. His aphorism on the dangers of mob rule—

> Evil it is when many rule. Let there be one lord,
> One king, to whom it is granted by Zeus—

was cherished by political thinkers for over two thousand years.

In this way by Athene's favour Odysseus not merely became the pivot of the whole plot of the *Iliad* for a while, but also first entered the main stream of European literature as an outstanding figure in political thought. In other words the serviceable negotiator of Book One has been promoted for a while to be the saviour of the Greek cause and the proto-evangelist of hierarchical order in European thought. The significance of the repeated references to 'gentle words' will become clear later.

Athene again intervenes notably to help Odysseus in the Night Raid in Book Ten. Autolycan aspects of the outwitting of Dolon in this episode have already been mentioned. But Homer makes it clear that Athene's influence predominates. As the heroes set out (after a passing reference to Autolycus) Athene sends them a good omen. Odysseus prays in reply: 'Hear me, daughter of Zeus, who dost ever stand by me in all my toils—no movement of mine escapes thee[3]—now show me thy special love, Athene, and grant that we may return again with glory and great success . . .' Diomedes prays to her as well (for she had befriended his father, Tydeus, in the famous attack on Thebes), but he prays only for his own safety, while Odysseus had prayed for them

---

[3] Odysseus's consciousness of Athene's constant surveillance, as expressed here, struck Epictetus (*Discourses* 1, 12, 3) as a notable example of religious faith.

both. After the killing of Dolon, Odysseus has no compunction in dedicating his armour to her with a pious prayer. When danger threatens later, it is Athene who warns the heroes to withdraw. Nestor clearly recognizes the benefits of her protection when the two heroes have returned in triumph. The episode ends with a picture of both heroes pouring a grateful libation to her. Homer could hardly have made her pervading influence plainer.

In this and in the Thersites incident Athene's main purpose is to promote the victory of the Greeks. Odysseus and Diomedes are employed as the best instruments[4] for her partisan policy. But Homer is not just playing a *Kriegspiel* with brightly coloured [27/28] puppets. In the second incident he allows us to see more of Odysseus's personality, as distinct from the public talents displayed in the Thersites affair. Odysseus's unusual modesty[5] both before and after the sortie has been explained in the previous chapter as a symptom of his constant effort to avoid Autolycan odium. That is its negative aspect. But seen in the light of Athene's influence a complementary reason emerges. It may be that Homer also wishes us to see how Odysseus, once he was conscious of Athene's special favour, was less susceptible to the normal heroic craving for public approval. Knowing now that he has won divine favour, he finds satisfaction in the action itself. He is eager to get to work without any flourish of trumpets, and when his work has been well done, to go to rest without such fulsome congratulations as Nestor offers. There is a foreshadowing here, too, of that spirit of *Non nobis, Domine, sed nomini tuo*, which becomes apparent towards the end of the *Odyssey*. In the later tradition this refusal to exult in his successes will turn to cynicism (as in the prologue to Euripides's *Philoctetes*) and disillusion (as in the epilogue to Plato's *Republic*); but there is no trace of these sophistications here.

The other notable feature of Odysseus's conduct in the Doloneia is his piety.[6] This is frequently emphasized elsewhere. Here Homer

---

[4] Apuleius, *De deo Socratis*, 18, remarks that in the Doloneia Odysseus is the intelligence (*consilium, mens, animus*), Diomedes the physical force (*auxilium, manus, gladius*) in this episode.

[5] The scholia A on *Il.* 10, 249, note Odysseus's modesty here, and explain the contrasting boastfulness of his self-description in Phaeacia (*Od.* 9, 19–20) as being necessary to win enough respect to be granted an escort home. His self-praise in *Od.* 8, 166 ff., is forced by Laodamas's direct insult. For his remarks to Sokos see later in this chapter.

[6] For the more formal aspect of Odysseus's piety see especially Zeus's testimony in *Od.* 1, 66–7. 'More than other mortals has he offered sacrifices to the immortal gods'. Odysseus's actions throughout the *Odyssey* illustrate his personal piety. Even in his worst sufferings he never blames the gods (except Poseidon whose wrath is admittedly justified) or accuses them of 'envy' as others do (e.g. in *Od.* 4, 181; 5, 118; 23, 211). His single moment of petulance against Athene in *Od.* 13, 316 ff. is discussed later in this chapter. Contrast Achilles's threats against Apollo (*Il.* 22, 20 ff.) and his defiance of the river-god Scamander (*Il.* 21, 130 ff.).

makes him unusually scrupulous. He calls on Athene three times with marked devotion and reverence—at the outset of the enterprise, after his first success, and when he has safely returned. Even in times of greatest stress in the *Odyssey* he is never as devout as this. Some modern readers may find this piety revolting in a man who had no qualms about deceiving a helpless enemy with a deliberate equivocation. But clearly Homer did not intend his hearers to feel any such revulsion.

Thus Athene's first intervention in Odysseus's Iliadic career resulted in a display of his superb skill in handling a major political crisis. Her second displayed his modesty and piety as well as his resourcefulness in a perilous, uncertain task. In both Odysseus serves as a means of advancing the Greek victory which Athene so ardently desires. In her third intervention at the Funeral Games he receives his reward in a personal and special way.

The circumstances are these. In the preceding wrestling match with Telamonian Ajax Odysseus had deftly tripped him and won a fall. After a second indecisive bout Achilles, perhaps fearing Ajax's *amour propre,* had intervened and proclaimed a draw. Odysseus did not protest though he had reason for feeling aggrieved. Next [28/29] came the foot-race. Normally Odysseus with his unusually short legs would have had very little chance of winning this, especially against Locrian Ajax, the swiftest of the Achaeans. However, he got off to a quick start and doggedly kept close behind Ajax until the last lap. Then just before the final sprint Odysseus prayed Athene to come to his aid. She had previously intervened to help Diomedes to win the chariot race. Now she gives strength to Odysseus's limbs and makes Ajax stumble ignominiously. Odysseus wins the cup. The last we hear of him (and of Athene) in the *Iliad* is Ajax's angry remark: 'Confound it, the goddess baulked my running, she who—and before this, too—stands by Odysseus and helps him like a mother'.

The words form an apt epilogue to Athene's care for Odysseus in the *Iliad,* and an apt prologue to her closer relationship with him in the *Odyssey.* It is hardly unreasonable to discern a careful arrangement here. Odysseus has advanced in the *Iliad* from being Athene's effective agent to being her special protégé. In the two earlier incidents she gave scope and assistance to his natural gifts of prudence, courage, versatility, and endurance. In the third she gives him supernatural strength to overcome his physical defects. Homer leaves it open to his audience to conclude that under such influence a grandson of Autolycus would become, if not a conventional hero, at least something nobler than a traditional Wily Lad. Yet it is significant, too, in view of Autolycus's reason for naming his grandson, that the last reference to Odysseus in the *Iliad* is an expression of odium at his success.

Troy has fallen before the *Odyssey* begins, so that Athene no longer has a military reason for prompting and guiding Odysseus. If

Homer had regarded Odysseus's relationship with Athene in the *Iliad* as being simply that between an agent and his director, he would probably have let the relationship lapse or become merely vestigial in the *Odyssey*. Athene had paid off Odysseus, so to speak, in the Funeral Games: he could now find his own way home. But Homer chose differently. He decided, instead, to intensify the relation between goddess and hero, and to transform Athene's military motives into motives of personal sympathy and affection. The implication of the words 'like a mother' at the end of her interventions on Odysseus's behalf in the *Iliad* become fully explicit before the *Odyssey* is concluded.

It is unnecessary to analyse all Athene's efforts for Odysseus's welfare in the *Odyssey*. She sets the plot in movement by persuading [29/30] Zeus to allow his return when the angry Poseidon is away in foreign parts. As soon as he has passed out of the sphere of fairyland by reaching Phaeacia, she is constantly at hand to guide, prompt, and help him. After this Homer apparently felt that such a special personal relationship between a divinity and a mortal needed a special explanation. In other cases of the kind the motive was generally either erotic passion (as with Aphrodite and Anchises) or some definite practical purpose. Athene had neither motive for favouring Odysseus in the *Odyssey*.

Homer devotes a whole scene to the answer. It occurs when Athene and Odysseus meet openly and undisguised for the first time in the *Odyssey*. Odysseus has just returned to Ithaca. Athene approaches him (*Od.* 13, 221 ff.) in the form of a young shepherd. In answer to his question she tells him that he is in Ithaca. He at once becomes wary, 'loyal as ever to his own crafty nature'. He pretends that he is a Cretan refugee, and extemporizes a fictitious story. Athene listens with amusement. She smiles, puts her hand on him in a gesture of friendly intimacy, and abandons her disguise. 'What a cunning knave it would take', she exclaims, 'to beat you at your tricks! Even a god would be hard put to it. And so my stubborn friend, Odysseus the arch-deceiver, with his craving for intrigue, does not propose even in his own country to drop his sharp practice and the lying tales that he loves from the bottom of his heart. But no more of this: we are both adepts in chicane. For in the world of men you have no rival as a statesman and an orator, while I am pre-eminent among the gods for invention and resource'. She goes on to refer to her constant protection of Odysseus and to advise him about his further trials.

Odysseus replies with some annoyance. He complains that Athene has neglected him during his sea voyages. He feels uneasy and suspicious. Has he really reached Ithaca, or is Athene merely mocking him? Athene's reply contains the kernel of the whole scene: 'How like you to be so wary! And that is why I cannot desert you in your misfortunes: *you are so civilized, so intelligent, so self-possessed.*'[7]

---

[7] I have used Rieu's translation in the last two paragraphs both for its liveliness and to avoid any risk of subjective interpretation to suit my own views.

The scene in general is full of sophisticated charm: it has been well compared[8] with the conversations of Benedick and Beatrice in *Much ado about nothing*. Nowhere else in early classical literature can one find such a graceful portrait of two wits, male and female, exchanging banter and reproaches without malice or scorn in this free and easy style. But Homer would hardly have composed the [30/31] scene for its charm alone. Its supple, effortless style carries the clue to the whole Odyssean relationship of Athene and Odysseus. She cannot desert him in his misfortunes because, cunning as he is, he is also 'civilized, intelligent, and self-possessed'. The Greek terms used are complex and deserve closer analysis.

The first epithet, *epētes*, is used only once elsewhere by Homer. When Amphinomos, the only likeable person among the Suitors, speaks kindly and compassionately to Odysseus in his beggar's disguise, Odysseus uses the same word in saying that he seems like a 'civilized' man. It implies personal attentiveness, kindness, and gentleness, in contrast with boorishness and selfish indifference to other people's feelings—a quality closely akin to that philosophic gentleness which Plato praises in his *Republic*. Athene was specially fitted to appreciate it in Odysseus for she herself had this gift, as Hera made clear in requesting her to check the Greek retreat in *Iliad* 2, 165—'You go and restrain each man with your *gentle* words'. Hence, perhaps, her indignation when, pleading again for Odysseus's home-coming at the second council of the gods in the *Odyssey* (5, 8–10), she bitterly exclaims 'Let there be no more deliberate gentleness and mildness among reigning kings, and no more justice; let them ever be harsh and lawless instead; since no one among the people that Odysseus once ruled as mildly as a father now remembers him'. One is reminded of Antony's speech to the Roman plebs:

When that the poor have cried, Caesar hath wept.

And it is significant that the first entrance of Odysseus into the main narrative of the *Odyssey* reveals him weeping tenderly for his home. Has Homer designed this to offset stories of Odysseus's callousness at the sack of Troy, obliquely making Antony's point?—

Ambition should be made of sterner stuff.

Yet Euripides will say he was ambitious. . . .

Others besides Athene found gentleness in Odysseus. When he met the ghost of his mother Anticleia in the Land of Shades she told him that the cause of her death had been her yearning for his thought-

---

[8] Hart, pp. 263 ff. Apropos of this scene he discusses Odysseus's freedom from the dominance of passion and his carefulness in considering possible courses of action, citing *Il.* 11, 401 ff.; *Od.* 5, 465 f.; 6, 141 ff.; 10, 151 ff.; 18, 90 ff. I cannot agree with his view that Odysseus is characteristically sceptical towards the gods here and in *Od.* 5, 173, 356, but prefer the explanation offered in chapter two. [The Hart essay is reprinted in this anthology. Ed.]

fulness and kindness (*Od.* 11, 202–3). There are further tributes in the *Odyssey* from relatives, subjects, and servants, to this mildness and kindness of his.[9] 'He was as kindly as a father.' Among the other Homeric heroes notably Hector (and to some degree his father Priam) had this endearing gift of civilized gentleness in thought, word, and deed; and it was the loss of this that Helen lamented most at Hector's death (*Il.* 24, 770–2). In a world [31/32] of heroic violence women would naturally appreciate this quality more than men. The cruder hero might despise it as weak and effeminate, for as Socrates insists (*Republic* 2, 375B), these high-spirited natures are apt to be savage with one another and everyone else. But, as Socrates adds, the ideal guardians of the commonwealth ought to be dangerous to their enemies and gentle to their friends, like a well-trained dog; and further, 'he who is likely to be gentle with his friends and acquaintances must by nature be a lover of wisdom or knowledge'.

'Dangerous to enemies and gentle to friends, like a well-trained dog'. One may note in passing that Odysseus had good reason to weep when he saw his dog Argos lying neglected and verminous while the Suitors roistered in his halls. But the main point is that to an ancient Greek Odysseus's civilized gentleness to friends was not incompatible either ethically or psychologically with his savage ferocity towards his faithless servants and towards even the best of the Suitors. As far as archaic ethics was concerned, usurpers and traitors were beyond the pale of kindness. And psychologically, allowance must be made for a much greater emotional resilience than can be expected in a modern 'civilized' hero. One must not be surprised at the contrast between Odysseus's tearfulness and his fierceness, nor be shocked that the preliminaries to Odysseus's tender recognition scene with Penelope are the ghastly massacre of the Suitors and the barbarous hanging of the disloyal maidservants. There is no schizophrenia here. One can find the same combination of sensibility and ferocity, of gentle courtesy and daemonic energy in Renaissance men like Raleigh or Essex, half pirate, half courtier, as well versed in Castiglione's *Courtier* and Spenser's *Faerie Queene* as in the latest type of thumb-screw. One should judge this aspect of Odysseus's character more in terms of the *Duchess of Malfi* than of *Westward Ho.*[10]

[9] *Od.* 2, 47; 2, 234; 5, 12. Other tributes of Odysseus's gentleness are to be found in *Od.* 4, 689–91; 14, 62–7; 138–9; 16, 443–4.

[10] Cf. G. M. A. Grube, 'The Gods of Homer' in *Studies in Honour of Gilbert Norwood* (Toronto, 1952), p. 9: 'Certainly, Odysseus cannot claim any outstanding moral rectitude; in fact, the slaying of the suitors and, in particular, of Amphinomus and Leodes, with the revolting massacre of the maidservants, is the most deliberately savage episode in the two poems'. While I agree in general with Grube's view that Homer's gods and heroes are mainly amoral, I question the view that Odysseus's slaughter of the usurping suitors and disloyal maidservants would have been regarded as particularly savage by Homer or his audience: cf. Agamemnon's view in *Il.* 6, 55 ff., and Achilles's in *Il.* 22, 346–8. O. did try to warn off Amphinomus, the only gentle suitor. [The Grube essay is reprinted in this anthology. Ed.]

The second word used by Athene, *anchinoos*, is not found again in Greek literature until Plato. Aristotle (*Nicomachean Ethics* 1142b, 2 ff.) explains it as a kind of 'skill in hitting the mark' which is quick in action and not dependent on logical thought. This meaning suits the Homeric context well. It implies a quality approximating to what is called feminine intuition, that gift of instantaneous insight into the essence of a complex matter, which both ignores and baffles logical analysis. Here, perhaps, is the secret of Odysseus's unusual promptness in action. Joined to his more masculine ability to work out careful plans, it made a formidable combination (as in [32/33] Aeschylus's Clytaemnestra). But it is not entirely clear just how it differs from Autolycan shrewdness; it is perhaps a purer, more spontaneous quality.

The third term, *echephron*, is much commoner, but with one exception Homer always applies it elsewhere to Penelope, the exception being when Achilles uses it of a man who is faithful to one woman. It is often rendered as 'sensible, discreet', but this hardly gives the right emphasis. Literally 'mind-restraining' or 'thought-controlling', it describes a self-possessed person who does not allow his impulses and thoughts to lead to wrong words or actions. Thus Penelope never allowed any thought of marrying another man—a natural thought for a woman uncertain of her husband's fate for nine years, and surrounded by many insistent wooers—to make her abandon her love for Odysseus. She is 'self-possessed' in this—the opposite of fickle, or flighty. It is in many ways the highest form of self-control. Homer doubtless intended it as a special tribute to Penelope when he gave her almost a monopoly of the epithet in his poems. By making Athene use it to describe Odysseus here he may have intended to imply that the marriage of Odysseus and Penelope was such a marriage of true minds as Shakespeare's sonnet describes—

> Love is not love
> Which alters when it alteration finds,
> Or bends with the remover to remove.

This self-possession could go further than this. In a negative sense it implied keeping one's own counsel. Where other heroes like Agamemnon and Achilles and Ajax, or other figures of Autolycan propensities like Thersites and the Cyclops, would blurt out their least prudent thoughts, Odysseus rarely spoke an unconsidered word even under the strongest provocation. It did not always take the form of mere silence. It consisted rather in saying just as much as the present purpose warranted, and no more. When necessary Odysseus could be as brutally frank to Agamemnon as to Thersites. On other occasions he would mix frank criticism with his characteristic courtesy of manner so that the listener could neither evade the indictment nor take offence at it. This form of restraint was the most typical of his better nature through the whole tradition. One finds him using it in Shakespeare's *Troilus and Cressida* and Giraudoux's *La guerre de Troie n'aura pas lieu*, as effectively as in the *Iliad* or *Odyssey*. One of its finest examples in the Homeric poems comes when an insolent young Phaeacian prince taunts Odysseus with [33/34] looking less like an athlete than a trader. Odysseus's reply has won a just tribute from that past-master of public oratory, W. E. Gladstone,[11] as teaching 'more than any composition with which I am acquainted, up to what a point emotion, sarcasm, and indignation can be carried without any loss of self-command'. A comparison with the interchanges between Achilles and Agamemnon in the first book of the *Iliad,* where self-interest, passion, and indignation are in complete control, would show how much this Ulyssean moderation differs from normal heroic conduct.

The most remarkable example of this kind of restraint (though here its motive is less politic and more philosophic) comes at the climax of Odysseus's career as a Homeric hero, the supreme triumph of his valour, patience, and wiliness—the slaughter of the Suitors. Their corpses now lie in heaps on the floor, a hundred and eight killed by one hero helped only by his son and two servants. This, if ever, is the time for Odysseus to boast and exult, and for Homer to write a triumphal song equal to those of Moses and Deborah after the defeat of the enemies of the Lord. But that is not Homer's, or Odysseus's, way. Instead, when Eurycleia is about to raise a cry of triumph, Odysseus prevents her: 'Rejoice only in your heart, woman, and restrain yourself; raise no triumphal shout. It is wrong to boast over slain men. It was destiny and their own stubborn deeds that laid these men low. They showed no reverence for mankind, good or bad, whoever came to them. Therefore by their own wanton folly they met a shameful fate.' This is a remarkably dispassionate pronouncement for a Homeric hero in his moment of success. It contrasts vividly with the vaunts of victorious champions in the *Iliad.* Odysseus completely ignores his own achievement. He sees himself only as the instrument of destiny in punishing harshness, inhumanity, and folly. It is partly the feeling of *Non nobis, Domine;* but there is a difference. The emphasis here is less theistic than humanistic: men reap what they sow. Zeus himself had preached on the same text in the opening scene of the *Odyssey:* 'How men blame the gods for their ills, when in fact it is by their own folly that they get woes beyond measure!' In so far as Homer has any moral message in the *Iliad* and the *Odyssey* it comes to this: only by Ulyssean self-control and moderation can men achieve victory in life. In contrast the wrathful, vainglorious Achilles, the arrogant, grasping Agamem-

---

[11] *Juventus Mundi,* p. 392. See also Gladstone's discussion of Odysseus's patience and endurance as an active quality based on moral courage (p. 389). At times this active self-control merges into dogged endurance (cf. the comparison with a dog in *Od.* 20, 13 ff.: Odysseus's self-control there is specially admired by Socrates in *Republic* 441B and *Phaedo* 94D). Odysseus is the only hero who is called τλήμων in the *Iliad* (5, 670, cf. 10, 231–2, where the quality is specially emphasized, and 498): see Geddes's study of this and similar terms, pp. 88–9 and 226.

non, the obstinate Ajax, the self-centred, unscrupulous Autolycus, paid their penalties.

For a moment here Odysseus touches on the deeper meaning of [34/35] life's suffering, and seems to speak for Homer himself. As the ancient commentators noticed, Odysseus was the first Greek to adopt the principle of 'Nothing in excess', which with its complementary principle of 'Know thyself' produced so much of what was best in Greek thought and art. He knew how easy it is to fall into excess and thence into destruction. He emphasizes this in his speech to the best of the Suitors, Amphinomus, who had spoken a kind word to him in his beggar's disguise (*Od.* 18, 125 ff.). Odysseus, as has been noted, recognized his courtesy and tried obliquely to warn him of the impending slaughter. There is nothing feebler in the world, he told him, than mankind. In his days of manly strength he thinks that he will never come to harm; but when the gods decide to change his fortune, willy-nilly he goes astray and suffers for it. (An unexpectedly Autolycan note is then struck for a moment in this moral and friendly discourse: Odysseus untruly states that he, in his beggar's misery, is himself an example of the miseries caused by foolish and unrestrained conduct.) The general tone of melancholy[12] and the suggestion that at times men are little more than the playthings of the gods reveal the darker side of an attempt to combine theism with even the most exalted utilitarianism. Generally Odysseus was too much involved in practical difficulties to have time to make philosophical pronouncements like these. By making Odysseus utter them here Homer gives a sombre depth to his hero's mind, even if he is partly using Odysseus to express his own view of life. Later writers on the Ulysses theme will explore this philosophic quality more thoroughly.

It seems, then, that Athene's favour for Odysseus depended partly on his value as an instrument for overthrowing Troy, partly on an affection for his personal qualities. It is the second motive that was unique. The only other relationship between a divinity and a hero which approached its intimacy and mutual understanding was that between Achilles and Thetis. But they were son and mother. Athene had no formal reason for picking out Odysseus as her favourite. Further, as the remarkable scene in *Odyssey* Thirteen reveals, her affection is for the whole of his complex personality. She recognizes his Autolycan qualities—his inveterate scheming, his deluding ways, and his wily words—with a genial tolerance because she, too, is 'an adept in chicane'. But what she admires most is his civilized courtesy and gentleness, his keen-wittedness, his firm self-possession. There is a steady deepening

---

[12] *Od.* 18, 130 ff. A similar melancholy pessimism is found in Glaucus's words to Diomedes in *Il.* 6, 144–9, and more markedly in Achilles's to Priam in *Il.* 24, 525–33; but the first makes no reference to the gods and the second accuses them of caring nothing for men's sufferings, while Odysseus accepts the divine will without criticism. Cf. n. 6 above.

in their relations from the time when she gives Odysseus his first great opportunity in the *Iliad* [35/36] until the end of his Homeric career. Significantly in the last scene of the *Odyssey* it is she who *restrains* both Odysseus and the hostile Ithacans and makes peace between them.

What did Homer mean by this continuous guidance and protection? Some may say, Nothing: the goddess is simply that part of Homer's divine machinery which manipulates the fortunes of Odysseus: Homer is a story-teller, not an allegorist. Certainly Homer is primarily a story-teller. But one has only to compare his poems with other heroic stories like the Burnt Njal Saga or the Nibelungenlied to see how much more he is than a mere chronicler or tale-teller. He is intensely interested in human personality and in the human qualities of his gods. The subtleties of the dialogue between Athene and Odysseus after his arrival at Ithaca would be entirely pointless, if Athene's function was simply to expedite the plot of the *Odyssey*. The physical events described in the *Odyssey* are not, as Homer makes clear in the first line, its subject. Its subject is 'the man of many turns', just as the subject of the *Iliad* is not primarily the siege of Troy or the exploits of the heroes, but 'the destructive wrath of Achilles'.

If, then, Athene is not simply a piece of divine machinery to keep his plots moving (an anachronistic emphasis on 'plot' has done much harm to Homeric studies), what is her significance? Can one detect the poet's own attitude to Odysseus behind her special patronage? Homer's artistic self-effacement prevents any certain answer here. One can only guess, and many guesses are possible. The favourite interpretation in antiquity was allegorical and moralistic. Athene, it was believed, was intended by Homer to represent the power of divine wisdom to guide and control men's lives. One can see this allegorical method confidently at work in the *Homer Allegories* of Heracleitos (of the first century A.D.: formerly confused with fourth-century Heracleides Ponticus). He exploits it ingeniously. According to him Athene represented the power of divine wisdom, guiding and controlling men's lives. Thus when she seizes Achilles by the hair of the head to restrain him from attacking Agamemnon (*Iliad* 1, 197), it is taken as an allegorical representation of the fact that the reasoning faculty, through which the divine wisdom works, is situated in the head (hence, too, the birth of Athene from the head of Zeus). Her relationship with Odysseus is to be explained in the same way, he thinks. He makes the striking claim that Plato (whose hostility to Homer he energentically denounces) derived his tripartite division of the soul from Homer. If one elaborates a little [36/37] on this last suggestion a neat equation can be framed to explain the problems of Homer's Odysseus. The Autolycan element in his character could be identified with the appetitive faculty in Plato's division, for, as Socrates explains (*Republic* 581A), 'if we were to say that the loves and pleasures of this . . . part were concerned with gain, we should then be able to fall back on a single notion, and might truly and intelligibly describe this part of the soul as loving gain or money'. (Autolycus, it will be remembered, devoted his wiles to cheating people for his own advantage.) Secondly, what one might call the Laertes element, that is, the conventional heroic qualities of Odysseus's environment, would then be represented by Plato's 'spirited element', which is 'set on ruling and conquering and getting fame'. Then, thirdly, Athene must stand for Plato's third principle, the rational element, controlling the dark horse of Autolycan self-seeking and the white steed of heroic spirit, like the charioteer in the *Phaedrus* myth. But Homer was hardly so good a Platonist as that.

Allegorical interpretations held the field in Homeric studies for over two thousand years, and they still pervade many discussions on Homer's meaning. The chief objection to them in the case of Athene is that they ignore the harsher features in Homer's characterization of the goddess and depend on categories of thought not to be found in the Homeric poems. In the *Iliad* Athene is far from being the urbane goddess of wisdom and industry who presided over the civilization of fifth-century Athens. She is essentially a partisan warrior-goddess intent on the destruction of Troy. When necessary she can be ruthlessly treacherous and deceitful. Her deception of Hector in his last encounter with Achilles is as brutal a piece of primitive partisanship as one can find anywhere in literature, inconceivable in a personification of divine wisdom. Secondly, the later moralists' conception of virtue and truth was not Homer's; and Homer never remotely suggests that Athene's ultimate purpose was to make Odysseus virtuous, good, or truthful in any sense. Nor did she favour him because he was specially righteous in his behaviour. No, she chose Odysseus first because he was the sharpest instrument for the overthrow of Troy, and secondly because she liked his personal qualities and had a fellow-feeling for his wiliness.

Yet somehow one is reluctant to abandon the moralistic interpretation entirely, at any rate in its less fantasic forms. It is so much a part of the European literary tradition—subtle Heracleitos was a favourite author in post-Renaissance times—that Homer would [37/38] seem impoverished by its rejection. Perhaps it is reasonable to hold that, though Homer was not deliberately inculcating such consciously moral lessons, he did at times write more moralistically than he realized.[13] This is, after all, the characteristic quality of transcendent genius, to give beyond its conscious powers.

But allegorical and moralistic interpretations are generally out of

---

[13] In giving this mere opinion I must apologize for not entering more deeply into the perplexing problems of Homer's theology. For a convenient discussion of recent views see Grube, loc. cit. in n. 10 above. Taking the view that Homer certainly does not intend the conduct of his gods to be a moral example, Grube does concede 'the very first glimmerings' of a moralistic attitude to divinity in his poems.

fashion among contemporary scholars. Some prefer to explain Athene's favour for Odysseus in terms of early religious cults. It might, for example, have originated in her early function as the protectress of the Mycenaean kings[14] (though this would not explain her special interest in Odysseus), or else from her rôle as Goddess of the Palace[15] (so that she would be zealous to secure the safe homecoming of a pious prince like Odysseus). Theories of this kind can illuminate the historical background to the Homeric poems, and they support the view that Athene's patronage of Odysseus was not an invention of Homer. But they fail to throw any light on the subtler and more personal relationship between the goddess and the hero. Another theory is based on the hypothesis that the early Greek divinities can be separated into Olympian and chthonic powers. Athene, it is suggested, represents the Olympian influence on Odysseus's career: Hermes (being the father of Autolycus according to post-Homeric sources) represents the chthonic influence. Odysseus's nature is 'polarized' between these two antipodal powers. This explanation presents an attractively clear schematization of the two main external forces on Odysseus's evolution, the hereditary influence of his maternal ancestry and the supernatural aid of Athene. But one may doubt whether so humanistic an author as Homer would be satisfied with a strictly theological rationale of this kind. Besides, despite the efforts of contemporary writers to keep terms like 'chthonic' from acquiring moral values, it seems a fundamental instinct of human nature, ancient and modern, to identify qualities like 'dark', 'underground', with cruelty and evil, and 'bright', 'heavenly', with kindness and goodness—which leads one back to a moralistic interpretation.

One could also explain Athene's rôle in terms of literary genre. In the previous chapter it was suggested that Autolycus represents a folk element in the Odysseus myth. Athene, as Homer portrays her, belongs to the loftier style of the epic. Her constant surveillance of Odysseus's career, especially in the *Odyssey*, does in a sense run parallel with Homer's constant efforts to prevent his princely hero from degenerating into a mere Wily Lad. But this can hardly be [38/39] more than an incidental, perhaps only an accidental, parallelism. His Athene is much

---

[14] Cf. E. R. Dodds, *The Greeks and the irrational* (Berkeley, 1951), p. 54, with a reference to Nilsson's *Minoan-Mycenaean Religion*, 2nd edn., pp. 491 ff. See also C. Ghislau, *Beschouwingen over de Athene figur bij Homerus* (Leiden, 1929), pp. 41–3.

[15] Cf. C. Seltman, *The twelve Olympians* (London, 1952), pp. 50–51, for Athene as Palace Goddess. On pp. 59–60 he admits some symbolism in the myth of Athene's birth from the head of Zeus but begs a large question in calling it the 'mind' and 'brain' of Zeus. He concludes: 'So Athene, sprung from the brain of Zeus, is the symbol and the patroness of *sophia*, which means "skill-plus-wisdom", and therefore is the protectress of every man and woman who is definitely keen on and good at his or her job'. This fits her attitude to Odysseus well, but Seltman is referring here to the fully developed post-Homeric concept of Athene. Chaignet, p. 192, discusses Athene's two aspects, as Πρόμαχος and as Μηχανῖτις, in connection with Odysseus.

more than a Muse, and it would be perverse, indeed, to try to find anything like a primeval Battle of the Books in his poems. Yet, it is not altogether impossible that tellers of folk-tales in Homer's time may have felt indignant at the slenderness of Autolycus's rôle in Homer's version of Odysseus's story, and may have seen Athene as a personification of the more sophisticated literature that would soon eclipse their art.

These moralistic, religious, and literary interpretations seem too rigid and limited to account for the fullness of Homer's comprehensive humanism. Homer is supremely interested in persons, both as individuals and in society. Everything in his poems is subordinated to the interests and fortunes of human beings. One fundamental problem seems to have challenged Homer as it challenged every great humanistic writer after him, the problem of human suffering. The conventions of the epic style prescribed an atmosphere of violence and suffering. Ostensibly an epic poet had to glorify war and slaughter, if he was to use the genre at all. Yet again and again Homer implies that he hated the effects of war and deplored the destructivenss of heroic passion and heroic folly. Whether Homer was in advance of his own time (as distinct from the Heroic Age) in this or was simply voicing a general reaction from archaic violence, one cannot tell. But undeniably there is a great difference between his attitude towards death and destruction and that implied in the early sagas of Western Europe.

It may be, then, that Homer used the Athene-Odysseus relationship to express his humaner instincts, his desire for a less violent order of society, within the militaristic conventions of the early epic. Odysseus had two supreme qualities, intelligence and gentleness. Intelligence *per se* is ambiguous. In an Autolycus it becomes greedy, selfish, and odious. But used to promote the common good of society it becomes the chief instrument of civilization. One cannot, indeed, say that the use Athene makes of Odysseus's intelligence is unreservedly public-spirited. Her favour is limited to the Greeks. Yet despite this partisanship, if one compares Odysseus's conduct under her guidance with the self-centred policy of an Autolycus there is some ethical progress here. Under Athene's influence Odysseus's cleverness is used *pro bono nostro* not merely *pro bono meo*. The highest use of intelligence—for the good of all mankind—had still long to wait for its fulfillment.

Thus one of the two qualities that Athene fostered in Odysseus [39/40] was the power of applying his hereditary intelligence to public service, through his innate self-restraint and patience. In this way she made him supremely serviceable for destroying Troy. Agamemnon's arrogance, Achilles's pride, Ajax's stolidity, Menelaus's lack of drive, rendered these loftier chieftains inadequate for her purpose. Here Athene seems to express Homer's own view of human society. The only kind of man that one can trust to bring a complex crisis to a safe conclusion is a man like Odysseus. Passionate heroism, glorious as it is, disrupts society and causes senseless destruction.

But what then does Homer intend by Athene's special liking for Odysseus's other outstanding quality, his gentleness and courtesy? Perhaps he implies something like this: intelligence, even when superbly under control and unselfishly directed to the public interest, is not enough to redeem a man or a society from knavery or savagery. Or, to look at it from the point of view of reputation rather than conduct, mere intelligence may win admiration but it will never win affection. Some warmer quality is needed. Homer's own poems illustrate this well; Virgil's even better. What eventually wins the reader's heart is not the impressive intellectual qualities of their style and design, but their pervading compassionateness, even tenderness, for suffering humanity. The quality that Athene admires in Odysseus is not so profoundly humane as this. But, whether one uses the terms 'civilized', or 'gentle', or 'courteous', for it, it does sometimes reach out towards that deeper compassion, as one sees in Odysseus's speech to Amphinomus. It is certainly an advance on the selfish indifference of an Autolycus or the angry arrogance of an Agamemnon.

Odysseus is not, indeed, the only Homeric hero to possess this quality of civilized gentleness. Nestor, with all his senile failings, is intuitively gentle: so is Menelaus. It is significant that these two with Odysseus are the only Greeks whom Homer portrays safe and happy at home again after the war. One other courteous and gentle knight had to die at the hands of a hero of the more primitive type. This was Hector. But Homer, perhaps, meant to imply that gentleness alone is not enough, either. One must be clever as well, clever enough not to fight an irresistible foe and not to let an Athene lure one to death. More probably, however, the reason was that, being a Trojan in a saga of Greek prowess, Hector had to die. He and his equally courteous and gentle father, Priam, are the two most tragic figures in the *Iliad*—civilized men doomed to fight and die in a barbaric conflict. (Shakespeare in his *Troilus and Cressida* makes [40/41] much of this.) Inescapably, Homer implies, in a world of hostile Greek and Trojan warriors there must be Andromaches who mourn gentle husbands, besides Penelopes who rejoice at their return. In the conventional framework of heroic poetry there must always be undeserving losers like Hector as well as deserving winners like Odysseus. Homer accepts this as an essential condition both of his literary genre and of all militaristic societies—but not without compassion.

Perhaps this is what Homer mainly meant or felt in his account of Athene's relations with Odysseus. As has been emphasized, it is not a static relationship. It grows and becomes more personal up to its psychological climax when Odysseus first sets foot on Ithaca again. What would be more natural than that this development expressed a development in the poet's own mind as he composed the poems? It would be a remarkable and unusual phenomenon for a poet to retain exactly the same conception of his chief hero in the course of composing nearly thirty thousand lines. Homer, as he described scene after scene of carnage and passion in the *Iliad,* may have felt a need for some symbol of faith in humanity, some hope of salvation from the Minotaur that lurks in the labyrinth of every man's dominant passion, if he was to escape despair. The final scene between Priam and Achilles in the *Iliad* provided one answer to the problem of pain and death. But its tragic resignation, for all its sombre magnificence, is desolate and hopeless. In contrast, the end of the *Odyssey,* with its promise of peace and reconciliation, is reassuring and confident. The pessimism of archaic heroism yields to confidence in an emergent humanism.[16]

Was this portrait of Odysseus and Athene drawn from contemporary figures and conditions known to Homer; or was it a prophetic anticipation of future trends in human destiny, like Dante's conception of Ulysses the explorer? Unfortunately the uncertainty of Homer's date, combined with ignorance about the personal qualities of people in archaic Greece, prevents any sure answer here. But it has always been a quality of poetic genius to discover potentialities in human nature as well as to describe its already active powers. It is possible that Homer in his development of Odysseus's personality, and especially in his development of Odysseus's relationship with Athene, saw qualities of the emergent Greek genius which were not yet established in contemporary society—in other words, that in Homer's Odysseus there is a foreshadowing of men like Solon, Peisistratus, Themistocles, and Pericles, who, under the [41/42] aegis of a less vindictive Athene, established the foundations of European civilization.

If this suggestion is valid it is not simply another form of allegorical interpretation. Allegory implies telling a story with an intentional second meaning, or, from the interpreter's point of view, seeing two meanings in one narrative. The process described in the previous paragraph is not allegorical in this sense. It is better described as creative symbolism, by which an artist arrives at a deeper understanding of his subject (which for Homer was human nature) by thought and intuition. Homer's Odysseus and Athene are obviously not *both* themselves *and* figures of later Athenian civilization, even to the extent that Circe can be interpreted as being both an actual person and an emblem of sensuality. Odysseus and Athene as Homer presents them are not emblems of anything. They are essentially persons acting in and acting on human society. But in their mutual relationship, as it grew in his

---

[16] For a different conclusion, but on similar lines, cf. Levy, p. 144: 'the shift of focus [between the *Iliad* and the *Odyssey*] from spiritual conflict to equilibrium seems rather to belong to the old age of the real or symbolic author of the Greek epics. At the conclusion of the dark era, it may be conjectured, the non-epic qualities came to be admired. The *Odyssey* represents an involuntary revolt against the bitter and joyful (?) heroism of the *Iliad,* on the part of an old man or a dying epoch'. And p. 145: 'The self-control of Odysseus makes him a hero no longer dependent upon *menos* or *mana*. He is without passion (?), like Rama and Aeneas, and so belongs to a new civilization. This is an epic of transition'.

imagination, Homer may have seen potentialities that could raise humanity above both the selfish trickeries of an Autolycus and the insensate pride of the average Achaean hero. [42]

Odysseus, the Inner Man

CHARLES H. TAYLOR, JR.

THE VITALITY OF ODYSSEUS' ADVENTURES DURING HIS TRAVELS HOME HAS always fascinated readers of the *Odyssey*. Their extraordinary diversity is generally thought today to derive from the collection in Books Five through Twelve of motifs from a wide range of folk tales. But a variety of sources for Odysseus' adventures does not prove an absence of unity among them. On the contrary, their artistic unity has been felt so strongly by some critics that they have developed elaborate arguments showing that these adventures form a logical progression in the moral and social education of the hero. Only after learning from them, they claim, is Odysseus fit to return to Ithaca. Such arguments are often enlightening in their interpretation of individual episodes, and Odysseus does gain from some of his adventures experience which is valuable to him later. Nevertheless, Odysseus is basically, as Cedric Whitman puts it, "a fixed personality," equipped from the beginning to manage almost any situation in which he finds himself. Unlike Achilles, Odysseus experiences no division of the will.

Yet we remain confronted with the feeling that these marvelous encounters, so many of them imbued with magic or the supernatural, have a consistent bearing on the hero's role in the poem. Instead of depicting primarily the progressive development of the hero, they reveal the nature of his already developed character. They enable us to understand why he is able to achieve what he does and what the meaning of that achievement is.

Odysseus' goal throughout his adventures is his destined return to Ithaca. W. B. Stanford distinguishes Homer's Odysseus from many of his followers in the Ulyssian tradition by terming him a "centripetal" hero. His basic urge, Stanford reminds us, is not to explore but to make his way home.

It has been pointed out frequently that this desire to return is motivated [569/570] by the Homeric hero's characteristic devotion to

Charles H. Taylor, Jr., "The Obstacles to Odysseus' Return: Identity and Consciousness in *The Odyssey*," *The Yale Review*, L (Summer 1961), 569–580. Copyright by Yale University. Reprinted by permission of the author and the publisher.

fame and reputation. Odysseus would always be honored for having been the cleverest of the Greeks at Troy, but only when he regains his place as King of Ithaca can he complete his fame as the most resourceful of men, equal to any challenge.

Intent on his reputation, Odysseus is naturally concerned with his name. In the Cyclops episode, his pride in his name leads him to taunt the monster with the identity of his conqueror, thereby enabling Polyphemus to call upon him the savage wrath of Poseidon. From this rash act, Odysseus learns that it is sometimes essential to keep his name to himself, as we see him do later both in his anonymous approach to the Phaeacians and in the disciplined maintenance of his disguise upon his arrival in Ithaca. But these disguises are only temporary sacrifices of his identity for the present in the interest of establishing it beyond compare for the future. Rash or cautious, Odysseus' dedication to his reputation always reflects his care for his identity.

Many of the extraordinary obstacles to Odysseus' return are in the form of temptations. Yet they are not so much temptations to sexual immorality or social irresponsibility as they are temptations to the surrender of his individual identity. The encounter with the Lotus-eaters epitomizes many of the temptations which follow. Feeding on the lotus makes Odysseus' men νόστου λαθέσθαι (IX, 97), "forget their homeward journey." They desire instead to live like vegetarian animals and resist being brought back to the world of human hardships and responsibilities. The eater of the lotus becomes like an infant who is well-fed and contented, for the environment supports him without demanding anything in return. The lotus-eater loses all consciousness of self, of being an individual with origins of his own. For a man of Odysseus' powerful intelligence this is an easy temptation to resist, easier than some of those which follow. He quickly recognizes that eating the lotus is self-destructive, for he tells the Phaeacians that it was not literal death which the Lotus-eaters planned for his men, but the narcotic effects of the lotus instead. That this holds no attraction for Odysseus underscores an important dimension of his heroic character. He is always conscious of who he is and of what he wants to achieve and is never willing to trade this consciousness for some kind of euphoria.

The most obvious menace to Odysseus' identity during his travels is [570/571] death by water. To drown at sea, Poseidon's constant threat, is to vanish utterly from the world of men. This is a fate far worse than death in battle, a natural end to a heroic career. More than once Odysseus wishes he had fallen at Troy, for thus at least he could have bequeathed his son a famous name. Facing instead what seems a hopeless struggle against Poseidon's awful power, he must resist many times the temptation to allow himself to die. Once, the temptation is explicit, when he debates whether he should drown himself after his companions have let the winds out of the bag, while on other occasions the temptation is implied in his expressions of dismay when he thinks he has been saved to no avail. His profound disappointment makes his knees quake when after swimming for two days and two nights he finds himself off the isle of Scheria only to discover that reefs and cliffs make the shore unapproachable. By this time, however, he has learned from Achilles in Hades that life, wretched as it may be, is always preferable to death. So, despite his misery and exhaustion, he weighs the alternatives with careful discrimination, trying to decide whether to attempt a risky landing or to expose himself again to the open ocean. He refuses to relax his intelligence and permit himself to disappear in the unknown depths of the engulfing sea.

In many of Odysseus' other adventures, the temptation to surrender his individual identity is perhaps less obvious, but no less real. Beautiful and soft, Calypso carries the appeal of the eternal feminine. She offers Odysseus much more than the lotus can: not only an escape from physical suffering, but lovely sexuality and eternal life as well. Not only will the environment nurture him like an infant in the womb—note the image of Calypso's cave—but, unlike the infant, he will retain his identity as a male and be able to share the pleasures of sexual differentiation with the goddess. But this is all he will retain of his identity, for with Calypso he can no longer be Odysseus the hero. If he accepts Calypso's offer, he will be no more than the consort of a minor goddess. Impervious to death he will remain, to be sure, but for that very reason he will be unable to run any of the risks which make survival a heroic achievement. Instead, he would have to surrender himself to the instinctual female principle, physically vital, but intellectually and spiritually lifeless. Odysseus' surrender to Calypso would involve the loss both of his outward identity as πολύτλας Odysseus, the man who suffers and endures, and of his inner identity as a separate [571/572] individual free to come to terms with life on his own. He would have no self, but would exist only as an appendage to the goddess, serving her desire.

Odysseus refuses Calypso's offer of bodily immortality for the same reasons that he resists bodily death: in neither case could he preserve his whole being as Odysseus. Fleshly immortality with Calypso is no more complete than the fleshless immortality so forcefully disparaged by Achilles.

Calypso, Athena tells Zeus at the beginning of the poem, is trying to make Odysseus forget Ithaca; the analogy with the temptation of the Lotus-eaters is clear enough. What is perhaps less clear is that Circe's charms are directed to the same end. She drugs Odysseus' men, not at once to turn them to swine, but ἵνα πάγχυ λαθοίατο πατρίδος αἴης (X, 236), "that they might quite forget their native land." Only after the drug takes effect does she strike them with her rod and pen them in her sties. The sequence of events is significant because it presents the metamorphosis as a corollary of forgetting one's native land. The transformation of man to animal is a vivid image of the lessening of human conscious-

ness which forgetting one's origins implies. Men who let themselves
be drugged into a lower level of awareness by the destructive power of
the enchantress, the story suggests, become no more than animals to
be kept as the woman's pets.

But for Odysseus the consequences of encountering Circe are very
different. Homer says that Hermes gave Odysseus the herb Moly as an
antidote to the enchantress' potion. Yet who has a better claim to divine
aid than Odysseus? Possessing more intelligence and will-power than
other men, he is ideally equipped to resist the hypnotic powers of
Circe's enchantment. She herself never complains that Odysseus has
been aided by a god; rather, her response to Odysseus' refusal to suc-
cumb to her potion is that he is a man whose mind is proof against
enchantment. Unable to subdue him, with characteristic womanly
duality she desires to surrender herself instead, imploring him to come
to her bed. He, in turn, is obligated to accept her offer, once he is
assured he can do so on his own terms. To avoid submission to Circe's
destructive power does not mean that her positive feminine values need
be rejected. On the contrary, Odysseus' heroic individuality is partly
defined by his capacity to encounter the essence of the female principle
without being overwhelmed by it. [572/573]

Circe, then, embodies both the destructive and the creative aspects
of the feminine, and Odysseus profits from the latter. It is scarcely surprising that he finds her exotic knowledge and complex sexuality more
interesting than Calypso's immortal ease. He enjoys her company so
much that even after a year he has to be prodded by his men into
continuing on his way.

Though Odysseus temporarily loses his sense of urgency with
Circe, there is never any question whether he intends ultimately to
resume his journey. There is, indeed, only one occasion when he consciously wishes to yield to a temptation, even though he knows it would
mean his destruction. Despite Circe's explicit warning of the mortal
danger, he wishes to stop and hear the Sirens' song. Since he takes the
precautions Circe has advised, he is unable to yield, but it is revealing
that this one time he wishes he could.

The unique appeal of the Sirens emphasizes once again Odysseus'
concern for his personal identity. Besides embodying the seductive
attractions of feminine allure and poetic song, the Sirens' words are
especially calculated to make Odysseus wish to yield. They appeal to
him in terms of their knowledge of his renown as "great glory of the
Achaeans," their appreciation of the heroes' suffering at Troy, and
their understanding of events to come. Thus it seems to Odysseus that
his conscious desire for identity, reputation, and knowledge is at one
with his masculine urge to enjoy the feminine. The irony is that this
illusory union of his higher and lower desires will mean in fact the loss
of his life and thus of the heroic identity for which he cares so much.
The apparent wholeness of the Sirens' appeal makes it an irresistible

temptation and temporarily causes Odysseus to lose control of his will.

But in the final trial before his return to Ithaca, Odysseus is magnificently aware of his true objectives. Though he is never personally moved by the possibility of marrying Nausicaa, he is careful not to preclude it as a possibility. Only after he has been guaranteed passage home and everything is prepared for his departure, does he reveal who he is. His opening address to Nausicaa when she comes upon him by the shore is a supremely subtle invitation to consider him as a potential husband, yet it does not commit him as an acknowledged suitor. Although she is not a goddess and cannot make him immortal, in one way Nausicaa is more attractive than Calypso. Because she is mortal, with [573/574] her Odysseus could take his place in a world in which heroic action and identity are achievable. Still, the utopian setting of Phaeacian life tends to vitiate the need for heroism. Once again the temptation is to escape from the struggle for survival which requires such alertness. With Nausicaa, Odysseus would not have to be subordinate to a woman (unless we feel that Arete's domination of Alcinous implies this possibility) but he would have to accept, without earning it, the unheroic relaxation which music, feasting, clean linen, and gregarious sociability encourage. Moreover, whatever reputation he might achieve in Scheria could never be of a piece with his fame as Odysseus the inventor of the Trojan Horse and Lord of the Ithacans. As Odysseus, he would not be eligible for Nausicaa's hand, having already a wife and obligations of his own. Concerned with his identity, he would naturally prefer to return, even to the enormous challenges which he knows will face him in Ithaca.

Thus it is clear that whether Odysseus faces a temptation or a threat, an opportunity to evade suffering or a danger of being crushed by it, the challenge is always to his survival as Odysseus. The essentially equivalent menace of the temptation to ease, on the one hand, and of the threat to life, on the other, is nicely suggested in the encounter with the Laestrygonians. There, Odysseus' ship alone survives because he refuses to be tempted by the smooth waters of the protected harbor. To seek the easier resting place is to invite destruction. By lying outside, although exposed to the discomforts of poorer protection from the weather, he is able to cut his cables and flee when the frightful attack of the man-eating Laestrygonians begins. Because he is willing to accept more suffering than other men, Odysseus avoids being swallowed up by the monstrous giants.

Despite the variety of situations which they present, then, Odysseus' adventures during his homeward journey repeatedly confront him with some kind of threat to his identity as hero. But they have more in common than that, for nearly every threat also manifests the forces at work in man's natural environment. Whether Odysseus is endangered by predatory monsters, narcotic herbs, feminine sexuality, or the violence of the sea, he experiences in each case the realm of nature and instinct. The strength of his opponents is rooted either in the external natural world or in the non-rational elements within human nature. [574/575]

Poseidon, Odysseus' greatest enemy, is only superficially detached from the natural environment by his designation as an Olympian deity. Of all the Olympians, he is the most immersed in the elements. Although he attends gatherings on Olympus, his sphere of action is the Mediterranean waters and his home is deep in the Aegean Sea. Three of his epithets tie him directly to the earth, for he is γαιήοχος, "earth-holder," and ἐνοσίχθων or ἐννοσίγαιος, "earth-shaker." Moreover, the most satisfactory explanation of his name is that he was once πόσις of Δήω, spouse of Da or Demeter, the earth goddess. The evidence now strongly suggests that he was chthonic in his origins, and it is therefore the less surprising that as he actually functions in the *Odyssey* he is still so—the god of a violent sea.

It has been remarked that the Homeric poems are remarkably free of the chthonic cults and powers which were widespread in contemporary popular culture. Of chthonic cults this is certainly true; in the *Odyssey*, even the earthbound deities Calypso and Circe are carefully subordinated to the Olympian system, as Hermes' errands show. Poseidon, as we have noted, is theologically an important part of the system, and the monstrous Polyphemus is given an Olympian heritage. But like Poseidon, Calypso in her cave and Circe keeping men as domesticated animals are indeed chthonic personalities.

Homer's recognition of the influence of these earthbound divinities never takes the form of ritual devotions, but it is respectful nevertheless. Odysseus must demonstrate his ability to withstand their powers, whether seductive or destructive, without scorning them. It is partly his contempt for Polyphemus which brings him so much pain at the hand of Poseidon. He suffers for foolishly supposing that a monster might behave like a civilized host and for taunting the brute whom he has duped. Only after he has lived out the consequences of this disdain and come to terms with many representatives of instinct and violence can he achieve his return.

It is noteworthy that in all Odysseus' adventures in Books Nine through Twelve, excepting the single intercession of Hermes on Aeaea, Odysseus receives no Olympian aid. His opponents, for all their nominal subjection to Olympian authority, are left to exercise their powers unopposed by champions of Olympian values. Indeed, Odysseus receives more aid from Circe, following his conquest of her, and from [575/576] the inhabitants of the underworld to which she directs him, than he does from anything but his own wits and determination. Thus we can say that chthonian powers are not so much absent from the *Odyssey* as they are subdued or brought into his service by the hero's extraordinary feats of will and intelligence.

The Olympian whose neglect of Odysseus during his travels is most conspicuous is Athene. When she reveals herself to him after he has been put ashore on Ithaca, Odysseus pointedly reminds her that she had showed him no favor during the years between his departure from Troy and his arrival at the land of the Phaeacians. Prior to leaving Ogygia, he had to manage without her aid. Yet when the poem opens, it is she who is urging Zeus to free him from Calypso so that he can pursue his homeward journey. He has assumed for her by this time a very personal value and she interests herself in all his subsequent adventures.

In their spirited conversation in Book Thirteen, Athena tells Odysseus that she reveres him because he is, in Rieu's words, "so civilized, so intelligent, so self-possessed" (ἐπητής, ἀγχίνοος, and ἐχέφρων, XIII, 332). These are the qualities which distinguish Odysseus from other men, including other heroes; they are the hallmarks of his identity. We see his intelligent self-possession again and again as he parries the threats and blandishments of his opponents. It is for this keen-witted firmness of mind that Athene becomes devoted to him.

Like Odysseus, Athene is intelligent, cunning, and strong-willed, possessing as a goddess the attributes which enable the hero to survive. When she comes to his assistance, she reinforces his strengths, but only after he has proven himself capable of survival without her aid. Rather than acting as the effective cause of his success, she stands instead as a symbol or projection of that already within Odysseus which makes him successful.

Hesiod tells us that Athene sprang full-grown from the head of Zeus. Conceived the daughter of Metis, her associations with wise counsel and the values of the head are as evident in her origins as in her adoption of Odysseus. She represents that intelligent awareness which characterizes the hero.

Probing the meaning of their alliance more deeply, we find Athene, Odysseus' genuinely Olympian advocate, in direct opposition to Poseidon [576/577] and the other essentially earthbound powers. Just as she emblems Odysseus' rational consciousness, the chthonic forces she opposes symbolize the non-rational core of man's nature. Projected as external threats and temptations, they image in reality the powers which menace the identity of the hero from beneath the surface of consciousness.

The analogy between these external forces and the biological foundations of human nature is suggested in the poem through the dangers of sleep. In the debacle with the bag of winds, Odysseus fails to reach Ithaca because sleep overcomes him. Though the body lives, the saving consciousness which defines the hero departs. It was "cruel sleep" (X, 68–69), Odysseus tells Aeolus, which was his undoing. Later, he is "in pitiless sleep" (XII, 372) when his comrades slaughter the Oxen of the Sun. Odysseus cannot be held responsible for the failure of his men on this occasion, for he has warned them fully.

Nevertheless, it is while he sleeps that the catastrophe occurs. Similarly, the youthful Elpenor loses his life because he has neither the will-power nor the intelligence to dispel the fogginess induced by wine and sleep. Unlike Odysseus, he is not proof against enchantment.

It is remarkable, too, how many of the specific threats to Odysseus suggest symbolically the magnetic attraction of the unconscious in the human psyche. The sea is an ancient emblem of the whole realm of the irrational, and drowning in the sea a compelling image of being over-whelmed from below, returning to the elemental. In the picture of Odysseus clinging doggedly to the fig tree above Charybdis' whirlpool we find a striking representation of the struggle between conscious determination and the downward pull of subconscious forces. Calypso's womblike cave and Circe's pet swine depict the appeals of returning to infancy or animality where one lives unaware of personal selfhood. Like Calypso, Polyphemus is an earthbound cave-dweller. As the son of Poseidon he is allied with the natural violence of the sea. Moreover, his identifying feature is his single eye, an arresting image of half-con-sciousness. With his primitive vision, he is naturally both hostile and vulnerable to Odysseus' civilized intelligence.

Thus it seems to me that Odysseus' struggles for survival and identity convey more than the recognized Homeric values of fame and reputation as their ends. To apply the metaphor both more personally and more broadly, part of the poem's appeal rests in the way it suggests the [577/578] struggle for individual consciousness against the forces for primitive absorption in the instinctual world. This is a fundamental meaning of nearly every hero story. It is a struggle we all experience as we strive to achieve a degree of genuine individuality and self-aware-ness. In Odysseus, the struggle displays a fixed personality more than a growing one because, unlike ourselves, he almost always wins.

Telemachus' gradual discovery of the meaning of his identity as his father's son, on the other hand, shows the normal growth of the youth-ful personality. As he puts away the youthful childishness of helpless daydreaming about his father's return, he becomes equipped by his own sea-journey to help Odysseus meet the greatest challenge of his heroic career. With determined cunning, they effect together the de-struction of the suitors. The poet emphasizes Telemachus' developing maturity by having him displace his mother as head of the household in his father's absence. While Telemachus outgrows subjection to the personal mother, Odysseus refuses to submit to the elemental forces of the whole domain of nature.

Bruno Snell insists that the abstractions which deal with the nature of the self are not present in Homer's vocabulary. But to note that it was not possible for Homer to discuss such problems abstractly does not mean that therefore they are not problems for him at all. It is widely acknowledged that one of Homer's ways of representing inner events, particularly those caused by non-rational impulses, is to project them by means of the divine machinery in his poems. My point is that the extraordinary encounters of Odysseus in his travels function in much the same manner.

E. R. Dodds shows that Homeric man believed what was not rational in his behavior was not really a part of himself, and the resulting projection of the irrational upon external powers produced a culture in which shame, not guilt, was dominant. The shift from shame-culture to guilt-culture in the centuries between Homer and Aeschylus he ascribes partly to progressive recognition that most of the evil men do, whether consciously determined or not, is actually generated from within themselves.

Increasing consciousness does bring with it increased moral awareness, and, often, a sense of sin. Yet, as I see it, another reason there is more guilt consciousness in the later writers is that they have more [578/579] to feel guilty about. Dodds himself conjectures that their sense of guilt is somehow related to the extremely patriarchal society which had by then evolved. Besides attributing the sense of guilt to repressed feelings of hostility toward the father-order, as Dodds does, I would assign it primarily to unconscious recognition that the earthbound and all it stands for have been undervalued. The powerful feelings of guilt are derived ultimately from undue disregard of the claims of the nonrational. An additional tension would be caused by rebellion against the consciously accepted patriarchy, but the Aeschylean "haunted, oppressive atmosphere" of which Dodds speaks springs essentially from the vengeance in the unconscious of the matriarchal Furies.

There is none of this atmosphere in the *Odyssey*. Although Odysseus, as we have seen, stands for the values of consciousness, there is not yet that contempt for the feminine and the irrational which brings with it a sense of guilt. This will come later because the trend of conscious development is patriarchal and is accompanied after a time by reduced esteem for the female. Erich Neumann observes that since the unconscious is generally given a feminine character, the depreciation of the unconscious in cultural development becomes confused with a belittling of feminine values. In the *Odyssey*, however, there is no such confusion. The characterizations of Helen, of Arete, of Nausicaa, and of Penelope, not to mention Athene, show each to be worthy of respect and admiration. Odysseus (or Telemachus) honors each appropriately and there is no hint that each, in her own way, is not at least the equal of her masculine opposite. Odysseus accepts the favors of Calypso and of Circe, even as he refuses to surrender his will to them. Although Poseidon is masculine, we have noted that he is closely related to the chthonic feminine. He too must be respected, as we see both in the dire consequences of wounding his son and in Teiresias' insistence upon Odysseus' duty to carry his homage to a people who think an oar a "winnowing fan."

Odysseus' quest for identity is in fact inextricably bound up with the feminine. In seeking the wholeness of his being, he passes through intimate experience with various embodiments of archetypal woman, each reflecting some aspect of what he as masculine hero lacks. The majority of these women pose the temptation of a return to the matriarchal order, where a man may be killed or be comfortable, but is [579/580] dead as a hero in either case. Athene's femininity alone is not earthbound and instinctual, for she is associated instead with those intellectual and spiritual values which distinguish civilized human beings. In their purest form these qualities are mysterious and reside as much above normal consciousness as the instinctual do below it. Thus they too have a feminine coloring and are frequently represented by women in the metaphors of art.

But for Odysseus throughout his journey, Penelope is the woman he seeks. For all her beauty, Athene's Olympian dignity offers no biological warmth and her immortality disqualifies her as a heroic consort. Only Penelope shares Odysseus' intellectual alertness and is yet so alluring that she can represent the feminine counterpart of his heroic individuality. Whether or not we agree with the argument that in their conversation by the fireside in Book Nineteen Penelope consciously recognizes Odysseus, we cannot doubt that at the least she senses intuitively the need to force a crisis with the suitors. Yet she will not acknowledge Odysseus later without testing him in her own terms; her equality as his partner is nowhere more convincingly displayed than in her subtle allusion to moving their bed. At the same time, there is no more vivid evidence of her spontaneous femininity than her touching surrender after Odysseus' angry response. Penelope embodies in attainable reality the combination of qualities which the Sirens imply in false illusion. Her depiction throughout the poem as Odysseus' loyal wife emphasizes that she alone can carry for him both the higher and the lower feminine values. In regaining Penelope, Odysseus reclaims something of his own soul and so makes meaningful his resistance to the wiles of all the other women he meets on his way home. Having avoided submitting to the powers of the unconscious in a way which would destroy his identity, he is able finally to relate to them in the only way which will complete it.

This achievement makes Odysseus one of the wholest men in literature. For Homeric man, both the spirit and the flesh are indispensable, and this is why Odysseus refuses the immortalities both of Calypso and of Hades. Put another way, man must be conscious to be human, but he must come to terms with the unconscious to be whole. Divided as we have been since Homer's time by our awareness of the duality of human nature, the *Odyssey* continues to impress us with its vital image of an integrated man. [580]

Telemachus

HOWARD W. CLARKE

IT HAS LONG BEEN STANDARD WITH ANALYSTS THAT IF THE *Telemacheia* is not by another hand, then it is certainly distinct enough in treatment and integration to deserve its special name.[1] Nor are the reasons urging its separateness only aesthetic. First of all, Telemachus' position in the *Odyssey* raises questions about the political structure of Ithaca, or at least indicates that Homer has left much unsaid about the conditions of royal tenure. Odysseus' father Laertes, who is generally a blank in heroic mythology, has withdrawn to the country in sorrow over the loss of his son, but even before his retirement he does not seem to have ruled as king.[2] If Odysseus assumed the kingship as next in line and primogeniture were the rule, we might expect that Telemachus would have clear title to the throne after Odysseus failed to return from Troy. Such is not the case. Instead, the kingship is to be awarded to whoever marries Penelope—hence the dynastic ambitions of the Suitors and their menace to Odysseus and Penelope.

The dilemma in which this situation involves the Ithacans is obvious. On the one hand the old king has been made unfit for kingship through infirmity; on the other hand Telemachus is unqualified by youth and inexperience. Ithaca is trapped in the weakness of its leaders, the weakness of old age and the weakness of youth, senility and adolescence.[3] Odysseus alone combines exuberance and experience, and he is desperately needed. It is noteworthy too that when he returns not only does he save his family and his land, but the vitality of

---

[1] This essay, in a somewhat revised form, was originally one chapter of a dissertation accepted in partial fulfillment of the requirements for the degree of Doctor of Philosophy in Comparative Literature at Harvard University (*The Lion and the Altar: Myth, Rite, and Symbol in the Odyssey*, 1960). I am indebted to Professors Finley and Whitman, who directed this dissertation.

[2] Stanford sees Homer, "suggesting a latent father-son antagonism," *The Ulysses Theme* (Oxford, 1954), p. 60. Certainly mythology abounds in examples of the feared son who will depose his father; there is even the un-Homeric account of Circe's son by Odysseus slaying his father.

[3] Strength and vigor seem the qualifications for rule in Ithaca. M. I. Finley, *The World of Odysseus* (New York, 1954), p. 93.

Howard W. Clarke, "Telemachus and the *Telemacheia*," *American Journal of Philology*, LXXXIV (April 1963), 129–145. Reprinted by permission of the author and The Johns Hopkins Press.

his presence extends to [129/130] his father and son. For Laertes there is a sudden and miraculous transformation.[4]

Athene herself intervened to increase his royal stature. As he stepped out of the bath she made him seem taller and sturdier than before, so that his own son was amazed when he saw him looking like an immortal god.

Athena's powers here show symbolically how the presence of his beloved son has revitalized the aged Laertes. Nor is the Telemachus Odysseus meets in Book XVI and fights beside in XXII the same young man Athena found in I; but his transformation has been gradual, for not even a goddess can immediately infuse into a young man the wisdom accumulated in a lifetime's experience as hero and king. Laertes needed only to be revivified; he had already known the meaning of the heroic life. The process of Telemachus' introduction into that life is one of the purposes of the four books (and part of Book XV) commonly referred to as the *Telemacheia*. In a society where kingship depends upon merit as much as inheritance, the candidate must be prepared to prove his worth, as Telemachus will in Book XXII, but before the test he must know what it is he is fighting for. Pylos and Sparta can offer him examples.

The *Telemacheia* properly begins after the Council of the Gods when Athena visits Ithaca to hearten Odysseus' son and urge him to call an assembly of Ithacans and then set off to Sparta and Pylos in search of news about his father. Here she finds a despairing Telemachus lost in the dream-world that has become his since the Suitors made the real world intolerable. He is hoping that somehow Odysseus will appear "from somewhere" (115). It will be Athena's purpose in the next few books to rid Telemachus of his melancholy, to show him how in the heroic world dreams are translated into realities. Naturally, the heroic paradigm is from the Agamemnon myth.[5] [130/131]

You are no longer a child: you must put childish thoughts away. Have you not heard what a name Prince Orestes made for himself in the world when he killed the traitor Aegisthus for murdering his noble father? You, my friend —and what a tall and splendid fellow you have grown!—must be as brave as Orestes. Then future generations will sing your praises.

Athena's encouragement is not without its effect, but Telemachus' adolescent attempts to take charge are a fiasco.[6] He shocks Penelope quite unnecessarily, even cruelly, and then turns on the Suitors in a tone that must have been totally unexpected by them, for they too are

---

[4] XXIV, 368–71. Translation by E. V. Rieu.

[5] I, 297–302. Translation by E. V. Rieu.

[6] Athena is impressed by Telemachus' physical resemblance to his famous father, but his insecurity is such that he is even unsure of his own identity. "My mother says that I am my father's son, but for myself I do not know" (I, 215–16). The burden of the next few books is to harmonize Telemachus' inner and outer selves.

taken aback. But the New Telemachus lapses back into the Old Telemachus as soon as Antinous has a chance to distract him. He discourses vaguely on the nature of kingship, then is so uncertain of his own position (if, indeed, he is to succeed Odysseus) that he concedes the claims of the other princes. He then concludes lamely that he intends at least to control his own house. Not a very convincing display of newly found authority, but in his confusion Telemachus has at least raised the great question which Odysseus will answer: who is to be king of Ithaca? He has also asked what kingship means; and his tentative answer—an enrichment of one's house and an increase of honor (392–3)—will soon be confirmed in the glory and wealth of the courts of Nestor and Menelaus. This awakening to royal prerogatives is critical, for it will be his initial preparation for the coming struggle to preserve the same privileges of rightful kingship in Ithaca. When the first book ends with the touching scene of Eurycleia tending Telemachus as he prepares for bed, Homer has completed the picture of Telemachus' surroundings. He is in some way subject to Penelope, although he has now dared to bridle at her authority; he is attended by an aged nursemaid; and he is bedevilled and oppressed by insolent Suitors. Odysseus is away, Laertes is off on his farm, and Telemachus has only two women to support him against the menace of 108 would-be usurpers.

Book II does little to convince us that Telemachus has profited by Athena's encouragement. His indictment of the Suitors and appeal to their non-existent sense of justice and his plea that [131/132] they regard Zeus and Themis is clearly not the kind of speech his father would deliver, and whatever faint effect it might have had on their consciences is dissipated when he concludes his words with a sudden burst of tears. The crowd pities him, less so the Suitors, particularly the cynical Antinous, who goes on to shift the blame to Penelope for her funeral shroud ruse. Once again Telemachus' attempts at oratory have been abortive and ineffective, but once again he has raised a central theme of the *Odyssey*: the justice of Odysseus, the injustice of the Suitors. Furthermore, the terms of his speech, just as in Book I, foreshadow elements of his experience in III and IV. He describes Odysseus' kingship as fatherly in its gentleness (47), and he will see gentle and exemplary fathers in Nestor and Menelaus; the food wasted by the Suitors in their revels in Ithaca (55–6) will be consumed in order and harmony in the feasts in Pylos and Sparta; the wine that intoxicates the Suitors in Ithaca (57) will become a tranquillizer in Sparta; and the weakness he protests here (60–1) will be overcome by confidence and resolve before he sees Ithaca again. Telemachus next commences his preparations for his journey, but runs into the astonished protests of Eurycleia: "But there's no need at all for you to endure the hardships of wandering over the barren seas" (369–70). This feminine attraction to place is partly what Telemachus must overcome by becoming acquainted with the ways of the heroes who did suffer hardships at Troy and then had to return over the seas to the great centers of the Mycenaean age. But for all Telemachus' determination, Eurycleia's objection still stands; and to assert that Telemachus must rid himself of his feminine inhibitions is not a very convincing justification for his trip. That Telemachus intends to go off on a junket at this crucial time was duly noted by Analyst critics and made one of their reasons for the original separateness of the *Telemacheia*. In this objection, however, they were anticipated by Homer himself, not only here but also by Odysseus in XIII, 417, and Eumaeus in XIV, 178. All stress that this is the worst conceivable [132/133] time for Telemachus to leave Ithaca, what with the Suitors getting impatient and Penelope at her wit's end. To them the answer is provided by Athena in XIII, 422. Yes, she could have told Telemachus the truth about his father, but she wanted him to make the trip to win *Kleos*. The fact is that nothing Athena *told* Telemachus would have any lasting effect; what he needed before meeting his father was experience in heroic society, and this journey to Pylos and Sparta was the only resort. Telemachus had to be baptized into the heroic life, commune with its leaders, and be confirmed in its values or he would never be a trusted ally to his father or a fit successor to the kingship. *Kleos* ranks with *arete* as an honorific word in the heroic vocabulary, and it is only in places like Pylos and Sparta that Telemachus can absorb their meanings and prepare himself to merit them. It is true that this is a critical juncture in the affairs of Ithaca, but far from impeding Telemachus, it makes his journey all the more necessary. For it is at the truly critical periods of man's life—when he is most exposed—that he must appeal to an extra source of strength. Hence Telemachus' journey is neither unnecessary nor unmotivated, although the necessity is Telemachus himself and the motive transcends the averred search for information.

    Book III brings the travellers to the first stage of their journey, Nestor's citadel at Pylos. Here we are in the heroic world and Telemachus does not know how to act, what to do, how to approach the great man. Athena encourages him as the libation is offered, and Telemachus manages nicely in his first bout with the social forms of a kingly court, though not as deftly as Nestor's son Peisistratus, who had, after all, the benefit of growing up within this mannered society.[7] Nestor then [133/134] delivers a long speech, luxuriating in the recollected sorrows of the Trojan War and remarking Telemachus' re-

---

[7] Elaborate form is part of the heroic life; and the *Odyssey* is, generally, a very polite poem. The emphasis of the *Telemacheia* on manners subtly indicates an extra dimension to the threat the Suitors embody. Not only do they want to marry Penelope and slay Odysseus and Telemachus, they also want to destroy the whole facade of heroic manners. Themselves without courtesy, regard, tact, restraint, they would utterly decivilize Ithaca. Manners are important; they buttress conduct and give life style, grace, and ease; in a formalized society they can heavily influence conduct by providing it with traditional and customary patterns of action. All of this the barbarism of the Suitors would despoil.

semblance to his famous father.[8] In reminiscing about Troy, Nestor passes from Achilles to Ajax to Patroclus and finally to his own son Antilochus. He praises Odysseus for his good sense, tells how out of allegiance and piety Odysseus stayed behind with Agamemnon, and does not forget to remind Telemachus approvingly of the sterling example of Agamemnon's son Orestes. Telemachus picks up the hint, but then awkwardly blurts out his despair of ever seeing his father again, for which he is promptly chided by Athena. In the fully integrated society piety and manners are identical and Telemachus must learn to trim his private doubts accordingly. Athena leaves that evening and Telemachus is received into Nestor's palace where he sleeps beside Nestor's son Peisistratus. The next day Nestor arranges an elaborate banquet for Telemachus' crew and even has his youngest daughter, Polycaste, give Telemachus a bath. This is almost a rebirth, for out of it Telemachus emerges, "looking like a god" (III, 468). Nestor then gives him horses and a chariot and sends Peisistratus to accompany him in his way to Sparta. Athena is no longer with him; but he has been accepted into Nestor's household, bathed by his daughter, and is now being accompanied by his son. For Telemachus this has been a tonic experience after the desperation of his life at Ithaca, and at last he is ready to break out of the shell of his depression and uncertainty and make his way in broad heroic society.

Book IV opens with a scene of feasting and family cheer (the marriages of Menelaus' son and daughter) in the splendid palace of Menelaus. Here is a prosperity, a security, and a family intimacy that Telemachus had never known in Ithaca and only lately met in Pylos. Indeed, Homer's choice of details to contrast Menelaus and Sparta with Odysseus and Ithaca is subtle and exact. The primary complication of the *Odyssey* proper is the disunion of a family, whereas here we have an immediate awareness of union (the marriages) and reunion (Helen). And compare the joy and harmony of Menelaus' banquet with the pointless carousing of the Suitors. Nor has anything in Telemachus' limited experience prepared him for the magnificence [134/135] of Menelaus' palace, and before it even Peisistratus is impressed. Nevertheless, Telemachus is making progress; at the beginning of Book III the mere sight of a hero panicked him; here he seems quite sure of himself before Menelaus, and he can be forgiven his awe before the royal palace (his father, who has seen everything, is no less impressed by Alcinous' palace in Book VII). Manners are once again stressed: Menelaus' anger that hospitality is refused strangers, and his embarrassment when Telemachus weeps as he reminisces of Odysseus. And in the stories Menelaus tells there are little morals which can also be of use to Telemachus. Proteus, for example, tells Menelaus that he should have sacrificed to Zeus before embarking; Ajax' fate is an example to those who would blaspheme; and when Proteus tells Mene-

---

[8] Note the continuing reference to faithful sons—Antilochus, Peisistratus, Orestes.

laus of what happened to Agamemnon and then urges him to hurry back to his land as quickly as he can, Homer shows us that the point is not lost on Telemachus. He refuses to protract his stay in Sparta, and when Menelaus offers him three horses he has the wit and temerity to ask for a gift he can carry, not horses which are so impractical on Ithaca. Menelaus is impressed.

The *Telemacheia* next picks up in Book XV when Athena again visits Telemachus, this time in Sparta, and urges him to hasten back to Ithaca. His reaction is almost as precipitate as it was in I, but Peisistratus checks him: after all, there are ways of doing these things, and "a guest never forgets a host who has shown him kindness" (54–5). Telemachus frets through Menelaus' moralizing and the rituals of gift-giving, but by now he is aware of his responsibilities and feels himself a man of action; now it is more than he can stand to have to return to Pylos and brave Nestor's oppressive hospitality. Telemachus has been schooled in the forms of the heroic life in Books III and IV; in XV he has earned the right to transcend them. He can dispense with social obligations, for his own are infinitely more demanding. He must be about his father's business.

The last scene of the *Telemacheia*, the Theoclymenus episode, is puzzling.[9] Why is Theoclymenus brought in? Perhaps to [135/136] palliate murder in the face of Odysseus' treatment of the Suitors? Certainly Theoclymenus, like Odysseus, can say, "It is my fate to wander about the world" (XV, 276), and he is being pursued by the kinsmen of the man he has slain. And for the rest of the poem this relic of heroic world feuds will hover uneasily in the background like Conrad's Leggat, the secret sharer in Odysseus' revenge and a disturbing reminder of the random violence and blood guilt of the heroic age. But for Telemachus this decision to accept Theoclymenus demonstrates his newly won authority, that he has the right to give asylum, even hospitality, if he wants, to a murderer. Through Theoclymenus Homer can underscore the identity of Telemachus, show that he is now coming into his own and can afford his father the assistance Odysseus might have received from another Achaean hero on the fields before Troy. In this sense it is appropriate that the *Telemacheia* end with Theoclymenus interpreting an omen, a hawk appearing on the right with a dove in its talons, which he sees as signifying that, "No family in Ithaca is kinglier than yours; you will have power forever" (533–4). As a professional performance this is indeed drab, and as a prophecy it is so vague as to be meaningless. But it is not a prophecy; it is an accolade, a ceremony to complete the *Telemacheia;* by marking Telemachus' attainment to true sonhood. His doubts about his right to his royal patrimony are allayed, and he is rewarded with an assurance of future success. Theoclymenus' words signal an access of power that Telemachus will need in the days ahead.

9 Page criticizes it as too long an introduction for so unimportant a person: *The Homeric Odyssey* (Oxford, 1955), p. 84.

After Telemachus returns to Ithaca his fortunes are subordinated to his father's. This somewhat diminishes the impact of Telemachus' personality and Homer is not always successful in giving him something to do. Although he is potentially his father's most powerful ally against the Suitors, even Odysseus seems to ignore him when he tells Athena, "I am alone" (XX, 40). Of course, Telemachus shows his mettle: only a nod from Odysseus in XXI keeps him from stringing the bow, and he seems to do his share in the fight with the Suitors. He is exceptional [136/137] in his mercy, checking Odysseus from slaying Phemius the minstrel and Medon the herald, and relentless in his revenge, personally stringing up the unfaithful serving women. But if Telemachus does acquire some of his father's heroism, it is at the price of his own individuality. Homer seems conscious of this and goes to great lengths to let us know Telemachus is still around. But the glimpses he gives us are often of the "old" Telemachus, laughing (XXI, 105), sneezing (XVII, 541), and absentmindedly botching his father's plans (XXII, 154); Telemachus speaks out of turn (XXIII, 97–103), parades in borrowed feathers.

One answer here seems to be that the second half of the *Odyssey* belongs to its hero alone. Odysseus must be alone in center stage if his presence is to have the startling effect appropriate to the return of the hero. But no sooner is Odysseus back in Ithaca than he finds himself implicated in an intrigue to disarm the Suitors and an alliance to slay them. This involvement could detract from the interest in Odysseus if Homer had not manipulated his characters in such a way as to enhance the personality of Odysseus. *His family becomes Odyssean.* Penelope can even restrain herself from rushing into the arms of her husband. Instead she tests him in proper Odyssean fashion, with a self-control and cunning that must have warmed Odysseus' wary old heart. This transformation also affects Laertes, who, as we have noted, is rejuvenated by Athena. Telemachus, for his part, becomes so like Odysseus that he is indistinguishable from him, being as much a replica of his father as his own name is—or sounds like—a title of Odysseus.[10] The problem Homer faced was technical: how to show the maturity, individuality, and heroism of Telemachus without detracting from the dominance of Odysseus. If his compromises were not always successful, it is largely because the pre-logical situations of myth will not readily conform to the logic of literature.[11] [137/138]

[10] Far-fighter? Cf. Astyanax and Hector. See G. Germain, *Genèse de l'Odysée* (Paris, 1954), p. 485, for a discussion and list of references.

[11] Mireaux sees Telemachus as the ritual successor of Odysseus, as Oedipus succeeded Laius and Aegisthus Agamemnon and, indeed, Telegonus Odysseus, but precluded by the exigencies of the myth—or Homer's version—from playing his sacral role. "Dans la légende odysséenne, il est vrai, Ulysse est vainqueur des prétendants; mais sa victoire, nous le savons, est celle de son fils qui a combattu à ses côtés, vaincu avec lui et peut ainsi lui succéder. Lui-même est obligé de s'exiler": *Les poèmes homériques et l'histoire grecque* (Paris, 1948–49), pp. 152–3.

Telemachus' fortunes may be checkered in the *Odyssey*, but in his own "epic" he can stand a thorough comparison with his more famous father. First, both Telemachus and his father make journeys, from which both must return home indirectly and in constant danger. Odysseus has to grapple with the world's perils and disorders and yet survive, preserving his identity and his purpose. For Telemachus the world is precisely the opposite: the well-ordered kingdoms of Nestor and Menelaus. Telemachus' progress is from the chaos of Ithaca to the cosmos of Pylos and Sparta; Odysseus seeks the stability of his home across the ragged edges of the world. But in their separate worlds there is an important difference between the two: Odysseus acts, Telemachus reacts. Although Odysseus more than once comes within an inch of his life, Telemachus' experiences (apart from the social) are vicarious: he listens, observes, absorbs. He learns about his father, not his whereabouts, but rather the full story of the Odyssean exploits at Troy. He can now better appreciate his father (particularly when it comes to infiltrating a hostile city), because he has learned of his derring-do from the greatest living authorities on heroic *arete*. It is important, therefore, that in this atmosphere of wartime heroism recollected in the tranquility of peace Telemachus do nothing, just as it is for Odysseus in Book XI. And yet, through his own faltering efforts to make this trip and share the memories of Nestor and Menelaus, Telemachus is able to rehearse privately many of the great crises of the *Odyssey*. The stories of the heroes fighting at Troy and returning to Greece prepare him for the coming struggle by expanding his knowledge, if not experience, of the world. He has the same vision of man's life as Odysseus sees projected in the Underworld: family (Nestor and Menelaus), moral (Ajax' blasphemy, Menelaus' delay), and women who suffered through [138/139] love (Helen). He hears a prophet (Proteus) who is at the same time a sea monster of the ilk that besets his father; and he too must hurry home at the warning of Athena to save Penelope from the Suitors. Homer has succeeded in packing a version of the *Odyssey* into a little more than two books, all in the passive voice.

The *Nekyia* [Book XI, Odysseus' visit to the Underworld] serves in other ways to define the special quality of the *Telemacheia*. Both of these episodes presume to show us the hero learning something vital to his future welfare, yet in each the information is either not forthcoming as supposed or else could have been acquired elsewhere. Further, it is only in the *Nekyia* that Odysseus assumes the stance of Telemachus in Books III and IV, that of the passive observer of an unfamiliar cere-

---

This is interesting, in that it offers an explanation for Odysseus' leaving Ithaca again, though this sort of explanation may seem no less mysterious than Tiresias' and even less central to the poem. The point worth emphasizing is that the archery contest and the massacre of the Suitors are essentially Odysseus' affairs, and his favored position as king makes Telemachus superfluous.

mony. However there are significant differences. Whereas Telemachus is introduced to the heroic tradition in the front parlors of the returned chieftains where manners saturate conduct, where worldly prudence and social maturity have a climactic importance, and where the storms and struggles of life seem comfortably remote; Odysseus on the other hand has to break through the world's surfaces, has to pass, indeed, from life to death. Telemachus hears about Agamemnon and Achilles; Odysseus goes to see them. Odysseus' fate is cosmic, hence he must penetrate to the mist-bound areas beyond this life. His living presence in Hades prefigures the life that he will restore to the stricken land of Ithaca. Odysseus must go beneath the levels of the world, the very levels which Telemachus must come to know with tact and nicety. Ordinarily Odysseus is satisfied with his knack of survival in a hostile and perplexing world, but in the *Nekyia* he is in touch with powers beyond his techniques and he is immobilized by them. He comes for specific information from Tiresias, but he stays to meet the representatives of the heroic Establishment. Odysseus needs no education in the ways of this world; now his experience has been deepened by exposure to the ways of the other world. But if the *Odyssey* in XI breaks through the forms, the *Telemacheia* is content to slide along their surface, initiating their hero into the rites of a faith in which he was born but never reared. Its high priest is Nestor, its catechism the legends of Troy.

Again, Odysseus is saddled for much of his return with the [139/140] burden of his company, the responsibility for their safety and the accountability for their lesser talents. Within his larger fate are subsumed the fates of his companions. With Telemachus, however, the situation is reversed. He is under the divine protection of Athena and the fraternal guidance of Peisistratus. Since Odysseus overshadows his men when accompanied or else travels alone, his personality everywhere dominates the action even when the forces opposing him are most critical or catastrophic. Telemachus does not dominate the action; instead, he is usually at its mercy. He finds himself in social impasses, situations where he fears that his training and experience are not adequate to cope with them. He is never alone; Athena and Peisistratus are ever with him, and his final character is shaped by their tutoring or example. Their salutary presence, their promptings, assurances, commendations are the background of his development.

From the time of Porphyrio, who called it a *paideusis*,[12] the [140/

---

[12] *Quaest. Hom.*, ed. H. Schrader (Leipzig, 1890), pp. 15–18, on I, 284. Whether or not Telemachus' exploits in aid of his father can be attributed to a change in his character, and whether or not this character change (or development) is directly induced by his trip to Pylos and Sparta or by Athena's appearance in Book I, has been much disputed. Favoring some sort of *Entwicklungsgang* are E. Drerup, *Homerische Poetik: Das Homerproblem in der Gegenwart*, I (Würzburg, 1921), p. 365, n. 3; J. A. Scott, "The Journey Made by Telemachus and Its Influence on the Action of the *Odyssey*," *C.J.*, XIII (1917–18), p. 426;

141] *Telemacheia* has sometimes been taken as a kind of *Bildungs-roman;* and it is true that all the elements are there. Telemachus is the callow youth, Pylos and Sparta are the paradigms of the princely court, Athena is the guide, and the result is Telemachus fighting with skill and courage beside his father against the Suitors. One distinction: the *Telemacheia* is not simply a schooling or an education; it is not something taught but something imparted; it is an experience, one young man's initiation into a world he has inherited and whose values he will soon have to defend by force.[13] And yet it is not a rite of initiation in the anthropological sense of a set of artificial dangers contrived to test a candidate's reactions.[14] Growing up [141/142] fatherless in a house full

---

H. Herter, "Telemachos" in *R.-E.*, A 5, 1, col. 351; E. Schwartz, *Die Odyssee* (München, 1924), p. 253; R. Pfeiffer, rev. of Schwartz, *op. cit.*, and of Wilamowitz, *Die Heimkehr des Odysseus* (Berlin, 1927), *Deutsche Literaturzeitung,* XLVIII (1928), pp. 2368–9; J. Geffcken, *Griechische Literaturgeschichte,* I (Heidelberg, 1926), p. 39; W. Jaeger, *Paideia,* I, trans. G. Highet (Oxford, 1939), pp. 28–9; K. Reinhardt, *Von Werken und Formen* (Godesberg, 1948), p. 47; R. Robert, *Homère* (Paris, 1950), p. 267; E. Delebecque, *Télémaque et la structure de l'Odyssée* (Aix-la-Provence, 1958), p. 137. Wilamowitz' final view was that character development is foreign to Greek literature and that there is no change in Telemachus in the later books of the poem, *op. cit.*, p. 106. F. Focke quotes Wilamowitz approvingly, but also claims that after his trip Telemachus "ist jetzt wer, eine vollwertige Persönlichkeit, von der 'man' mit Achtung spricht," *Die Odyssee (Tübinger Beiträge,* XXXVIII [1943]), p. 60. Cf. the view of Luigia Stella, that Telemachus is an unimportant character and the *Telemacheia* only a pretext to reinsert into the *Odyssey* the great figures of epic legend, *Il poema d'Ulisse* (Florence, 1955), p. 88.

Be he changed or developed, transformed or matured, and whatever his incidental difficulties in helping his father (like leaving the storeroom door open in Book XXII), the Telemachus whom Odysseus meets in XVI has been abroad in the heroic world and has come to appreciate personally the glories of a settled kingdom enjoying the benefits of order and prosperity. This, at any rate, is a kind of knowledge he did not have before visiting Pylos and Sparta; but whatever the trip might have done for Telemachus' character, its vision of the heroic world at peace with itself certainly enriches the poem and extends its meaning.

[13] What one would most expect to happen fails to materialize, namely that either Nestor or Menelaus would volunteer to send off a detachment of their palace guard to Ithaca to restrain the Suitors, protect Penelope, and confirm Telemachus in his patrimony. Instead, they seem to assume that this is exclusively the problem of Telemachus and Odysseus.

[14] Insofar as the *Telemacheia* does suggest such a rite of passage, its truest correspondent in the *Odyssey* is the inserted account of Odysseus' naming in Book XIX, 392–466. Here Autolycus visits his son-in-law and daughter on the remote island of Ithaca and invites them to send the young Odysseus to Parnassus. In time Odysseus visits the land of his fathers, takes part in a hunt with Autolycus' sons, is wounded by a boar, and returns home laden with presents. This hunt seems less an incidental episode than a rite of initiation, wherein the young man participates in an adult act of bravery superintended by his elders, suffers the ritual wound, sheds the symbolic blood, and then returns home, his success ratified by his many presents. This is paralleled by Telemachus' experience, bloodlessly of course, because his initiatory trial operates on the social surfaces and his participation in bloodshed—Troy and the *nostoi*—is vicarious, filtered through the accounts of Nestor and Menelaus.

of scheming Suitors has given him a taste of peril; now in the *Tele-macheia* Pylos and Sparta demonstrate to him the possibilities of peace, and the example of Nestor and Menelaus expose him to the precedents of *arete*.

The worlds Telemachus is exposed to—Ithaca and Pylos-Sparta—and the social images they offer him extend beyond the *Odyssey*; like so much of Homeric poetry they are archetypes of our literary consciousness. That the details of the *Telemacheia* are not wholly arbitrary and that they have a high literary convertibility can be demonstrated by a cursory comparison with a modern analogue, William Faulkner's long short story *The Bear*. Faulkner's story of Ike McCaslin's initiation into the mysteries of the wilderness through participation in a hunt for a bear named Old Ben touches Homer's work in detail and theme. The ritual element of *The Bear* is explicit, with Faulkner saying of his hero at the beginning of the story, "He entered his novitiate to the true wilderness" (p. 195),[15] and at the end, "Sam led him into the wilderness and showed him and he ceased to be a child" (p. 330). And like Telemachus in Pylos-Sparta, Ike in the big woods is more spectator than actor. "*So I will have to see him,* he thought . . . *I will have to look at him*" (p. 204, Faulkner's italics). And for the term of their preparation each is assigned a guardian. For Ike it is the appropriately named Sam Fathers, half Negro and half Indian, "childless, kinless, peopleless" (p. 246); for Telemachus it is Athena, herself half native and half intruder, also childless and kinless, and appearing as Mentor, a name also used by Faulkner to make the educative meaning of his story evident. There is also a resemblance in movement between the two stories. Each has two general episodes or stages, the *Telemacheia* moving from Nestor's Pylos to Menelaus' Sparta, while Faulkner's hero first downs a buck under Sam Father's tutelage before he is worthy to face Old Ben.[16] It is interesting that the end of the first stage in each account is sealed by an accolade. Ike's face is bathed with the buck's blood. "Sam Fathers marked his face with the hot blood which he had spilled and he ceased to [142/143] be a child and became a hunter and a man" (p. 178). For Telemachus, too, the departure from Pylos is solemnized by a bath given him by none other than Nestor's own daughter, from which he appears, "looking like a god" (II, 468). There are other details. When Ike finally sees Old Ben and is so reverent before its "furious immortality" (p. 194) that he is immobilized, we recall Telemachus so awestruck by Nestor that he tells Athena, "Looking at him I think I am beholding immortality itself" (III, 246). Then when General Compson, himself a kind of Nestor, lets Ike take his horse Katie, one thinks of the horses Nestor gives Telemachus to continue his jour-

---

[15] Page references are to the Modern Library edition of *Go Down, Moses* (New York, 1955).

[16] Actually recounted in *The Old People*, the story preceding *The Bear* in *Go Down, Moses,* but recalled twice (pp. 210, 323) in the latter story.

ney. And as Ike protects the repellent Boon Hogganbeck when his cousin McCaslin accuses him of shooting Sam Fathers, so Telemachus accepts the murderer Theoclymenus and later spares Phemius and Medon in the slaughter of the Suitors. The planter aristocracy which helps instruct Ike may also be compared with the feudal aristocracy of the late Mycenaean age as represented in the *Telemacheia* by Nestor and Menelaus. Finally, the names of the two boys have a symbolic dimension. Faulkner first calls his hero "the boy" or "he," then "Ike"; but it is not until the end of the story that Faulkner identifies him as, "An Isaac born into later life than Abraham's and repudiating immolation" (p. 283). In the same way, Telemachus' aspiration to the conditions of heroism is suggested by his name, so apt for this young Ithacan who in the future will be the kind of fighter his father can trust and admire.

Both Telemachus and Ike lost their fathers in early childhood and both grew up in worlds where they felt they did not belong. For both these abandoned children the trial they will ultimately face is the effort to prove themselves by worthy deeds, to demonstrate before their elders and peers that they are truly the sons of their fathers. For Ike the preparation is the bear hunt, and for Telemachus, the journey to the heroic world. These are experiences in which each is received into a timeless world, ceremonies of attainment in which they are secluded from distraction and released from the entanglements of the present, journeys into the exemplary past where historical pageant can already be made to yield a moral parable. For Telemachus the meetings with Nestor and Menelaus are sacraments, the visible means to the graces of heroism. Hence his search is for more [143/144] than news of his father: he seeks the social and family assurance of the heroic age, where sons are like their fathers because they have grown up in their shadows, as Antilochus was like Nestor, or where sons inherit their fathers' bravery and defend their memories, as Orestes avenged the death of Agamemnon. Telemachus has never had a father to provide the scenes and cues for his glory, and so this journey is not only for information but, as Athena admits (XIII, 422), to win him his first *kleos*. But like *The Brothers Karamazov* it deepens the search for the physical father into the profounder theme of the spiritual condition of children deprived of faith and security. For both young men this trip "into the new and alien country" (p. 207) is a maturing and purifying experience, although in its results the *Telemacheia* extends into an heroic deed the action which for Faulkner's hero culminates in renunciation. Whereas Ike leaves "the settled familiar land . . . the childish business of rabbits" (p. 171), penetrates the elementary and numinous wilderness, sees the bear, learns in his bones its greatness of courage and defiance and endurance, Telemachus on the other hand leaves the menace of the Suitors behind in Ithaca, experiences the harmony and stability of Pylos and Sparta, and then returns to help his father purge the contaminated land and restore justice and the social conventions. Ike is sequestered from society, Telemachus is exposed to it. Yet in each story the "heroic" world, whether it be a Mycenaean court reflecting recent glories or the big woods sheltering a bear who is proud of his liberty and ruthless to defend it, is opposed to the suffering homeland where the natural inheritance has been disrupted and power is passing into the hands of the dispossessors and the exploiters. Ike is tragically aware of his share in this corruption; his position is more ambiguous than Telemachus' and his opportunity for action more limited. So he repudiates his patrimony and becomes a carpenter without children or property. Telemachus' experience, in contrast, is more social; renunciation is a luxury he and his parents can scarcely afford —and so he joins his father and fights to restore his rights and ensure his succession.

It does not really matter that Old Ben, the bear, is a hunted animal, while Nestor and Menelaus are Telemachus' father's friends and allies. Both the animal and the heroes embody the [144/145] pride and assurance and skill that mark maturity and assure survival. And both are destructive; for heroic self-assertion also has its toll of grief (as Iphigeneia reminds us) and its besetting sins of bloodlust and predatory pride. These are perhaps clearer in the *Odyssey*, where the brief glories of the Trojan War are dimmed by time and by their entailments of loss and suffering, and where the action culminates in the bloody impartiality of the *Freiermord*. And if the Suitors represent the heroic age's inevitable historic successors, seizing power through an oligarchic *stasis*, then this notion is not too far from Ben's ultimate destruction by the dog Lion, "an animal almost the color of a gun or pistol barrel" (p. 216), owned by Boon Hogganbeck, "a violent, insensitive, hard-faced man" (p. 220). In Faulkner's story more than in Homer's the obsolescence of the heroic order is explicit, and Faulkner himself has underscored its significance: "That is a change that's going on everywhere, and I think that man progresses mechanically and technically much faster than he does spiritually, that there may be something he could substitute for the ruined wilderness, but he hasn't found that."[17] This is also the point of the logging operations in Part 5 of *The Bear*, a noisy and ruinous attack on the life of nature that effectively matches the idle destructiveness of the Suitors in Ithaca. Granted the old, wild, heroic order cannot forever afford the costs of its glories; yet if it must pass, it deserves worthier successors than Antinous and Eurymachus.

Thus the wilderness Ike penetrates and the heroic society Telemachus traverses are not wholly dissimilar. Each is an enclosed world with its own laws and conventions, its own mystique of wisdom and virtue, and its own concept of honor. It is in this "other world" that the

---

[17] *Faulkner in the University*, ed. Frederick L. Gwynn and Joseph L. Blotner (Charlottesville, 1959), p. 68.

young novices are absolved of the corrupting burdens of the historical world and born again of courage and truth and humility. Faulkner tells us that it seemed to Ike that, "at the age of ten he was witnessing his own birth" (p. 195). This is also the final purpose of the *Telemacheia:* the birth of a hero. As such it parallels in its way the *Odyssey,* which presents the return of the hero (and with Laertes, the rebirth of a hero), and thereby completes the picture of heroic life which the *Odyssey* celebrates. [145]

Penelope

J. W. MACKAIL

JUST TWO HUNDRED YEARS AGO, POPE WROTE, IN THE POSTSCRIPT TO HIS own translation, "The *Odyssey* is a perpetual source of poetry." That is as true now as it was then; and even more so, because our means of being able to appreciate the *Odyssey* are much larger than his or those of his age. In spite of all translations, popularisations, commentaries, the *Odyssey* itself is for each fresh reader a new miracle. The study of one of its great central and vital figures to which I invite you will have fulfilled its purpose if it sends those of you who have learnt or are learning Greek to Homer, and if it arouses, in those who have not, desire to drink at the fountain themselves. One word of warning, which is never superfluous, must be given: to listen to lectures is not to study the Classics; nor is it any substitute for that study.

Penelope is one of the great women of history. If at first sight she seems remote from, or even contrary to, modern ideals, a larger and more intelligent view will alter that misconception. She will reveal herself as no obsolete type, but as an individual figure, of extraordinary fineness and complexity, and intensely human because portrayed, or created, by a consummate artist.

In a sense, she has become obscured by her [54/55] own fame. She is universally known, but in a slovenly, superficial way. From being typical, she has tended to dwindle into a mere type, part of the defaced currency passed on from hand to hand. The type, as thus degraded, is that of the housewife—bloodless, tearful, incompetent, occupied in endless complainings and everlasting needlework. *Domum servavit, lanam fecit,* the phrase of one of the noblest and most touching of Roman epitaphs, has become debased, for her as for others, into

J. W. Mackail, "Penelope in the *Odyssey*," in *Classical Studies* (London: John Murray, 1925), pp. 54–75. Reprinted by permission of the publisher.

a sort of sneer: into a description of the woman without brains, who must be always clinging and whose constancy is habit, not virtue.

The first touch of this—for it is no new thing—comes in the *Odyssey* itself; in the half-mocking, half-angry spurt of jealousy with which Calypso speaks of her. It is answered there by the grave and beautiful reply of Odysseus. But always afterwards it has tended to recur with aggravations. It is fully developed in Bacon's cynical sentence in the essay "Of Marriage and Single Life": "Grave natures, led by custom, and therefore constant, are commonly loving husbands, as was said of Ulysses, *Vetulam suam praetulit immortalitati.*" On this it may be noted, first, that it was not said; the words to which Bacon alludes were said not of Penelope, but of the "little nest among the rocks," his own island of Ithaca; secondly, that it is dishonouring alike to Homer and to humanity; and thirdly that *vetula*, "old woman," is a wilful falsification. The whole thing is an instance of the Elizabethan vulgarity which is so constantly mixed up with high thought and splendid imagination in that age. But all that [55/56] makes it still more worth while to get back to the real Penelope, the Penelope of Homer.

The real Penelope? some one may say; one of the great women of history? Surely you mean, not of history, but of poetry? Here we touch on the secret of art. Whether the actual Penelope ever lived at all—probably she did—does not matter. It would not make her less real if she were as much of an imaginative invention as the Bradamante of Ariosto; nor more real, if she were presented with the same minute historical accuracy as the Gudrun of the Laxdaela-saga. Poetry is the highest and ultimate expression towards which history is perpetually reaching.

Further, there is more in poetry (as one might state the case) than the poet put there, that is, than he consciously meant or planned. In some of the detail which follows in this sketch, you may reasonably ask, But did Homer have this in his mind? The answer is, Yes and No. He certainly did not, in the sense of a set of data on which he worked, but vital creation from within outwards has an instinctive or "inspired" knowledge. The poet tells "what the Muses teach him." Think of all the implied background to Hamlet, say, or to Imogen. They are so real, so living, that they create all round them a sort of world of reality, or if we prefer to say so, of super-reality. Not only do they exist, but their detailed environment exists, takes shape, comes alive.

Those who read and delight in the *Odyssey* as a masterpiece of poetry are often, and very naturally, so enthralled by its fascination as a story, its splendour of construction and brilliance [56/57] of handling, that they fail to appreciate fully other qualities no less remarkable, its subtle psychology, its pathos and humour, its insight into the springs of human nature. The best Greek art—and in this respect at least, Homer is thoroughly Greek—is so delicate, so reserved, so free from insistence and display, that it only yields its secret to the most careful study and to a corresponding fineness of apprehension. We feel its beauty, its charm, its magic potency; but we feel all these indistinctly. Even to handle it seems sometimes a sort of profanation. Art cannot be explained, any more than it can be analysed. But at least we may attempt to appreciate it better. And that is not hard. "Nature, purity, perspicacity, and simplicity," in the fine words which I quote again from Pope, "never walk in the clouds; they are obvious to all capacities, and where they are not evident, they do not exist."

One of the foolish things said in antiquity about the *Odyssey* was that Homer composed it for women after composing the *Iliad* for men. One of the foolish things said about it by a brilliant but eccentric modern writer was that it was written by a woman. What originated notions like these is the large part played in it by women. That marvellous picture-gallery includes half a dozen figures of the first rank, fully and finely drawn; Circe and Calypso, Arete and Nausicaa, Helen, Eurycleia (several of these, Helen and Arete especially, have outstanding gifts of capacity and intellect), but above all, Penelope herself. Round her, and her relation to Odysseus and Telemachus, the whole poem circles. From her first appearance in the Hall [57/58] at Ithaca Book I., where the keynote is firmly struck in the phrases by which she is introduced—περίφρων Πηνελόπεια, δῖα γυναικῶν—to the final reunion in Book XXIII., we are never allowed to forget her. She passes in and out of the scene like a phrase in music or a gold thread in a woven texture. Gradually, as we study the poem more closely and let its poetry sink into us, she takes shape as a creation largely and delicately modelled, extraordinarily true to life, fascinating alike in her strength and weakness, and like a character of Shakespeare's in the way that she is created from within, vitally.

First, then, who was Penelope? What is the background of facts, as one might say, upon which the artist produces his living figure? We may neglect here all the odds and ends of local tradition or antiquarian invention; for we cannot say whether, or how far, any of them belonged to the story as it was known to the poet, and there is nothing more dangerous than to read them into the poem.

Of her own family we learn this from the *Odyssey* itself: her father Icarius is still alive somewhere on the mainland; and she has brothers, who are only mentioned once, casually; both father and brothers are outside of the story. She has also a sister Iphthime, married to Eumelus of Pherae in Thessaly, far away. There is no mention of her mother. This much is stated in the poem itself: but we may add to it another very important fact, from the general and unvarying main outlines of the heroic cycle, as they had already become fixed before the age of Homer: namely, that Icarius was the brother of Tyndareus, [58/59] and hence that Penelope is first cousin of Helen and Clytemnestra. This is in a sense the key to the whole structure of the poem.

From her home overseas she was married young to Odysseus.

Telemachus was a newborn baby when Odysseus went to Troy: and the return is uniformly spoken of as in the twentieth year. Consequently when the action of the *Odyssey* opens he is nineteen, and she, if she married at fifteen, would be thirty-five or thirty-six—in any case, under forty, and at the "dangerous age." She is still in mature and unimpaired beauty, which is overpowering in its splendour whenever she can throw off the weight of anxiety and cloud of gloom. This beauty the poet leaves to be felt by its effects, without any formal description; we do not know even if she was dark or fair, though the ivory-coloured face of XVIII. 196 suggests a dark complexion. When Athena has beautified her in her sleep—when, as we should put it in our more prosaic and unimaginative way, she is looking her best—the suitors cannot contain themselves for admiration.

But her beauty, great as it is, is almost eclipsed by a sort of impressiveness, mingled of skill, wisdom, and character. She is δῖα γυναικῶν, "the bright of women," but her constant epithets are περίφρων, "exceeding wise," and ἐχέφρων, "self-controlled"; a word which conveys the combined notions of chastity and of a sort of power held in reserve. The whole matter is summed up, early in the poem, in the magnificent praise of Antinous (II. 116):

> —Athena has bestowed on her
> Wisdom of mind and excellence of skill [59/60]
> In beautiful devices manifold
> Beyond all others, such as is not told
> Even of those renowned in former time,
> Achaean women lovely-tressed of old.

Eurymachus crystallises this, a little later, into two words, τῆς ἀρετῆς, "the excellence of her." No English, it may be added, can convey the magical beauty of the Greek line, τάων αἱ πάρος ἦσαν ἐϋπλοκαμῖδες Ἀχαιαί.

It is quite of a piece with this that she says she hates Antinous most of all the suitors; that young prince, though he had a pretty gift of speech, was something of a fop, and a good deal of a fool; and he expressed his admiration too openly. The plausible Eurymachus never imposes on her for a moment. Amphinomus was the one who pleased her best, "because he was quick of understanding." Herself she shows unusual intellectual power when she allows it play; but it has been stifled by circumstance, and the necessity of rigid and cruel self-control. She had but one passion, her love for Odysseus, and that had been starved: and her wisdom only made her feel her weakness and helplessness more keenly.

The position of a young wife left alone while only a girl in a strange house for many years was difficult at best, and became harder as years went on. Her mother-in-law, Anticleia, had been kind to her; but she was dead. Telemachus while a child engrossed her, with that jealous mother's love which often makes such difficulties when the boy grows up and begins to assert his own personality. She had her household duties, the needlework in which she was so accomplished, her poultry in which she took great delight (XIX. 537); [60/61] the old family nurse loved her deeply; Eumaeus, the foster-child of the house, "the man who was loyal to his lords," has a real affection for her. But she had no companions of her own age, no real friends, no one to whom she could pour herself out unreservedly. The burden of her life became slowly too great for her to bear. While the war at Troy went on, life was possible, however anxious. But then came the slow sickening years of hope deferred. Anticleia died of a broken heart. After her death Laertes aged rapidly, gave up control of the house and buried himself at his little country farm. She was among old people. Odysseus' sister Clymene had married and gone to live in another island, Same. The suitors began to pour in, treated the house as their own, and became more and more intolerable, taxing all her wit and self-control to the utmost. Except for them, it was a household of women. Eumaeus was away at the hill farm; she used to send for him often at first, but by and by ceased even to do that. News was brought to her of Odysseus again and again; it all proved false. She was thrown in more and more on herself, on silence and brooding. Telemachus became a problem: a sort of jealousy insensibly grew up between them in spite of her love for him and his real affection for her; it was perhaps accentuated by his startling likeness to his father, which was so strong that Helen at Lacedaemon, who had never seen him, recognises him by it at once. She felt the reins slipping from her; and her control of the household, though she knew it to be ineffective, was for her a sacred trust. The policy of compromise she was forced into with [61/62] the suitors as they grew more insolent and masterful caused a chill of misunderstanding between mother and son; and neither of them spoke out. Even Telemachus must not take the place that she was desperately keeping open for Odysseus. She resented any attempt of his at self-assertion; she would keep him a child. For more than one reason she would not let him have any control over the women; indeed, the less he had to do with a young woman of the type of Melantho, the better. But she did not quite understand him; nor he her. When Antinous says that she is acting simply for her own vainglory, Telemachus does not contradict him.

This is the state of things at the opening of the *Odyssey;* it is all set out before us by delicate touches in Books I. and II. The fluid situation is precipitated by the visit of Athena. It is well to bear in mind that throughout, Athena, while a goddess, is also the inner god-prompted wisdom—the conversations in which she takes part must be read in this double light.

Almost in his first words Telemachus lets the unconscious friction appear. When Athena asks, "Are you really Odysseus' son?" his answer, with a curious accent of petulance, is "My mother says I am." And

immediately after, when Athena has gone, and Penelope comes into
the hall and asks the minstrel to sing another lay, not of the woes of
Troy, Telemachus, apparently for the first time, snaps at her in public,
and asserts that he is head of the house. He is finding himself, but, like
a boy, is not very nice or considerate about it. She makes no answer, but
slips away, disconcerted and astonished. After a night's thinking, [62/
63] he announces to his nurse in Book II. his intention of going to seek
for his father. In his confidences with Eurycleia one sees the mixture
in him of suspicion and tenderness: Penelope is not to be told, really
that she may not have any opportunity to interfere, but also, as he adds
in a mood between malice and affection, ὡς ἂν μὴ κλαίουσα κατὰ χρόα
καλὸν ἰάπτῃ, "that she may not spoil her lovely complexion with crying."

So he slips off in the night; and the next of Penelope is when she
hears of his being gone from Medon the herald. This scene, and the
episode of Penelope's dream after it, give a complete picture of her;
and we may notice that here, as wherever she is excited and kindled
out of her dull misery, her qualities of intellect come out, and her
language is of extraordinary richness and beauty. Notice too with what
a firm subtle touch it is brought out here that it is Odysseus that she
cares for most; she has just been saying that her anxiety is greater for
her son than for "that other," but as soon as the phantom says it is sent
by Athena, she at once turns her inquiry to him, with a new passion of
eagerness. It is an index of her loneliness that her sister's appearance
even in a dream unlocks the frozen fountains of her heart. It is the first
lifting of the darkness.

This astonishingly beautiful scene, with its subtle psychology and
its thrilling emotion, is the noble close to the prelude of the *Odyssey*,
Books I.–IV. Penelope does not reappear till Book XVI.; but she is
kept in the picture meanwhile by repeated references; in the scene of
Calypso's uneasy taunt (Book V.) and Odysseus' adroit and dignified
answer (Odysseus is never at a loss how to deal [63/64] with women—
Nausicaa, Arete, Circe, Calypso, Penelope herself except once): in the
strange pathos of the speech of Anticleia's ghost (Book XI.) that
begins and ends on her; καὶ λίην κείνη γε, "surely and over-surely she
abides and awaits you," and "mark this" (the pageant of dead Queens
which was to pass before him), "that you may tell it to your wife
hereafter": and perpetually in the expressed or implied contrast between her and her cousin Clytemnestra which is a recurring keynote
from the beginning of the poem to the end.

The return to her is led up to, with incomparable skill, in the
passage describing Telemachus' thoughts during his sleepless night at
Lacedaemon, put (according to the epic formula) in the shape of
counsel given by Athena.

> Take heed now therefore lest against your will
> She bear away your substance, knowing still
> What kind of heart is in a woman's breast,
> That ever she is fain his house to fill

Who weds her: and the children whom she bore,
And him who was her wedded lord before,
From her remembrance, after he is dead,
She blots, nor asks about them any more.

Towards the end of Book XVI. the scene shifts back to the palace of Ithaca. Penelope reappears; she approaches Antinous bitterly with the plot to kill Telemachus. He is taken aback and speechless, but Eurymachus, always ready with his quite unconvincing falsehoods, makes a glib reply: "There is no danger for him while I am alive; I will protect him at the risk of my own life." She is too miserable to make any answer, but goes away and cries herself asleep. She is very near breaking point. [64/65]

Early next morning Telemachus returns; and her welcome, weeping and clinging to him and kissing him, has no trace of jealousy or reproach. But he is rather short with her: "Do not break me down," he says. "The word took not wing from her"; she goes silently away. But later in the day, when he comes in again with Theoclymenus to give him dinner, she is spinning by the doorway and makes a touching appeal to him; then at last he tells her the story of his voyage, still with reluctance, hurriedly, and constrainedly. There is a wonderful touch here. "Nestor," he tells her, "sent me on to Lacedaemon to Menelaus: there I saw Argive Helen." Not a word more about her; he keeps back Helen's fondness for him ("darling child" she had called him); and her gift of the embroidered gown "for your wife to wear on her wedding day; till then let your mother keep it for you in her chamber." Penelope would hardly have welcomed this trust. Herself she makes no reference to Helen, either here or elsewhere. The constraint between mother and son has come back. All the comfort she gets at this interview is from Theoclymenus.

Later on the same day Odysseus himself comes, and slinks into the hall in his beggar's disguise; Antinous throws a footstool at him, which shocks even the suitors. Penelope hears the tumult; she sends for Eumaeus into her bower and tells him to bring the beggar to her: she has just seen him through the doorway, and even that unrecognising glimpse has moved her strangely; she actually laughs, the only time she does so. When Eumaeus brings back word that the stranger thinks it wiser not to have his interview till night has fallen and [65/66] the suitors have left, she answers quite contentedly: "He seems to be no fool, whoever he may be." From this point on, to the *Niptra* [The reunion of Penelope and Odysseus], the dramatic tension of the story increases and centres about Penelope.

In Book XVIII. (after the episode of Irus) she speaks to Eurynome. "My heart moves me, as never heretofore, to show myself among the suitors." This was "the counsel of Athena to make her more precious than before to her husband and her son." It was what we should call an unconscious cerebration. Eurynome, who is no witch, advises her to wash and anoint herself first: adding that "it is no use weeping for ever, especially now when you have such a fine grown son." This was not the kind of comfort Penelope wanted: she answers a little testily, "Do not talk like that; the gods have made my beauty fade." Then Athena casts sleep upon her and increases her beauty in it: when she awakes, it is as a new woman. The suitors' "knees are loosened with desire of her." For the first time in the poem she speaks to Telemachus firmly and with authority, "When you were a child you had more sense than now"; and he, for the first and last time, answers humbly and deprecatingly. The splendour of her beauty moves Eurymachus to compliment her: "You excel all women in loveliness and stature and inner wisdom." In her answer to him there is a new accent of strength, and then she goes on to taunt the suitors with meanness and tell them to show their love by gifts. "Odysseus was glad, because she enchanted them with soft words, but her mind purposed otherwise." He read her like a book.

Now comes a great scene. Night has fallen: [66/67] Odysseus and Telemachus have removed the armour, Telemachus has gone to bed in his own room across the court, and Odysseus is left alone. Then Penelope comes back into the fire-lit hall. Her women clear away the supper, and go. Odysseus and Penelope are alone, with the old nurse Eurycleia in the background. She asks him who he is.

Odysseus begins by fencing with her and paying her magnificent compliments, as to a strange queen. This sort of thing generally made her shrink up into herself; now it unlocks her; she positively chatters to him, pouring her soul out to him as she had never done to any one; she tells him all about herself; they sit talking for hours. With a pretty touch of coquetry she says at last that it is time to go to bed. "How shall you know, guest, that I excel other women in wisdom, if you are not bathed and clad well in my house?" The ice about her heart is unfrozen:

> —This embalms and spices
> To the April-day again.

During the feet-washing Penelope sits in a sort of dream, and notices nothing. Then he draws up to her again and she comes to herself, and breaks out in the most marvellous of all her speeches, with the incomparable nightingale-passage in which the lyric note at its highest and purest is caught and merged in the epic structure. She can hold nothing back from this stranger: and ends by telling him how she means to set the contest of the axe-heads. She can hardly tear herself away, but at last goes. Odysseus cannot get to sleep for a long time. When he does at last, Penelope is [67/68] just awaking from a dream of him. Her exaltation of the night before has faded away from her in the grey light of the morning, but has still left her highly strung: her prayer to Artemis, beginning:

> Goddess and mistress, fain were I that thou
> Wouldst pierce my bosom with thine arrow now
> And take my life from out me, Artemis,
> Daughter of Zeus, to whom in prayer I bow:
>
> Or that a whirlwind from the earth might tear
> And hurl me forth upon the ways of air,
> To fling me where the backward-flowing tide
> Of the Ocean-River leaves the seabanks bare:
>
> Even as the daughters born to Pandarus
> Of old were taken by the whirlwinds thus,
> Whose parents by the gods were slain, and they
> Left orphans in the palace perilous,

is ineffable in its beauty: this, and the nightingale speech, are her high-water mark, and almost, if not quite, the high-water mark of the *Odyssey*.

As always, her thoughts and heart are all with Odysseus; she says nothing of Telemachus. And he on his side is incurable. That same morning he asks Eurycleia whether the stranger has been properly treated: "My mother for all her wisdom is a desperate one for treating an inferior man with distinguished courtesy and sending a noble one away without honour." He does not know that Eurycleia knows. She does not undeceive him; her answer begins with a dignified rebuke. "Do not lay blame where no blame is to be laid," she says, and then she adroitly launches on a long account of the supper and bed that Odysseus had. She silences him thus, and then turns to her work, bidding the maids bestir to prepare the hall: "the suitors will be here early, for this is their high day." [68/69]

There follows a long episode or sèries of episodes, making a prelude of calculated delay before the climax, and ending with the insulting conduct of the suitor Ctesippus and the terrible second-sight of Theoclymenus: and, just at the end of Book XX., we are told Penelope was sitting opposite and heard it all. After dinner (Book XXI. now), she brings out the bow: there is a touch of tenderness almost passing into weakness, when she sits with it on her knee in the treasure-chamber, crying for a long time: then she recovers herself, goes into the hall and carries out the action that she had so carefully rehearsed; her speech to the suitors is almost verbally repeated from what she had said to Odysseus the night before. In Telemachus' taunting speech to the suitors there is still a little edge of temper against Penelope: "The prize is a wife such as there is not in the Achaean land: you know it; why should I praise my mother? Yet, if I could perform the feat, she might leave the house with any of you and I should not grieve much."

She stands by the doorway while the suitors one after another try to string the bow, and fail. Odysseus asks to be allowed to try, and

Antinous rates him. Then Penelope for once asserts herself and intervenes. Eurymachus, as before, takes up the word and apologises. But Telemachus, also strung up to high tension, turns on her almost angrily: "I am master here, and give or refuse the bow to whom I please; go away." It is more than she can stand: she goes away silently, and becomes again the Penelope of Book I., crying herself to sleep. She sleeps all through the slaying of that awful [69/70] afternoon. When it is over, Odysseus calls Eurycleia, but does not allow her to awake Penelope until the bodies have been removed and the hall purified. Then she goes up with her news. Penelope thinks she has gone mad at first: and when she repeats, with detail, the incredible story, still will not believe: "Some god has done this; it is difficult to fathom the devices of the immortals." She descends, to see for herself.

By this time it is almost dark. She sits down opposite Odysseus in the firelight, but keeping a long way off, against the wall, and stares at him where he sits by one of the pillars round the hearth. Neither speaks. It is more than Telemachus can bear. Μῆτερ ἐμὴ δύσμητερ, he breaks out, "ever your heart is harder than stone." She answers quite gently: "My child, if it is he, we shall know each other." Odysseus smiles: "Let your mother try me: soon she will know better." But still she stares silently; till at last even he, for the only time in the whole *Odyssey*, seems to lose control of the situation; he angrily bids Eurycleia prepare a separate bed for him. Then Penelope's chance is come; she tells her to bring out the bed from the bridal-chamber. For once Odysseus is outdone at his own craft, and gives her the sign she has been waiting for. It has come at last, the full assurance; she bursts into tears, rushes to him and flings her arms round him.

This is the end of the *Odyssey* according to the ablest Alexandrian critics; and certainly the remaining 624 lines are in a different key, and look like the work of a continuator, for whom the story had come to mean more than the epic treatment, [70/71] handling perhaps, as Professor Bury thinks, a draft-sketch left unfinished at the poet's death. Yet even here there are two or three fine touches; her making no reply to her husband's directions to keep still indoors and ask no questions when he leaves her in the morning: Laertes' lament that she had not mourned over him and closed his eyes: and the eager question of Dolius when Odysseus has made himself known, "does wise Penelope know you are come, or shall we send to inform her?" "She knows already," is the answer; "no need to concern yourself about that." The single line sounds almost unfeeling; really it is the brief expression of complete and triumphant confidence.

In this Epilogue to the *Odyssey*—for such in any case it is, whether it be the work of the same poet or not—the central point is the scene of the "Second Nekyia" [second scene in the Underworld]. It is very splendid, but it does not belong to the main structure and is almost "out of the picture." It can only be got in by ignoring what is an apparent absurdity, that the ghosts of Achilles and Agamemnon are sup-

posed to be meeting and conversing for the first time, though they had
had opportunity of doing so for nine years or more. It is of course
devised, and devised with high dramatic skill, to lead up to a final and
emphatic reaffirmation of the contrast between Penelope the good, and
Clytemnestra the evil wife. The narrative of the slain suitor Amphimedon, summarising the story of the whole poem, is followed by the
formal and explicit contrast placed in Agamemnon's mouth between
the two women, and the memorials they leave to mankind for ever:
[71/72]

> Thereat the son of Atreus' ghost begun
> And said: O fortunate Laertes' son
> Odysseus many-counselled, who a wife
> So virtuous and excellent have won!
>
> How rightly minded from of old was she,
> Icarius' child, unblamed Penelope!
> How well remembered she her wedded lord
> Odysseus! therefore undecayed shall be
>
> Her fame for worth, among mankind so long
> Shall the immortals make a lovely song
> Of chaste Penelope, not like to her,
> Tyndareus' child, who plotted deeds of wrong,
>
> Slaying her wedded lord; with loathing fraught
> Shall be her lay upon the earth, who brought
> Ill fame on the whole sex of womankind,
> Even on such as righteousness have wrought.

It is the moral of the *Odyssey*, and is given almost expressly as
such. But an epic poem transcends this way of looking at a story; it
has not a moral; or if it has, it does not state it formally. The dramatic
contrast has been emphasised from the beginning, and kept before us
throughout by repeated touches. Though the force and splendour of
this passage are admirable, yet the *Odyssey*, as a poem, does not need
it. A moral is a comment on a poem; it is no part of the poem itself.

What I have tried to put before you is the poetical evolution of a
wonderful figure under the handling of a great poet. The initial *motif*
is given by the contrast between the two cousins. This develops into
the studied portraiture of a perfect wife. And the perfect wife is a
term of large extent. It covers, for instance, in Shakespeare, both
Imogen and Lady Macbeth. But [72/73] further, the Homeric Penelope
is a special type. The contrast, expressed and implicit, is not merely
of the two cousins, but of the three. For the Helen of the *Odyssey* is
also a perfect wife, though she had not been so always. It is not only
Menelaus who finds her so; readers of the *Odyssey* who are perfectly
frank with themselves would not have a moment's hesitation in choosing whether they had rather have known Helen in Lacedaemon or
Penelope in Ithaca. So secure is a great artist of his work, that he can

afford to let the heroine of his story be outshone, even in a sense eclipsed, by a figure who is secondary in the construction. Helen speaks kindly and affectionately of her cousin; Penelope cannot even bear to let Helen's name pass her lips.[1] Penelope has all the virtues, except perhaps—dare we say?—magnanimity; but Helen has what is more potent than virtue, that magical, overpowering charm which has made the generations of mankind, from the elders of Troy downwards, in love with her. The crowning triumph of the poet of the *Odyssey* is that he has got both, constructionally and vitally, upon his canvas; and as regards Penelope, that under his vivifying imagination, Penelope herself has become flesh and blood. In his subtle, loving, understanding delineation, with its delicate humour and restrained pathos, she has ceased to be a special type, and become an individual, a living woman, with her nobilities and her weaknesses; like one of Shakespeare's women.

There is an instinctive and inevitable tendency [73/74] to wonder how the story went on, and to try to fill it up in imagination; the more so, the more that one appreciates the vivid reality of Penelope's figure. A poem ends, but life does not. "Which of us is happy in this world? which of us has his desire, or having it, is satisfied?" How did she bear the coming on of age? Did death come to her also, as it was to come to her husband, "very peacefully," far away from the sea? Poetry is more real than history; but is its reality, after all, only a strange illusion? It is part of this illusion that one can hardly help feeling and regretting, as in actual life, the misfits in families. Helen understood Telemachus in a way that makes one sure that she would have been a perfect mother to a son of her own; but she had none. And if Penelope had only had a daughter, it would have made all the difference to her. Even now, after so many centuries, she makes us try to get beyond the picture, as though it went on behind the frame, or if we looked at it long enough and steadily enough, would step out of the frame on to the floor. So difficult is it to realise that, out of the *Odyssey*, the Penelope of the *Odyssey* does not exist at all.

This is the power of art, and beyond all, of poetry.

> He will watch from dawn to gloom
> The lake-reflected sun illume
> The yellow bees in the ivy bloom,
> Nor heed nor see what things they be,
> But from these create he can
> Forms more real than living man.

But the instinctive desire to look behind the frame is one from which the artist himself is not always exempt. In the Epilogue to *War and* [74/75] *Peace*, Tolstoi (that great artist who hated and despised

[1] The passage, XXIII. 218–224, which would make an exception to this statement, was recognised by Aristarchus as an interpolation.

art) wrenches, as it were, a corner of the frame back; he shows us the lovely, brilliant, and passionate Natasha Rostov become, a few years later, a commonplace middle-aged woman, dully absorbed in her husband and children, exacting, tiresome, and unreasonably jealous. Tolstoi might (he certainly did, here and elsewhere) do as he chose. But the author of the *Odyssey* also did as he chose, and we had better be grateful for his choice and leave it so:

—Be it as it was,
Life touching lips with immortality. **[75]**

HOMER'S UNIVERSE

The Human World of the
Odyssey

M. I. FINLEY

IN THE SECOND BOOK OF THE *Iliad* THE POET CATALOGUES THE CONTEND-
ing hosts, in the case of the Greeks by the names of their chief leaders
and the number of ships each brought with him. "But the multitude
(i.e., the commoners) I could not relate nor name, not if I had ten
tongues, nor ten mouths."[1] The list totals 1186 ships, which, at a minimum computation, means over 60,000 men, a figure as trustworthy as
the 400,000 Saracens of *The Song of Roland*. The world of Odysseus
was a small one in numbers of people. There are no statistics and no
ways of making good guesses, but the five-acre sites of the archaeolo-
gists, together with what is known from later centuries, leave no doubt
that the populations of the individual communities were to be reckoned
in four figures, often even in three, and that the numbers in the poems,
whether of ships or flocks or slaves or nobles, are unrealistic and invariably err on the side of exaggeration.

One of the smallest contingents in the catalogue of ships was led
by Odysseus, a mere twelve (Agamemnon had one hundred and
provided sixty others for the inland Arcadians). He is announced as
king of the Cephallenians, who inhabit three [46/47] adjacent islands in
the Ionian Sea, Cephallenia, Ithaca, and Zacynthus, together with two
sites apparently on the nearby mainland. But it is with Ithaca specifically that he is always directly identified. And it is on the island
of Ithaca, not in the Never-Never Land through which he later wandered, that the world of Odysseus can chiefly be examined.

The island population was dominated by a group of noble families,
some of whose men participated in the expedition against Troy, while
others remained at home. Among the latter was Mentor, to whose
watchful eye Odysseus entrusted his young wife, Penelope, who came
from another land, and his only child, his newborn son Telemachus,
when he himself went off. For twenty years there was a strange hiatus

---

[1] *Iliad* 2.488–89.

in the political leadership of Ithaca. Odysseus' father, Laertes, did not resume the throne, though still alive. Penelope could not rule, being a woman. Mentor was no guardian in any legal sense, merely a well-intentioned, ineffectual figure, and he did not function as a regent.

For ten years a similar situation prevailed throughout the Greek world, while the kings, with few exceptions, were at war. With the destruction of Troy and the great homecoming of the heroes, life was resumed in its normal ways. The fallen kings were replaced; some who returned, like Agamemnon, ran into usurpers and assassins; and the others came back to the seats of power and its pursuits. But for Odysseus there was a different fate. Having offended the god Poseidon, he was tossed about for another ten years before he was rescued, largely through the intervention of Athena, and permitted to return to Ithaca. It was this second decade that perplexed the people at home. No one in all Hellas knew what had befallen Odysseus, whether he had died on the return journey from Troy or was still alive [47/48] somewhere in the outer world. This uncertainty laid the basis for the second theme of the poem, the story of the suitors.

Again there is trouble with numbers. No less than 108 nobles, 56 from Ithaca and the other islands ruled by Odysseus, and 52 from a neighboring mainland kingdom, says the poet, were paying court to Penelope. She was to be forced to choose Odysseus' successor from among them. This was no ordinary wooing, ancient style or modern. Except that they continued to sleep in their own homes, the suitors had literally taken over the household of the absent Odysseus and were steadily eating and drinking their way through his vast stores; "not twenty men together have so much wealth," according to the swineherd Eumaeus.[2] For three years Penelope defended herself by delaying tactics, but her power of resistance was wearing down. The ceaseless carouse in the house, the growing certainty that Odysseus would never return, and the suitors' open threat, made publicly to Telemachus, "to eat up your livelihood and your possessions,"[3] were having their effect. Just in time Odysseus returned, disguised as a wandering beggar. By employing all his craft and prowess, and a little magic, he succeeded in slaughtering the suitors, and, with the final intervention of Athena, in re-establishing his position as head of his household and king in Ithaca.

Abroad, Odysseus' life was one long series of struggles with witches, giants, and nymphs, but there is none of that in the Ithacan story. On the island we are confronted with human society alone (including the ever-present Athena, to be sure, but in a sense the Greek gods were always a part of human society, working through dreams, prophecies, oracles, and other signs). The same is true of the *Iliad*. For the story of the few days between the insult by Agamemnon and the death of [48/49] Hector at the hands of Achilles, as for the main plot

[2] *Odyssey* 14.98–99.
[3] *Odyssey* 2.123.

of the Ithacan theme, the nobility provides all the characters. The *Odyssey* parades other people of the island, but largely as stage props or stock types: Eumaeus the swineherd, the old nurse Eurycleia, Phemius the bard, the nameless "carvers of the meat," the sailors and housemaids and miscellaneous retainers. The poet's meaning is clear: on the field of battle, as in the power struggle which is the Ithacan theme, only the aristocrats had roles.

A deep horizontal cleavage marked the world of the Homeric poems. Above the line were the *aristoi*, literally the "best people," the hereditary nobles who held most of the wealth and all the power, in peace as in war. Below were all the others, for whom there was no collective technical term, the multitude. The gap between the two was rarely crossed, except by the inevitable accidents of wars and raids. The economy was such that the creation of new fortunes, and thereby of new nobles, was out of the question. Marriage was strictly class-bound, so that the other door to social advancement was also securely locked.

Below the main line there were various other divisions, but, unlike the primary distinction between aristocrat and commoner, they seem blurred and they are often indefinable. Not even so simple a contrast as that between slave and free man stands out in sharp clarity. The word *drester*, for example, which means "one who works or serves," is used in the *Odyssey* for the free and the unfree alike. The work they did and the treatment they received, at the hands of their masters as in the psychology of the poet, are often indistinguishable.

Slaves existed in number; they were property, disposable at will. More precisely, there were slave women, for wars and [49/50] raids were the main source of supply, and there was little ground, economic or moral, for sparing the lives of the defeated men. The heroes as a rule killed the males and carried off the females, regardless of rank. Before offering up his prayer for his son, Hector, who knew his own doom, said to his wife: "But I care not so much for the grief of the Trojans hereafter . . . as for yours, when one of the bronze-clad Achaeans will carry you off in tears; and you will be in Argos, working the loom at another woman's bidding, and you will draw water from Messeis or Hypereia, most unwillingly, and great constraint will be laid upon you."[4]

Hector did not need Apollo's aid in foretelling the future. Never in Greek history was it otherwise; the persons and the property of the vanquished belonged to the victor, to be disposed of as he chose. But Hector showed gentle restraint, for his prophecy was not complete. The place of slave women was in the household, washing, sewing, cleaning, grinding meal, valeting. If they were young, however, their place was also in the master's bed. Of the old nurse Eurycleia, the poet

---

[4] *Iliad* 6.450–58.

reports that "Laertes bought her with (some of) his possessions when she was still in the prime of youth . . . but he never had intercourse with her in bed, and he avoided the anger of his wife."[5] It was the rarity of Laertes' behavior, and the promise of his wife's wrath, that warranted the special comment. Neither custom nor morality demanded such abstinence.

It is idle to seek for numbers here. Odysseus is reported to have had fifty female slaves, but that is surely a convenient round figure, used for the household of King Alcinous of the Phaeacians too. A few men were also in bondage, such as the swineherd Eumaeus, an aristocrat by birth, who had been kidnaped when a child by Phoenician traders and sold into [50/51] slavery. Like the women, the male slaves worked in the home, and in the fields and vineyards, never abroad as servants or orderlies.

Of the Ithacans who were not slaves, the free population who were the bulk of the community, some were surely independent householders, free herders and peasants with their own holdings (although the poet tells us nothing about them). Others were specialists, carpenters and metal workers, soothsayers, bards, and physicians. Because they supplied certain essential needs in a way that neither the lords nor the non-specialists among their followers could match, these men, a handful in numbers, floated in mid-air in the social hierarchy. Seers and physicians might even be nobles, but the others, though they were close to the aristocratic class and even shared its life in many respects, were decidedly not of the aristocracy, as the treatment and behavior of the bard Phemius attest.

Eumaeus, we remember, called these specialists *demioergoi*, literally "those who work for the people" (and once Penelope attached the same classificatory label to the heralds). From the word, used in the Homeric poems only in these two passages, it has been suggested that the *demioergoi* operated in a way well known among primitive and archaic groups, the Kabyle of Algiers, for instance: "Another specialist is the blacksmith, who is also an outsider. The villagers lend him a house, and each family pays him a fixed portion of his yearly salary in grain and other produce."[6] Unfortunately the evidence for the world of Odysseus is far from clear or decisive. Once when Nestor, at home, wished to make sacrifice, he ordered his servants, " 'Bid the goldsmith Laerces come here, that he may gild the horns of the cow'. . . . And the smith came, with the smith's tools in his hands, the instruments of his crafts, anvil [51/52] and hammer and well-made fire-tongs, with which he worked the gold. . . . And the old horseman Nestor gave gold, and the smith then skillfully gilded the horns."[7] Neither the status

    [5] *Odyssey* 1.430–33.
    [6] Carleton S. Coon, *Caravan: The Story of the Middle East* (New York: Henry Holt and Company, 1951), p. 305.
    [7] *Odyssey* 3.425–38.

of the goldsmith nor even his domicile is indicated here, unlike the passage in the *Iliad* about the great "unwrought mass of iron" which Achilles offered from his booty for a weight-throwing contest. The iron was to be both the test and the prize for the winner. He will have it, said Achilles, "to use for five full years, for neither the shepherd nor the plowman will have to go into town for lack of iron, but this will furnish it."[8]

Although nothing is ever said about remuneration, it does not necessarily follow that each family in the community gave the smith, or the other *demioergoi*, a fixed annual maintenance quota. They could have been paid as they worked, provided only that they were available to the public, to the whole *demos*. That availability would explain the word well enough.

Eumaeus indicated still another special quality of the *demioergoi* when he asked "who ever summons a stranger from abroad . . . unless he be one of the *demioergoi*" (again with a parallel among the Kabyle). Were they, then, traveling tinkers and minstrels, going from community to community on a more or less fixed schedule? Actually the logic of Eumaeus's question is that all invited strangers are craftsmen, not that all craftsmen are strangers. Probably some were and some were not, and, of those who were, none need have worked on a circuit at all. The heralds were certainly permanent, regular, full-scale members of the community. The bards may have wandered a bit (in the poet's own day they traveled all the time). Regarding the others, we are simply not informed.

Indispensable as the *demioergoi* were, their contribution to [52/53] the quantity of work performed on an estate was a very small one. For the basic work of pasturage and tillage in the fields, of stewardship and service in the house, there was no need of specialists: every man in Ithaca could herd and plow and carve, and those commoners who had their own holdings worked them themselves. Others made up the permanent staffs of Odysseus and the nobles, free men like the unnamed "carvers of the meat," who were an integral part of the household. Still others, the least fortunate, were *thetes*, unattached, propertyless laborers who worked for hire and begged what they could not steal.

"Stranger," said the leading suitor Eurymachus to the beggar (Odysseus in disguise), "would you be willing to work as a *thes*, if I should take you in my service, on a farm at the border—you can be sure of pay—laying walls and planting tall trees? There I would furnish you ample grain and put clothes on your back and give you shoes for your feet." Ample grain and clothes and shoes made up the store of a commoner's goods. But Eurymachus was mocking, "creating laughter among his companions" at the direct inspiration of Athena, who "would

8 *Iliad* 23.833–35.

by no means permit the arrogant suitors to refrain from heart-rending scorn, so that the pain might sink still more deeply into the heart of Odysseus son of Laertes."⁹

A little of the joke lay in the words, "you can be sure of pay." No *thes* could be sure. Poseidon once angrily demanded of Apollo why he of all the gods should be so completely on the side of the Trojans. Have you forgotten, Poseidon asked, how, on order from Zeus, "we worked as *thetes* for one year, for an agreed-upon pay," for Laomedon, king of Troy, building the wall around the city and herding cattle? And how, at the end of the year, Laomedon "deprived us of our pay and [53/54] sent us off with threats?"¹⁰ The real joke, however, the utter scornfulness of Eurymachus's proposal, lay in the offer itself, not in the hint that the pay would be withheld in the end. To see the whole point, we turn to Achilles in Hades rather than to Poseidon on Olympus. "Do not speak to me lightly of death, glorious Odysseus," said the shade of Achilles. "I would rather be bound down, working as a *thes* for another, by the side of a landless man, whose livelihood was not great, than be ruler over all the dead who have perished."¹¹

A *thes*, not a slave, was the lowest creature on earth that Achilles could think of. The terrible thing about a *thes* was his lack of attachment, his not belonging. The authoritarian household, the *oikos*, was the center around which life was organized, from which flowed not only the satisfaction of material needs, including security, but ethical norms and values, duties, obligations, and responsibilities, social relationships, and relations with the gods. The *oikos* was not merely the family, it was all the people of the household and its goods; hence "economics" (from the Latinized form, *oecus*), the art of managing an *oikos*, meant running a farm, not managing to keep peace in the family.

Just what it meant, in terms of customary or legal obligation and in a man's own familial life, to be a permanent but free member of the *oikos* of another is by no means clear. Negatively it meant considerable loss of freedom of choice and of mobility. Yet these men were neither slaves nor serfs nor bondsmen. They were retainers (*therapontes*), exchanging their service for a proper place in the basic social unit, the household—a vicarious membership, no doubt, but one that gave them both material security and the psychological values and satisfactions that went with belonging. Altogether the chief [54/55] aristocrats managed, by a combination of slaves, chiefly female, and a whole hierarchy of retainers, supplemented by *thetes*, to build up very imposing and very useful household forces, equipped to do whatever was required of a man of status and power in their world. The hierarchy of retainers, it should be added, reached very high indeed. As a child Patroclus was forced to flee his home. Peleus received him in his palace

---

⁹ *Odyssey* 18.346–61.
¹⁰ *Iliad* 21.441–52.
¹¹ *Odyssey* 11.489–91.

and "named him retainer" of young Achilles.[12] The analogy that comes to mind at once is that of the noble page in some early modern court, just as "lord Eteoneus, the ready retainer of Menelaus" who met guests at the door and poured the wine for them, might well have been the counterpart of a Lord Chamberlain.[13]

A *thes* in Ithaca might even have been an Ithacan, not an outsider. But he was no part of an *oikos,* and in this respect even the slave was better off. The slave, human but nevertheless a part of the property element of the *oikos,* was altogether a nice symbol of the situation. Only twice does Homer use the word that later became standard in Greek for a slave, *doulos,* which seems etymologically tied to the idea of labor. Otherwise his word is *dmos,* with its obvious link with *doma* or *domos,* a house; and after Homer and Hesiod *dmos* never appears in literature apart from a few instances of deliberate archaizing as in Sophocles and Euripides. The treatment of the slaves was essentially milder and more humane than the pattern familiar from plantation slavery. Eumaeus, a favorite slave, had even been able to purchase a slave for himself. To be sure, a dozen of the slave girls were hanged in the midst of the carnage of Odysseus' successful return, but it was the method of their execution alone that distinguished them from the lordly suitors, who died by the bow and the spear. [55/56]

There was little mating of slave with slave because there were so few males among them. Nearly all the children born to the slave women were the progeny of the master or of other free males in the household. Commonly, in many different social systems, as among the Greeks later on, such offspring were slaves like their mothers: "the belly holds the child," say the Tuareg nomads of the Sahara in explanation. Not so in the world of Odysseus, where it was the father's status that was determinative. Thus, in the fanciful tale with which Odysseus sought to conceal his identity from Eumaeus immediately upon his return to Ithaca, his father was a wealthy Cretan, his mother a "bought concubine." When the father died the legitimate sons divided the property, giving him only a dwelling and a few goods. Later, by his valor, he obtained to wife the daughter of "a man of many estates."[14] The slave woman's son might sometimes be a second-class member of the family, but even then he was part of that narrower circle within the *oikos* as a whole, free and without even the stigma of bastardy in our sense, let alone the mark of slavery.

Fundamentally the difference between the ordinary landowner and the noble lay in the magnitude of their respective *oikoi,* and therefore in the numbers of retainers they could support, which, translated into practical terms, meant in their power. Superficially the difference was one of birth. At some past point, remote or near in time, either conquest or wealth created the original separation. Then it froze, con-

---

[12] *Iliad* 23.90.
[13] *Odyssey* 4.22–23.
[14] *Odyssey* 14.199–212.

tinued along hereditary lines, was given divine sanction through genealogies that assigned every noble family a god for an ancestor, and was called a blood-distinction.

The nature of the economy served to seal and preserve the class line. Wherever the wealth of the household is so decisive, [56/57] unless there is a measure of mobility in wealth, unless the opportunity exists to create new fortunes, the structure becomes caste-like in its rigidity. This was the case in Ithaca. The base of the *oikos* was its land, and there was no way, under normal, peaceful conditions, to acquire new land in the settled regions. Hypothetically one might push to the frontier and take up vacant land, but few men actually did anything so absurd and foolhardy, except under the most violent compulsions. It was not out of mere sentiment for the fatherland that banishment was deemed the bitterest of fates. The exile was stripped of all ties that meant life itself; it made no difference in this regard whether one had been compelled to flee or had gone from home in the search for land by free choice.

The primary use of the land was in pasturage. To begin the story of his adventure among the Cyclopes, which he told at the court of Alcinous, Odysseus underscored the primitive savagery of the one-eyed giants. First of all, they had not learned the art of agriculture: "they neither plant anything nor till."[15] Nevertheless, Odysseus' own world was one of pasturage, not of tillage (unlike the Greek world at the time of Homer himself and of Hesiod, when agriculture had moved to the fore). Greek soil is poor, rocky and waterless, so that no more than twenty per cent of the total surface of the peninsula can be cultivated. In places it once provided excellent pasturage for horses and cattle; virtually all of it is still, in our day, good for the smaller animals, sheep and pigs and goats. The households of the poems carried on a necessary minimum of plowing and planting, especially on orchard and vineland but it was their animals on which they depended for clothing, draft, transport, and much of their food.

With their flocks and their labor force, with plentiful stone [57/58] for building and clay for pots, the great households could almost realize their ideal of absolute self-sufficiency. The *oikos* was above all a unit of consumption. Its activities, insofar as they were concerned with the satisfaction of material wants, were guided by one principle, to meet the consuming needs of the lord and his people; if possible by the products of his estates, supplemented by booty. But there was one thing which prevented full self-sufficiency, a need which could neither be eliminated nor satisfied by substitutes, and that was the need for metal. Scattered deposits existed in Greece, but the main sources of supply were outside, in western Asia and central Europe.

Metal meant tools and weapons, but it also meant something else, perhaps as important. When Telemachus had concluded his visit at the

---

[15] *Odyssey* 9.108.

palace of Menelaus in Sparta, in search of news about his father, his host offered him, as a parting gift, "three horses and a chariot-board of polished metal and . . . a fine goblet." The young man demurred. "And whatever gift you would give me, let it be treasure. I will not take horses to Ithaca. . . . In Ithaca there are neither wide courses nor any meadowland."[16] The Greek word customarily rendered by "treasure" is *keimelion*, literally something that can be laid away. In the poems treasure was of bronze, iron, or gold, less often of silver or fine cloth, and usually it was shaped into goblets, tripods, or caldrons. Such objects had some utilitarian worth and they could provide aesthetic satisfaction too, but neither function was of real moment compared to their value as symbolic wealth or prestige wealth. The twin uses of treasure were in possessing it and in giving it away, paradoxical as that may appear. Until the appropriate occasion for a gift presented [58/59] itself, most treasure was kept hidden under lock and key. It was not "used" in the narrow sense of that word.

When Agamemnon was finally persuaded that appeasement of Achilles was absolutely essential to prevent the destruction of the Achaean forces, he went about it by offering amends through gifts. His offer included some to be presented at once, others on conditions of victory. And what a catalogue it was: seven cities, a daughter to wife with a great dowry "such as no one ever yet gave with his daughter," the girl Briseis, over whom the quarrel had broken out, seven captive women from Lesbos skilled in crafts, twelve prize-winning racehorses, and his choice of twenty Trojan women when the war was won. These, apart from the horses, were the utilitarian gifts. But Agamemnon began with none of them; first came "seven tripods that have never been on the fire and ten talents of gold and twenty glittering caldrons," and further on, from the anticipated Trojan spoils, as much gold and bronze as his ship would hold. That was treasure, and its high importance is marked by the care with which it is enumerated here and again later in the poem. Menelaus's gift to Telemachus, all treasure, reappears four more times in the *Odyssey*, in three different books.

Whatever its purpose or its source, metal created for the individual *oikos* a special problem in the distribution of goods. For the most part distribution was internal and hence no problem at all. Since there has never been a world of Robinson [59/60] Crusoes, the simplest human groups perforce have a mechanism, and it is the same one that served, with some extension, even the most elaborate princely *oikos*. All the productive work, the seeding and harvesting and milling and weaving, even the hunting and raiding, though performed by individuals, was carried on in behalf of the household as a whole. The final products, ready for consumption, were gathered and stored centrally, and from the center they were redistributed—in the authoritarian household, by its head at a time and in a measure he deemed appropriate.

[16] *Odyssey* 4.590–605.

It made no difference in essence whether the family members within the household were no more than a husband, wife, and child, or whether the *oikos* was that of King Priam of Troy, with his fifty sons and their wives, twelve daughters and their husbands, and his uncounted grandchildren; or the more reasonable example of Nestor at Pylos, with six sons and some sons-in-law. The sons possessed arms and treasure of their own, from gifts and booty, as the wives and daughters had their fine garments and jewels. But unless the males left the paternal household and established their own *oikoi*, their personal property was an essentially insignificant factor. Normally, the poems seem to say, although the evidence is not altogether clear and consistent, the sons remained with their father in his lifetime.

Architecturally the heart of the system was the storeroom. Preparing for his journey to Pylos, Telemachus "went down to his father's spacious, high-ceilinged storeroom, where gold and copper lay piled up, and clothing in chests, and fragrant oil in plenty; and there stood jars of wine, old and sweet, filled with the unmixed divine drink, close together in a row along the wall."[17] And of course it contained arms and grain in quantity. More than three hundred years after Homer the [60/61] Athenian Xenophon, a gentleman farmer and no tribal chieftain or king, still placed proper care of the storeroom high on the list of wifely virtues.

It was when distribution had to cross *oikos* lines that the creation of new and special devices became necessary. Wars and raids for booty, indistinguishable in the eyes of Odysseus' world, were organized affairs, often involving a combination of families, occasionally even of communities. Invariably there was a captain, one of whose functions was to act as the head and distribute the booty, all of which was first brought to a central storage point. Division was by lot, much like the division of an inheritance when there were several heirs. For example, not all of Odysseus' homecoming adventures were tragic. Two or three times he and his men had the pleasant opportunity to raid. "From Ilion," he began the account of his wanderings, "the wind bore me near to the Cicones, to Ismarus. There I sacked the city and killed the men; taking the women and many goods, we divided them, so that no one might go cheated of his equal share through me."[18]

Forcible seizure, followed by distribution in this fashion, was one way to acquire metal or other goods from an outside source. Some scholars think that the kernel of historical truth in the tale of the Trojan War is precisely such a mass raid for iron supplies. Whether they are right or not, there were surely many smaller Trojan wars to such a purpose, against Greeks as well as against barbarians. But the violent solution was neither always feasible nor even always desirable; if the

---

[17] *Odyssey* 2.337–42.
[18] *Odyssey* 9.39–42. The final line also appears in the *Iliad*, 11.705.

aggrieved party were strong enough it invited retaliation, and there were times and conditions when even the fiercest of the heroes preferred peace. An exchange mechanism was then the only alternative, and the basic one was gift-exchange. This was [61/62] no Greek invention. On the contrary, it is the basic organizing mechanism among many primitive peoples, as in the Trobriand Islands, where "most if not all economic acts are found to belong to some chain of reciprocal gifts and counter-gifts."[19]

The word "gift" is not to be misconstrued. It may be stated as a flat rule of both primitive and archaic society that no one ever gave anything, whether goods or services or honors, without proper recompense, real or wishful, immediate or years away, to himself or to his kin. The act of giving was, therefore, in an essential sense always the first half of a reciprocal action, the other half of which was a counter-gift.

Not even the parting gift was an exception, although in this one instance there was an element of risk. The last of the recognition scenes in the *Odyssey*, between the hero and his aged father, began in the customary fashion, with Odysseus claiming to be someone else, a stranger from another land in search of information about "Odysseus." Your son, he said to Laertes, visited me about five years ago and received the proper gifts. "Of well-wrought gold I gave him seven talents, and I gave him a bowl with flower designs, all of silver, and twelve single cloaks and as many carpets and as many fine mantles, and as many tunics besides, and in addition four pretty women skilled in excellent work." Laertes wept, for he had long been satisfied that his son had perished, and he could think of no better way to reveal that fact to the stranger than by commenting on the gift situation. "The countless gifts which you gave, you bestowed in vain. For if you had found that man still alive in the land of Ithaca, he would have sent you or your way well provided with gifts in return."[20]

Then there is the interesting scene in the opening book of the *Odyssey*, in which the goddess Athena appeared to Telemachus [62/63] in the shape of Mentes, a Taphian chieftain. When she was ready to part, the young man followed the expected custom: "Go to your ship happy in your heart, bearing a gift, valuable and very beautiful, which will be your treasure from me, such as dear guest-friends give to guest-friends." This created a very delicate situation for the goddess. One did not refuse a proffered gift, yet she could not accept it under the false pretense of her human disguise. (Gods as gods not only accepted gifts from mortals, they expected and demanded them.) Being the cleverest of the gods, Athena unhesitatingly found the perfect solution. "Do not detain me any longer as I am eager to be on my way. The gift, which

---

[19] Bronislaw Malinowski, *Crime and Custom in Savage Society* (New York: Humanities Press, 1952), p. 40.
[20] *Odyssey* 24.274-85.

the heart of a friend prompts you to give me, give it to me on my return journey that I may carry it home; choose a very beautiful one, that will bring you a worthy one in exchange."[21]

Telemachus had said nothing about a counter-gift. Yet he and "Mentes" understood each other perfectly: the counter-gift was as expected as the original gift at parting. That was what gift-giving was in this society. The return need not be forthcoming at once, and it might take several forms. But come it normally would. "In a society ruled by respect for the past, a traditional gift is very near indeed to an obligation."[22] No single detail in the life of the heroes receives so much attention in the *Iliad* and the *Odyssey* as gift-giving, and always there is frank reference to adequacy, appropriateness, recompense. "But then Zeus son of Cronus took from Glaucus his wits, in that he exchanged golden armor with Diomedes son of Tydeus for one of bronze, the worth of a hundred oxen for the worth of nine oxen."[23] The poet's editorial comment, so rare for him, reflects the magnitude of Glaucus's mistake in judgment. [63/64]

There was scarcely a limit to the situations in which gift-giving was operative. More precisely, the word "gift" was a cover-all for a great variety of actions and transactions which later became differentiated and acquired their own appellations. There were payments for services rendered, desired, or anticipated; what we would call fees, rewards, prizes, and sometimes bribes. The formulaic material was rich in such references, as in the lines with which Telemachus and twice Penelope responded to a stranger's favorable interpretation of a sign from the gods: "Stranger, would that these words be fulfilled! Speedily should you become aware of friendship and many gifts from me, so that whoever met you would congratulate you."[24]

Then there were taxes and other dues to lords and kings, amends with a penal overtone (Agamemnon's gift to Achilles), and even ordinary loans—and again the Homeric word is always "gift." Defending himself for having lent Telemachus a ship with which to sail to Pylos and Sparta seeking information about Odysseus, a young Ithacan noble made this explanation: "What can one do when such a man, troubled in heart, begs? It would be difficult to refuse the gift."[25] In still another category payment for service was combined with the ceremonialism necessary to an important event. There is much talk in the *Odyssey* about the "gifts of wooing," and the successful suitor, who reminds one of nothing so much as the highest bidder at an

---

[21] *Odyssey* 1.311–18.

[22] Marc Bloch, in *The Cambridge Economic History*, ed. by J. H. Clapham and Eileen Power, vol. 1 (Cambridge, England: Cambridge University Press, 1941), p. 262. Bloch is discussing the early Germanic world described by Tacitus.

[23] *Iliad* 6.234–36.

[24] *Odyssey* 15.536–38, 17.163–65, 19.309–11.

[25] *Odyssey* 4.649–51.

auction, in turn received his counter-gift in the dowry, without which there could be no marriage. The whole of what we call foreign relations and diplomacy, in their peaceful manifestations, was conducted by gift-exchange. And even in war occasions presented themselves, as between Diomedes and Glaucus, for example, or Ajax and Hector, when heroes from [64/65] the two contending sides stopped, right on the field of combat and before the approving eyes of their fellow heroes, and exchanged armor.

Odyssean trade differed from the various forms of gift-exchange in that the exchange of goods was the end itself. In trade things changed hands because each needed what the other had, and not, or only incidentally, to compensate for a service, seal an alliance, or support a friendship. A need for some specific object was the ground for the transaction; if it could be satisfied by other means, trade was altogether unnecessary. Hence, in modern parlance, imports alone motivated trade, never exports. There was never a need to export as such, only the necessity of having the proper goods for the counter-gift when an import was unavoidable.

Laertes bought Eurycleia "with (some of) his possessions . . . , and he gave the worth of twenty oxen."[26] Cattle were the measuring stick of worth; in that respect, and only in that sense, cattle were money. Neither cattle, however, nor anything else served for the various other, later uses of money. Above all, there was no circulating medium like a coin, the sole function of which was to make purchase and sale possible by being passed from hand to hand. Almost any useful object served, and it is noteworthy that the measure of value, cattle, did not itself function as a medium of exchange. Laertes bought Eurycleia for unspecified objects worth twenty oxen; he would never have traded the oxen for a slave.

A conventional measuring stick is no more than an artificial language, a symbol like the X, Y, Z of algebra. By itself it cannot decide how much iron is the equivalent of one cow, or how much wine. In Adam Smith's world that determination was made through the supply-and-demand market, a mechanism [65/66] utterly unknown in Troy or Ithaca. Behind the market lies the profit motive, and if there was one thing that was taboo in Homeric exchanges it was gain in the exchange. Whether in trade or in any other mutual relationship, the abiding principle was equality and mutual benefit. Gain at the expense of another belonged to a different realm, to warfare and raiding, where it was achieved by acts (or threats) of prowess, not by manipulation and bargaining. Gain from trade was "greedy gain."

The implication that exchange rates were customary and conventional seems unavoidable. That is to say, there was no constituted authority with the power to decree a set of equations—so much of X

[26] *Odyssey* 1.430–31.

for so much of Y. Rather the actual practice of exchange over a long period of time had fixed the ratios, and they were commonly known and respected. Even in the distribution of booty, where a central authority, the head of the *oikos* or a king or commander-in-chief, took charge, he was obviously bound by what was generally deemed to be equitable. The circumstance that no one could punish him for flouting custom, as in the conflict between Agamemnon and Achilles, is irrelevant to the issue. For the very fact that just such a situation gave the theme for the *Iliad* illustrates how dangerous the violation could be. In this world custom was as binding upon the individual as the most rigid statutory law of later days. And the participant in an exchange, it may be added, had the advantage over the passive participant in the distribution of booty. He could always refuse to go through with the transaction if the rules were manifestly being upset, or if he merely thought they were.

None of this is to say that no one ever deliberately profited from an exchange. But the exceptional instance is far less noteworthy [66/67] than the essential point that, in a strict sense, the ethics of the world of Odysseus prohibited the practice of trade as a vocation. The test of what was and what was not acceptable did not lie in the act of trading, but in the status of the trader and in his approach to the transaction. So crucial was the need for metal that even a king could honorably voyage in its search. When Athena appeared to Telemachus as Mentes, the Taphian chieftain, her story was that she was carrying iron to Temesa in quest of copper. That gave no difficulties, and her visit ended with the colloquy regarding costly gifts between guest-friends.

A stranger with a ship was not always so welcome or so free from suspicion. He might have been Odysseus before Ismarus, or Achilles: "Twelve cities of men have I destroyed from shipboard and eleven on foot, I say, in the fertile region of Troy; from all these I took out much good treasure."[27] No wonder that some Greeks eventually objected to Homer as the teacher of the Hellenes. Glorification of piracy, disapproval of theft (seizure of goods by stealth), and encouragement of robbery (seizure of goods and persons by physical prowess)—truly this seemed a world of mixed-up moral standards. "Theft of property is mean," protested Plato, "seizure by force shameless; none of the sons of Zeus delighted in fraud or violence, nor practiced either. Therefore, let no one be falsely persuaded by poets or by some myth-tellers in these matters."[28]

Yet there was a pattern and a consistency in the moral code; and it made sense from the premises. The distinctions rested on a specific social structure, with strongly entrenched [67/68] notions regarding the proper ways for a man to behave, with respect to property, toward

---

27 *Iliad* 9.328–31.
28 *Laws* 941B.

other men. Upon his arrival among the Phaeacians, but before he had identified himself and told of his wanderings, Odysseus was entertained by King Alcinous. Following the feast, the younger nobles competed in athletics. After a time the king's son Laodamas approached Odysseus and invited him to participate.

"Come, stranger and father, you enter the games, if perchance you are skilled in any; you seem to know games. For there is no greater fame for a man, so long as he is alive, than that which is made by foot and hand."

Odysseus asked to be excused, pleading the heavy burden of his sorrows. Another young aristocrat then interposed. "No indeed, stranger, I do not think you are like a man of games, such as there are many among men; but like one who travels with a many-benched ship, a master of sailors who traffic, one who remembers the cargo and is in charge of merchandise and greedy gains."[29]

The insult was unbearable under all circumstances, and to Homer's audience it must have carried an added barb when directed against Odysseus. There was something equivocal about Odysseus as a hero precisely because of his most famed quality, his craftiness. There was even a soft spot in his inheritance: his maternal grandfather, the goodly Autolycus, "surpassed all men in thievishness and the oath, for that was a gift to him from the god Hermes."[30] Later the doubts of many Greeks turned to open contempt and condemnation. "I know full well," says Philoctetes in the Sophoclean play, "that he would attempt with his tongue every evil word and villainy."[31] What saved the Homeric Odysseus was the fact that [68/69] his guile was employed in the pursuit of heroic goals; hence Hermes, the god of tricks and stealth, may have given him the magic with which to ward off Circe the witch, but it was Athena who was his protector and his inspiration in his heroic exploits. To the insult in Phaeacia he first replied with an indignant speech, but Odysseus, of all men, could not establish his status with words. Having finished his reply, he leaped up, seized a weight greater than any the young men had cast, and, without removing his garment, threw it far beyond their best mark.

Possibly there were men, a very few from among those who were not men of games, living in the interstices of society, who traveled in many-benched ships and trafficked. Yet there is no single word in either the *Iliad* or the *Odyssey* that is in fact a synonym for "merchant." By and large, the provisioning of the Greek world with whatever it obtained from the outside by peaceful means was in the hands of non-Greeks, the Phoenicians in particular. They were really a trading people, who sailed from one end of the known world to the other, carrying slaves, metal, jewelry, and fine cloth. If they were motivated by gain—

29 *Odyssey* 8.145–64.
30 *Odyssey* 19.395–97.
31 *Philoctetes* 407–408.

"famed for ships, greedy men"[32]—that was irrelevant to the Greeks, the passive participants in the operation.

The need for metal, or any similar need, was an *oikos* affair, not an individual matter. Its acquisition, whether by trade or by raid, was therefore a household enterprise, managed by the head. Or it could be larger in scale, involving many households acting cooperatively. Internally, the situation was altogether different. Trade within the household was impossible by definition: the *oikos* was a single, indivisible unit. Because a large sector of the population was enmeshed in the great households, [69/70] it too was withdrawn from any possibility of trade, external or internal. The *thetes,* finally, were absolutely excluded; having nothing, they had nothing to exchange.

That leaves the non-aristocratic, small-scale herders and peasants. In their households shortages were chronic, if not absolute as a consequence of a crop failure or a disaster to their flocks, then partial because of an imbalance in the yield. Their troubles are not the subject of heroic poetry, and neither the *Iliad* nor the *Odyssey* is informative in this regard. The inference is permissible, however, that some of their difficulties were alleviated by barter, primarily with one another, and without the instrumentality of a market or fair, absolutely unknown in this world. They exchanged necessities, staples, undoubtedly on the same principles of equivalence, ratios fixed by custom, and no gain.

Herders and peasants, including the *thetes,* always had another resource to draw upon. They could work. As with trade, so with labor, the society's moral judgment was directed not to the act itself but to the person and the circumstance. Back in Ithaca, but still disguised as a beggar, Odysseus, in reply to Eurymachus's mocking offer of employment, challenged the suitor to a plowing contest—just as, in his proper guise, he boasted of his superior bowmanship or his weight throwing. But Odysseus was not required to plow in order to live. In fact, it is obvious that, though he knew how to till and herd and build a raft, he rarely did any work on his estate except in sport. That was the great dividing line, between those who were compelled to labor and those who were not. Among the former, the men with the inspired skills, the bards and the metalworkers and the others, were an elite. Above all, the test was this, that "the condition of the free man is that he not live [70/71] under the constraint of another."[33] Hence there was a sharp line between those who, though they worked, remained their own masters, the independent herders and peasants, and on the other side the *thetes* and the slaves who labored for others, whose livelihood was not in their own hands. The slaves, at least, were usually the victims of chance. The *thes* was in that sense the worst of all: he voluntarily contracted away his control over his own labor, in other words, his true freedom.

32 *Odyssey* 15.415–16.
33 Aristotle, *Rhetoric* 1.9, 1367a32, writing with specific reference to labor.

Much of the psychology of labor, with its ambivalence between admiration of skill and craft and its rejection of the laborer as essentially and irretrievably an inferior being, found its symbol on Olympus. Having humanized the gods, the bard was consistent enough to include labor among the heavenly pursuits. But that entailed a certain difficulty. Zeus the insatiable philanderer, Apollo the archer who was also a minstrel, Ares the god of battle—these were all embodiments of noble attributes and activities, easily recreated in man's image. But how could the artisan who built their palaces and made their weapons and their plate and their ornaments be placed on equal footing with them, without casting a shadow over the hierarchy of values and status on which society rested? Only a god could make swords for gods, yet somehow he must be a being apart from the other gods.

The solution was neatly turned, very neatly indeed. The divine craftsman was Hephaestus, son of Hera. His skill was truly fabulous, and the poet never tired of it, lingering over his forge and his productions as he never sang of the smith in Ithaca. That was the positive side of the ambivalence. The other was this: of all the gods, Hephaestus alone was "a huge limping monster" with "a sturdy neck and hairy chest."[34] Hephaestus was born lame, and he carried the mark of his [71/72] shame on his whole personality. The other gods would have been less than human, in consequence, were Hephaestus not to be their perennial source of humor. Once, when Zeus and Hera were having a fearful quarrel, the limping god attempted the role of peacemaker, filling the cups with nectar for all the assemblage. "And unquenchable laughter was stirred up among the blessed gods as they watched Hephaestus bustling about the palace."[35] And the social fabric of the world of Odysseus was saved.

In fact, the mirror-image on Olympus was still more subtle. In art and craftsmanship, Athena was frequently linked with Hephaestus, as in the simile in which a comparison is drawn with a goldsmith, "a skillful man whom Hephaestus and Pallas Athena taught all kinds of craft (techne)."[36] But there was absolutely nothing deformed or the least bit comical about Athena, deservedly her father's favorite among the gods. It was unnecessary to apologize for Athena's skill with her hands, for the pattern with respect to work differed somewhat for women. Denied the right to a heroic way of life, to feats of prowess, competitive games, and leadership in organized activity of any kind, women worked, regardless of class. With her maids, Nausicaa, daughter of the Phaeacian king, did the household laundry. Queen Penelope found in her weaving the trick with which to hold off the suitors. Her stratagem, however, of undoing at night what she had woven in the

34 *Iliad* 18.410–15.
35 *Iliad* 1.599–600.
36 *Odyssey* 6.232–34.

day, repeated without detection for three full years until one of her maids revealed the secret, suggests that her labor was not exactly indispensable. The women of the aristocracy, like their men, possessed all the necessary work skills, and they used them more often. Nevertheless, their real role was managerial. The house was their [72/73] domain, the cooking and the washing, the cleaning and the clothesmaking. The dividing line for them was rather in the degree to which they performed the chores themselves—between those who supervised, working only to pass the time, and those whom circumstances compelled to cook and sew in earnest. [73]

The Divine World of the
Odyssey

G. M. A. GRUBE

THE PROBLEM OF THE HOMERIC GODS IS HOW TO RECONCILE "THE COSMIC gods and the comic gods."[1] The great Olympians often behave in a manner which is both frivolous and, in the widest sense, immoral;[2] yet they are the mighty powers which rule the universe and largely control the destiny of men. As such they inspire genuine religious feelings. Their irresponsible ways were condemned by Heraclitus and Xenophanes and have puzzled commentators ever since. In the light of later religious feelings, the gods of Homer present an insoluble paradox.

Modern scholars have for the most part not attempted to reconcile these incompatible aspects of the gods. Many have taken them to represent different religious or irreligious phases of thought perhaps centuries apart; such differences are then used as but another instrument to dissect the Homeric poems.[3] Others have suggested that to Homer

---

[1] The phrase is G. M. Calhoun's in "Homer's Gods: Prolegomena," *TAPA* 68 (1937) 21. The whole article is an interesting statement of our problem.

[2] Throughout this article I use the words moral, morality, immoral in their true sense, not in the debased and restricted modern fashion excellently illustrated when one of our learned judges, addressing the jury in a recent murder trial, said: "This, I repeat, is not a case of morals but of murder; morality has nothing to do with it." His lordship was of course referring to the sexual immorality of the accused.

[3] Proponents of this view, among others, are P. Cauer, *Grundfragen der Homerkritik* (Leipzig 1923) 376–406; Wilamowitz, who discovers several strata of development and degeneration, *Die Ilias und Homer* (Berlin 1916) 316–355;

G. M. A. Grube, "The Gods of Homer," *The Phoenix*, V (1951), 62–78. Reprinted by permission of the author and the publisher.

and his audience mythology had nothing to do with religion; sometimes they depict Homer, rather surprisingly, as both a sceptic and a
religious reformer.[4] Others again have found in the epics two quite
separate religions: that of the characters and that of the poet.[5] Attempts
have also been made to explain the inconsistencies by the convenient
theory that Homer's mind was so primitive that glaringly incompatible
ideas could dwell in it at the same time.[6]

Not one of these theories is convincing. If the *Iliad* is to be carved
up, differences of belief are far too uncertain and too entangled to lead
to a clean operation; nor is there any agreement among the surgeons
as to what is early and what late, or indeed when is early, when late.
Homer was a poet, not a theologian, and passages that are not logically
consistent may well be by the same hand—even theologians are not
always logical; but to regard mythology and religion as completely
separate is against the whole spirit of the poems, they are in any case
too closely enmeshed. Nor do I believe that Homer had a primitive
mind. He may well be blind to implied contradictions which will become explicit in the light of later thought, but that is quite another
story. Finally, those who seek to differentiate the religion of the poet
from that of the characters overemphasize certain expressions and
ignore a good deal; no such two religions would ever strike a reader
who was not looking for them. [62/63]

Let us rather re-examine the deeper question: is there any real in-
compatibility; are the gods not the same gods throughout, and such as
we might well expect them to be at the stage of development Homer

---

G. Finsler, who has an earlier stage of unrelated gods whom men revere, and
a later stage when Olympus has become a state of the gods and the poet hates
them as cruel and selfish, *Homer* I (Leipzig and Berlin 1924) 1.168–169 and
2.207–215; Gilbert Murray, who distinguishes four different strata, *The Rise of
the Greek Epic* (London 1934) 267. Interesting criticisms of this whole point of
view will be found in E. Drerup, *Das Homerproblem in der Gegenwart* (Würzburg 1921) 226–231 and 414–422, G. M. Calhoun's "The Higher Criticism on
Olympus," *AJP* 58 (1937) 257–274. J. M. Duffy, in his dissertation, reviews the
evidence to show that the gods are the same throughout: *A Comparative Study
of the Religion of the Iliad and the Odyssey* (Chicago 1937).

[4] So C. M. Bowra, *Tradition and Design in the Iliad* (Oxford 1930) 215–233,
Calhoun also separates the gods of ethical thought from those of myth in *TAPA*
68 (1937) 17. Andrew Lang, *The World of Homer* (London 1910) 120–127, and
Drerup 416–422.

[5] In particular E. Hedén, *Homerische Götterstudien* (Uppsala 1912) speaks
of a deeper religion, that of the characters, tinged with scepticism but closely connected with ritual, and that of the poet which is purely mythical and poetic. But
the most "religious" passage of the *Iliad* (16.386–393, see below) is in a simile.
Hedén's theory is discussed by E. Ehnmark, *The Idea of God in Homer* (Uppsala
1935) 64–70; M. P. Nilsson, *A History of Greek Religion* (Oxford 1949) 162–179.

[6] B. E. Perry, "The Early Greek Capacity for Viewing Things Separately,"
TAPA 68 (1937) 415–418; and J. A. Notopoulos, "Parataxis in Homer" *TAPA* 80
(1949) 8–9. Here more openly stated, some such mental parataxis is implied in
most discussions of Homer's gods.

represents? To find an answer it is necessary to clear from our minds the associations of the corresponding modern words, and also the associations which the Greek words themselves acquired in later times. The gods of Homer may help to explain the gods of Plato, but the gods of Plato can only hinder our search for the gods of Homer. More surprisingly, we must clear from our minds also the more primitive notions that seem to emerge from the archaeological evidence of pre-Homeric times, even though many earlier practices survived long afterwards; it has long been recognized that Homer is, in matters of religion, peculiar and unique.[7] It will be possible here only to indicate the lines along which the solution can be found; we shall largely restrict ourselves to the great Olympians, for they are the main difficulty. What are these gods?

The Homeric gods are immortal, and they are powerful. The greatest of them live as a family on Olympus, with Zeus as the father of the family or clan.[8] They are not creators, but have wrested the divine powers from an earlier generation. These older gods are now relegated to Tartarus, and have little dramatic or religious significance. The present generation is solidly established and their collective power is absolute. They have the capacity to see everything and to know everything when they care to use it, when their attention is engaged.[9] There are no other powers beyond or behind but only below them. Where Homer uses more abstract terms such as Fate—Moira, Aisa

---

[7] Wilamowitz, *Der Glaube der Hellenen* (Berlin 1931) 317; T. D. Seymour, *Life in the Homeric Age* (London 1907) 392–395; Jane Harrison, *Mythology* (Boston 1924) xvi–xx; Gilbert Murray, *Five Stages of Greek Religion* (Oxford 1925) 24–32; Nilsson, *A History* 135–146. While many of the details of Homer's representation of his gods can be accounted for by earlier evidence, and Athena may be called γλαυκῶπις because she was once an owl-goddess, this is of little help in interpreting the Homeric Athena. We shall therefore find little to help us in the many interesting books on the *origins* of Greek religion.

[8] M. P. Nilsson's theory that Homer's Olympus was created after the pattern of the Mycenaean kingship is well known; *Homer and Mycenae* (London 1933) 266–277, *The Minoan-Mycenaean Religion and its Survival in Greek Religion* (Lund 1950) 30. Finsler too speaks of Olympus as a kingdom, but G. M. Calhoun has shown that Zeus is much more like a patriarch than a king, he is never, for example, called βασιλεύς; see "Zeus The Father in Homer," *TAPA* 66 (1935) 1–17. Calhoun's other interesting theory that there is no real nobility of birth in Homer may also be noted here: "Classes and Masses in Homer," *CP* 29 (1934) 192–208 and 301–316.

[9] The qualification is important, for if all the gods knew everything, and could do everything, all the time, life on Olympus could not be of much dramatic interest. So the poet solved the difficulty by letting the attention of the gods wander, even that of Zeus. This dramatic necessity should offer no difficulty and is hardly worth learned discussion. So also the gods can move very quickly, but they have chariots and make at times elaborate preparations for a journey they could have accomplished as quickly as thought (*Il.* 5.711–791; 8.381–396; 13.17–28). Poseidon is away among the Ethiopians at the beginning of the *Odyssey* (1.22) as Zeus is at the beginning of the *Iliad* (1.423). The gods can also hide from one another (*Il.* 5.844; 13.352). For the omniscience of the gods see *Od.* 4.468; 10.306, 573; 14.443.

and the like—they are but another way of referring to the power of the gods, or else they represent subordinate functions.[10] Twice Zeus gets out his golden scales to weigh the fate of heroes, once that of the Trojans and Achaeans generally (Il. 8.66–67), once that of Hector and Achilles in particular (Il. 22.209–214); in both cases the decisions are already taken, known both to Zeus and to us. The scales are but the concrete symbol of a decision and, like an oath, make it irrevocable, so that even Apollo abandons Hector after the weighing, and in the former instance the gods are all on Olympus by order of Zeus, where they stay for a while at least. Consecrated by the scales, the decision must be accepted.

There is no hint in these passages of any other power over Zeus. The jars of Zeus, from which he distributes good and evil to mankind in any way he pleases, are of the same kind (Il. 24.527–533).

The name of Zeus, as that of the greatest god, is often used as equivalent to the power of the gods in general. No other name is so [63/64] used, though that collective power can also be referred to in more general terms as "the gods" or "a god." This is mostly because individual men, unlike the poet who is inspired by the Muses, have no special knowledge of what particular god is responsible. Such usages therefore occur mostly in reported speech.[11]

[10] Moira or Fate appears sometimes alone sometimes along with Zeus, sometimes as explicitly sent by the gods. Surely the poet need not repeat whence it comes every time it is mentioned, provided there is no suggestion of any other agency, and we have no right to pick out the places where it occurs alone to build on them a theory of an independent power. W. C. Greene, *Moira* (Harvard 1944) 14, says "there is no essential conflict" between Moira and Zeus, but he continues: "even the gods are under the stern power of the Erinyes." Actually the Erinyes too perform their function under Zeus. The two passages where the gods are under their power are Il. 21.412, where Athena warns Ares he may suffer the Erinyes of his mother Hera, and Il. 15.204 where Iris warns Poseidon of the anger of Zeus, "for the Erinyes always follow the elders." In those cases the Erinyes would obviously be acting for Hera and Zeus, and represent their anger. In other passages the Erinyes are another expression for the will of the gods which they execute (Il. 19.418; 19.258–260 where they punish perjurers and are immediately equated with the gods at 264–265; cf. Od. 2.135). The same is true of Atê who also is sent by Zeus (Il. 19.87–94). Jane Harrison, *Themis* (Cambridge 1927) 481, claims that "Themis is beyond all the other gods," but the Themites come from Zeus also (Od. 2.67), and Themis is clearly a subordinate when he orders her to call an assembly of the gods (Il. 20.4) as much as Iris when she is sent on an errand; it is foolish to say that Zeus could not call the assembly himself. All these concepts were to develop later, some had an earlier history, but in Homer they are subordinated to the great gods, particularly Zeus. If this is thought to be an over-simplification, it is Homer who simplifies. For other views see Greene's *Moira* 10–28, Bowra, *Tradition* 230–231; Ehnmark, *The Idea* 78–80. The fullest discussion of the evidence for Moira in Homer is still Nägelsbach, *Homerische Theologie* (Nürnberg 1861) 120–148.

[11] This generalized use of the name of Zeus, and the vaguer expressions θεός, οἱ θεοί, is excellently discussed by O. Jörgensen in "Das Auftreten der Götter in den Büchern ι-μ der Odyssee," *Hermes* 39 (1904) 357–382. He shows how these expressions naturally occur in direct speech and makes short work of the elaborate theories that ignore this simple fact in the story told by Odysseus. Hedén (above,

Zeus' power is also supreme within the divine family, but it is not uncontested. There have been rebellions in the past, and one of these has given Thetis a claim on Zeus which he so fatefully recognizes in honouring Achilles. Rebellion is still possible, as Hera says to Poseidon who recoils from the suggestion (*Il.* 8.202). Though Hera does not really believe such rebellion would be successful, she points out that Zeus would have a poor sort of life on Olympus all by himself. She is the privileged consort, but Zeus himself admits that, if Poseidon rebels, it will be a hard fight, and Poseidon yields only on condition that the agreed destruction of Troy shall finally take place; if Zeus goes back on that, there will be war in heaven (*Il.* 15.113 –141).

So the divine father has to respect the traditional give and take among the gods, as is natural in any family, even though he has the ultimate power. When, after the duel of Paris and Menelaus, Zeus suggests that they might now stop the war altogether, he does not really mean it, but Hera's furious answer argues that such a decision would be contrary to the agreed Trojan doom (*Il.* 4.1–67). Because Zeus is sorry that Sarpedon must die and suggests he might save him (*Il.* 16.431–461), commentators have assumed that he could not interfere with fate or *moira* (434). Yet Hera should know, and her anger is based on the contrary assumption: she warns him that all the other gods will disapprove, every god will want to save his favourites from death, and confusion would follow. The position before the death of Hector is of the same kind. The decisions have been taken and Zeus must stick to them (πάλαι πεπρωμένον αἴσῃ. *Il.* 16.441). There is no suggestion that the original decision was not that of the gods, or that Zeus has not the power to change it, only that he should have more sense. He is persuaded in both cases.

It is towards his own family that he has to assert his power forcibly and repeatedly in order to be obeyed at all, as every reader of the *Iliad* knows (e.g. 8.1–40; 15.1–235). As long as they yield in the end, Zeus, like any other wise paterfamilias, thinks it wise to overlook even provocative disobedience, though he loses his temper now and again. And he has to respect the prerogatives of the other gods. There is no discord in heaven in the *Odyssey* because all the gods (except Poseidon) are sorry for Odysseus; so Zeus expresses the hope that Poseidon will give away to this unanimous family opinion (1.77–79); no other weapon [64/65] is suggested. Even so, Poseidon's anger has to work itself out after all the others have decided it should end (5.282). Moreover, as Athena tells Odysseus herself (13.341), she too has to respect her uncle's anger while it holds the field.

The gods, then, have to respect each other's rights and powers.

---

n. 5) then exploits this discovery less happily for his own purposes. See also G. F. Else, "God and Gods in Early Greek Thought," *TAPA* 80 (1949) 24–36, and Ehnmark, *The Idea* 80–85.

That much is essential to any community life, human or divine. The final authority belongs to Zeus. In this way we may well see the beginning of a divine world-order, provided we do not claim for it a moral basis which does not exist. If Homer emphasizes the overriding power of Zeus, we should remember that he is writing for an audience of polytheists and is one himself, and the basic assumption of polytheism is the limitations on any one power. The insistence is therefore very necessary. We read the epics against a background of many centuries of monotheism and are too eager to convert Homer to it also. If Homer could have dreamt of expressing his ideas to us, he might have made Hera and Poseidon use even stronger language.

In any case, the father of gods and men must have the greatest power, since it is power that makes the gods divine. They are personifications of forces that are active in the lives of men and which men cannot control. This is quite obvious in the case of the lesser gods and spirits, and even among the greatest Olympians the majority are clearly a natural, social, or psychological power which we recognize still. Zeus himself is the weather and sky-god; Aphrodite, the goddess of sexual passion; and the modern world should have little difficulty in recognizing the power of Ares, god of war.

There were gods before Homer, and these must have been thought of as powers, spirits, animal or human persons in a general way, but the clear anthropomorphism which endowed the gods with human form, mind, and personality was almost certainly elaborated by the epic poets themselves. While this process was going on and the great Olympians, as other gods in varying degrees, became individual persons with a life of their own, there can have been for some time no thought that the conduct of the gods had any moral or religious significance. Such a concept could only arise *after* the anthropomorphic gods had been established long enough for men to reflect upon the implications and consequences of conceiving their gods as persons. While the process was actually going on, the poet could, in describing the life of these newly individualized gods, give entirely free rein to his imagination precisely because this individuality was not then the essence of their divinity, which remained vested in their power. The gods, if we may so put it, were anthropomorphized *poetically but not yet theologically*. The religious or theological problems which were [65/66] bound to *follow* full anthropomorphism could not then be realized; they arose later when the divine persons largely created by the poets became objects of worship as persons, their power then becoming secondary as their divinity became vested in their persons. At the stage of development we find in the epic, the force is divine, the personality secondary.[12]

---

12 One is reminded of Wilamowitz' profound remark that, in Greek, θεός is a predicative notion, "ein Prädikatsbegriff," *Der Glaube* 17–20.

Hence it would never occur to Homer that the conduct of his gods, their family life, could in any sense affect their divinity, or that it should be depicted as a pattern for humans to follow. It is significant that no one in either epic ever tries to justify his own conduct by pointing to similar conduct among the gods; that belongs to a much later order of ideas.[13] For the epic poets, poetic imagination was free from any religious implications in filling in the picture of the personal life of the gods, and it naturally took its material from the only place it could: human life as it would be if freed from the fears and inhibitions of mortality.

This purely imaginative anthropomorphism could not last. When the divine powers with human personalities had become divine persons with certain powers—an inevitable development already at work in the epics—reflection would follow and, with it, theological implications that had to be faced, such as the moral consequences of divine conduct. That stage was not reached by Homer who never had to justify the ways of the gods to men; his gods did not need to conform to the human code of honour in order to be worshipped.

Homer does not give us any catalogue of the gods and their powers; even the family on Olympus is not clearly defined. Some of them, Hera for example, represent a power at which we can only guess; and the gods (not only Zeus) encroach on each other's powers. Yet we should not conclude that these were as vague as they are to us; a good deal of what Homer does not say he takes for granted. However, in so far as the powers of certain gods have become vague and less functional, this only means that the divine persons have emerged. So the dignity of Zeus' position forces a certain remoteness upon him, a certain humaneness as well as humanity, at least in his dealings with men, though it does not yet compel him to be uniformly either just or truthful. His dealings with his family are still quite irrelevant.

Once the implications of full anthropomorphism were faced— which man surely could not do till anthropomorphism was fully a fact—the Homeric laughter at the gods could only survive on licensed occasions, on the comic stage for example, but it remained an integral part of the Greek attitude to the gods. Fortunately, it has never quite died out. [66/67]

In the Homeric epic, fear and laughter walk side by side.[14] Homer can laugh at his gods without making their divinity ridiculous precisely because that divinity resides in their power, not their persons. While the gods are often funny on Olympus, when they come down to exercise their power over the lives of men, they are not a matter for

---

[13] Homeric characters blame their misfortunes on the gods, e.g. *Il.* 19.87–94; they even blame the gods when they are not responsible (*Il.* 19.270; *Od.* 4.261) but they do not excuse their conduct by that of the gods.

[14] Drerup reminds us (417) of what is far too often forgotten, that Homer does not hesitate to laugh at his heroes too.

laughter at all. Moreover, Olympus itself is at one and the same time both the never-never land of poetic imagination where the gods lead their highly irresponsible and remarkably human lives, and also the awesome dwelling-place of the terrifying powers which the gods represent, which limit human freedom and control human life. No one is less afraid of war because Ares is amusingly caught in bed with Aphrodite. The gods laugh irresponsibly and so do we. Even a modern reader is more shocked by Zeus when he sends a lying dream to Agamemnon than by all his bickerings with Hera and all his amours. Rightly so, for the way the gods use their power towards men is a serious matter; how they behave to each other is a matter for poetry.

Nor is it hard to understand why Homer's audience enjoyed the picture of life on Olympus. We all do, but they could enjoy it without misgivings. They enjoyed seeing the great of the universe making fools of themselves, somewhat in the same spirit perhaps as they or their ancestors must often have looked upon the head of the clan. The Old Man might at times behave ridiculously, even badly, but his power, for all that, could not be trifled with. So Agamemnon behaves more than once like a fool, and sometimes rather badly, but he is still the king of kings, the supreme commander whose power and position not even Achilles can defy with impunity. Every soldier who enjoys stories about the private life of his superior officers, every adolescent in his ambivalent attitude towards the head of the family, has something of the attitude of the Homeric hero towards his gods. Besides, men still, in our much more theologically sombre age, enjoy funny stories about their gods or at least about their saints; and it is the believer who enjoys them most, not the atheist.

The trouble, however, is not only that the gods are funny, or misbehave among themselves; they are also bad. They do not seem to conform to any code of morality that any self-respecting human being, Homeric, classical, or modern, could accept as his own; and that is also true of their behaviour towards men. Viewed morally, the motivation of their actions is not only selfish, it is often vicious. That they punish beyond all reason any lack of respect shown towards themselves was perhaps a natural and inevitable inheritance from those less personalized beings whom they replaced,[15] but Hera's fierce hatred of Troy and the Trojans is both excessive and hardly accounted for;[16] [67/68] Poseidon's anger against Odysseus for blinding the Cyclops, that cannibalistic brute, in pure self-defence, is just as bad, and his vengeance on the Phaeacians disgusting. So is Helios' revenge upon the companions of Odysseus for slaying a few of his cattle after a

---

[15] To insist that honour be paid to them is as characteristic of other than Homeric gods; the Jehovah of the Old Testament is just as insistent.

[16] There is only a casual reference to the judgment of Paris at *Il.* 24.25–27, which should remind us of how much may be taken for granted that we do not know.

month's starvation brought upon them by Zeus.[17] The picture of world forces represented by these gods has little order and no morality. Even much later than Homer, the word θεός does not connote goodness but power[18] and Homer certainly does not depict his gods as moral rulers of the world. Of such a later conception there are only faint traces. It has been said that Homer's ethics are nobler than his theology.[19] That is very true. His heroes have a code of honour of considerable nobility; his gods have none. That is natural enough; men had lived in communities which required an ethical code for centuries; the gods had only just begun to do so, relatively speaking. We are accustomed to think of human conduct as deriving from, or at least sanctioned by, religion; for the Olympian religion, at least, the truth is the other way around. It was the human moral feelings which forced morality upon the gods, once they had become persons. Man's concepts of goodness developed, and the Olympians were always lagging behind. This process, in Homer, was only just beginning. To try, from a few stray passages, to make the Homeric gods the defenders of right and justice, is to force upon them a mould that simply does not fit, and to generalize a few faint hopes into ruling principles.[20]

Neither do the sons and favourites of the gods claim any special moral merit. Achilles is no better, morally, than Hector, Priam, Nestor, or Diomede; indeed he behaves worse than any of these; but he is the son of a sea-nymph who has a claim on Zeus. The poet makes Achilles greater, but not better. Menelaus is promised eternal life specifically because he is the son-in-law of Zeus (*Od.* 4.569). Certainly, Odysseus cannot claim any outstanding moral rectitude; in fact the slaying of the suitors, and, in particular, of Amphinomus and Leodes, with the revolting massacre of the maidservants, is the most deliberately savage episode in the two poems.[21] The maids are not punished for sexual immorality—that, from Odysseus, would be too absurd—but from an outraged sense of property.

---

[17] *Od.* 12.370–390; 13.125–187; we may also compare Poseidon's anger at the building of the Greek wall in *Il.* 7.442–463 and the ugly give and take of *Il.* 4.40–90. I can see no evidence for considering Zeus as "a high philosophical conception of the world-conscience" in the *Odyssey*, Jaeger, *Paideia* (Oxford 1945) 1.54.

[18] I have discussed the meaning of θεός also in *Plato's Thought* (London 1935) 150–153 and in *The Drama of Euripides* (London 1941) 41–44.

[19] Greene, *Moira*, 11.

[20] Typical of this point of view are W. E. Gladstone, *Homer* (London 1878) 66–67; Andrew Lang, *The World of Homer* (London 1910) 120–122; L. R. Farnell, *Outline of Greek Religion* (London 1920) 19–20.

[21] It will be recalled that Leodes is killed by Odysseus while a suppliant (*Od.* 22.310–329) although his claim to have been a restraining influence upon the suitors is endorsed by the poet himself (*Od.* 21.146–147). Telemachus kills Amphinomus (*Od.* 22.89) although it was he who had dissuaded the suitors from killing Telemachus (*Od.* 20.242–246). Amphinomus was also kind to the beggar Odysseus who in fact tried to warn him, but Athena saw to it that the warning should be ineffective (*Od.* 18.118–156). The conduct of Athena throughout these books is quite as objectionable as anything in the *Iliad*.

To say that the gods have no interest in morality does not mean that men have none, but it is quite independent of the gods.[22] In a very few particulars, however, the process of imposing this human code upon the gods, and looking to them to defend it, has begun. One of these is the sanctity of oaths. Agamemnon expects Zeus to punish the Trojans after the victory of Menelaus in the duel with Paris (*Il.* 3.160–167).[23] He later swears he never touched Briseis, by [68/69] Zeus, Earth, Helios "and the Erinyes who punish men, whoever breaks his oath." The gods, he continues, punish perjurers (*Il.* 19.255–265). In the *Odyssey*, too, oaths are expected to be kept, even by Calypso and Circe (5.178–187; 10.343). But how about the gods themselves? It is Athena who directs the spear that kills Pandarus (*Il.* 5.290–296), but it was also Athena, sent by Zeus for the purpose, who instigated him to break the truce (*Il.* 3.72–73). Hera does not hesitate, after her escapade on Ida, to perjure herself before Zeus by Earth, Heaven, Styx, Zeus' sacred head, and their own marriage. Zeus smiles, he doesn't really believe her, but nothing happens. Men attach great importance to oaths; but even here the gods have not quite caught up with them, either in their behaviour towards men or towards each other.

Then there is the protection which Zeus is expected to give to strangers and suppliants. This is more frequent in the *Odyssey*, for there are no strangers in the *Iliad*. The belief that strangers are under his protection is frequently expressed.[24] As we do not often meet Zeus himself in the *Odyssey*, we cannot conclude anything from his silence on the matter, but he singularly fails to protect the Phaeacians, those excellent hosts, whom Poseidon hates for this very reason; in fact, Zeus hands them over to him without a qualm.

There is beautiful personification of Litai or Prayers in the appeal of Phoenix to Achilles (*Il.* 9.496–512). Prayers are the daughters of Zeus, wrinkled and squinting though they be, and they follow after Atê, so strong and swift. If not listened to, they pray to Zeus to send Atê to him who did not listen, that he may be punished. The whole passage is a beautiful poetic image of a human hope, but it is only a hope: Zeus may or may not listen. Certainly, this expresses an aspiration towards divine justice, but that justice is not established. It is perhaps significant that in the story of Meleager which illustrates Phoenix' point there is no divine intervention on behalf of mercy; it is simply an example of the principle that mercy is often the best policy.

[22] A very striking brief account of the code of the hero and its relation to the gods is that of René Schaerer, *La Morale grecque dans Homère* (Lausanne 1934, inaugural lecture).
[23] It is interesting to find Idomeneus (*Il.* 4.270–271) saying that punishment and death will come to the Trojans for breaking the oath, without mentioning the gods. That is the general feeling that honesty is the best policy, before it is linked with the gods.
[24] *Od.* 6.207; 7.165, 180; 9.268, 478; 13.203; 14.57, 284, 388; 16.422; 17.484.

There is only one other passage in the whole *Iliad* which speaks of moral retribution from the gods, this time more definitely and spoken in the poet's own person, in a simile (16.384–386). The flight of the Trojans before Patroclus is compared to a flood "sent by Zeus when he is angry and presses upon men who by violence give crooked judgments in the market-place and have chased away justice (δίκην), without care for visitation from the gods." Thus once and once only in the *Iliad* do we find Zeus and the gods spoken of as defenders of "justice."[25]

The exact meaning of even this passage, however, is interesting. Δίκη in Homer is never used in the wide sense of justice; it usually [69/70] means lot or portion or legal decisions which give everyone his due. This is also the meaning here, as the reference to crooked judgments makes clear. The same sense is implied in various passages of the *Odyssey* where the belief is expressed that the gods will punish the suitors, whose *hubris* consists precisely in their wasting another man's property. And Odysseus' motive in punishing them is also an outraged sense of property, which in him was highly developed.

The most elaborate of these passages is where the pious Eumaeus speaks of the retribution from the gods which awaits the suitors; here δίκη still has the same meaning. He says to Odysseus in his cottage (14.80):

Eat, good stranger, of this pork which is available to us servants; the fatted hogs are for the suitors who have no thought of visitation from the gods, and have no pity. Yet the blessed gods like not deeds of excess; they honour each man's lot (δίκην) and deeds in accordance with fate.[26] Even the harsh and implacable men who attack the land of others, when Zeus has granted them booty, return to their ships and, when they have filled them, go home. Great fear of divine visitations comes even upon their minds; but these suitors must have heard some message from the gods that a dreadful death has come upon my master; they will not do their wooing in the accepted manner (δικαίως) nor go back to their own, but without let or hindrance they devour my master's possessions without mercy.

Eumaeus then enumerates the possessions of Odysseus that are being wasted. The illustration of pirates is significant. So wherever anyone

---

[25] We might declare at least 386–387 a later interpolation, but that way lies chaos. While we are not told that punishment always follows crooked judgments (which it obviously does not), the implication that crooked judgments are punished by Zeus is there, even if the punishment is rather indiscriminate. The sentiments are closely parallel in Hesiod, *Works and Days* 219–264. It is wiser to let this passage remind us that we are not dealing with static ideas about the gods. Human rewards for the best judgment are found in *Il.* 18.507–508.

The expression ὄπις θεῶν is usually translated as the wrath of the gods, but that is too strong a word. The word ὄπις seems to mean the attention of the gods, cf. Διὸς δ' ὠπίζετο μῆνιν/ξεινίου (*Od.* 14.283–284). It was used later in both a good and a bad sense.

[26]   οὐ μὲν σχέτλια ἔργα θεοὶ μάκαρες φιλέουσιν,
ἀλλὰ δίκην τίουσι καὶ αἴσιμα ἔργ' ἀνθρώπων.

expresses the hope that the suitors will be punished, the hope is tempered by the knowledge that the gods are unpredictable.

Apart from such occasional passages[27] which contain the seed of the later concept of divine justice, the gods are not presented, either in their own conduct or in the minds of men, as the protectors of order and justice. They are, of course, capable of the gentler emotions as well as the more violent. Some of them feel pity, usually for their own favourites, as when Apollo resents the treatment of Hector's body by Achilles, or Athena the prolonged sufferings of Odysseus. In both cases they persuade Zeus and the majority, but not all of the others, that something should be done about it. We should not, on such occasional better feelings, build any theory of the humaneness of the gods; it is simply part of their humanity.[28] For Homer's gods are human; they are often bad, but not one of the great Olympians is uniformly devilish.

The gods give of good and evil to the good and the evil at their own sweet will; man must endure whatever they send. This does not mean, however, that man is merely the plaything of the gods, without freedom of action or responsibility for his own life. Far from it. The dependence on the gods is much more immediate and complete in the [70/71] *Odyssey*, because there we find ourselves in the realm of folklore and marvellous adventure with the gods, mostly Athena, in constant attendance like a familiar spirit. If there is less divine supervision in the story as told by Odysseus himself (9–12), it is because he, like other mortals, is less aware of this supervision than the poet who knows all the details. That is also why there is a freer use in those books of the more general terms—Zeus, the gods, etc.

Yet it is also in the *Odyssey* that Zeus tells us that men by their own obstinacy bring much evil on themselves beyond the fate set by the gods (ὑπὲρ μόρον 1.35). He gives the example of Aegisthus; now if Aegisthus' fate did not include his living with Clytemnestra and the killing of Agamemnon, then surely the fate set by the gods left a great deal to the humans themselves. We remember Achilles' choice of a short but glorious life. The *Iliad* certainly leaves this impression of a wide area of freedom within the limits set by fate, for the heroes are there anything but puppets.

The poet expresses this freedom dramatically by leaving a great

27 We should perhaps add to them *Od.* 11.73, Elpenor's request that he be buried lest he provoke the anger of the gods against Odysseus; and *Od.* 18.130–142 —the famous passage on the wretchedness of men, where Odysseus (in his warning to Amphinomus) says that man must bear bravely what the gods send, for even his thoughts depend upon the lot Zeus sends him, and that man must not be ἀθεμίστιος but bear the gifts of the gods in silence. The ethical implications, however, are very faint.

28 *Il.* 24.23–64; *Od.* 1.44–47. One should, of course, not include the pity which the lying dream says Zeus feels, for there the whole point is that he doesn't, but pity is also felt by Zeus at *Il.* 15.12; 17.201, 441, 648; 19:340; 22.169.

deal of the action, some of it most important in its consequences, without any divine intervention upon the purely human plane. Apollo sends the plague and Hera puts it in Achilles' mind to call the assembly, but the actual quarrel between Achilles and Agamemnon is a matter of human temperament entirely until Athena comes to prevent it from going too far. Later, Achilles sends Patroclus into the Greek camp of his own accord; it is Nestor who first suggests that Patroclus should join the battle in Achilles' armour. This last chain of events has been cryptically forecast by Zeus (*Il.* 8.476) and is later sanctioned by him (*Il.* 9.796) but only human factors are involved. The same is true of the embassy to Achilles. Nor do the gods ever interfere with, or inspire, tactical decisions such as Nestor's advice to build a wall, to fight by phratries (*Il.* 2.364) or to send spies into the Trojan camp at night. And the same is true on the Trojan side (*Il.* 12.88; 15.287–299).

Not only will the Homeric hero act independently when the gods are absent; he will continue to fight when he knows that the gods are on the other side. Ajax says any fool can see that Zeus is helping the Trojans, but he then calls upon his friends to see what they can accomplish by themselves (αὐτοί *Il.* 17.634) and he utters his famous prayer to Zeus at least to let them die in the light. When the Greek envoys come to Achilles, they plead for his help precisely because Zeus is helping the Trojans (*Il.* 9.236–239), and Odysseus appeals to Diomede in the same manner (*Il.* 11.319). This is partly because, as the gods represent actual forces, to say that Zeus helps the Trojans is only [71/72] to emphasize the fact of Trojan success; partly because the gods are changeable, and men hold on in the hope of such a change; it is mostly because men must follow their own code of honourable conduct whatever the gods may do. The Phaeacians give a superb example of this: they know perfectly well that they are incurring the wrath of Poseidon by saving his victims; they have been warned of the dreadful fate that awaits them if they persist, but they live up to their code of behaviour in spite of it all (*Od.* 8.565–570). The gods may wound a hero, they may kill him, they can never break his spirit. When you die is a matter for fate and the gods; how you die, and what kind of a man you are while you live, is your own responsibility.

Such is, in part, the heroic code. In this sense men must endure, bravely and without flinching, whatever the gods may send, be it one's general fate or the result of unpredictable interventions on specific occasions.[29]

The manner of these interferences sometimes offers considerable difficulty to readers of a later age, even to those who can accept the amorality and frivolity of the gods in general. The more remote inter-

---

[29] Obedience to the gods is part of virtue, but it is largely voluntary: *cf. Il.* 1.207 and 216. Nor does the Homeric hero hesitate to curse his gods: *Il.* 3.365; 9.17–25; *Od.* 20.201–203.

ventions, such as the Apollo who sends the plague, are easier: he is a great power that has been offended; his anthropomorphism, in spite of the beautiful picture of his descent, does not here obtrude. Nor do we feel any direct discomfort about the scenes on Olympus once we accept the mythological apparatus; the visits of Thetis to Zeus and Hephaestus are of the same kind.

It is when the contact with mortals is more direct that we are disconcerted. In the battle of the gods (*Il.* 20 and 21) the Olympian family moves to earth in a body, with the exception of Zeus, and they bring with them both aspects of Olympus, the home of awful powers and the never-never land of poetic fancy. The intention obviously is to underline the importance of the final battle to come between Achilles and Hector (*Il.* 20.1–74). After their descent, accompanied by thunder and earthquake, the rest of the book is on the human level, with only the customary help from individual gods. Then, as the corpses choke the river Xanthus, we are prepared for the battle between Achilles and the river-god; soon, despite warnings, Achilles leaps into the river itself in pursuit and the battle is on. This struggle is not grotesque, as it has been said to be:[30] except that he is a god and speaks with a human voice, all the physical manifestations of this struggle are those of a river in flood which overpowers the reckless Achilles and drives him away as its swollen waves pursue him over the plain. Weird and wonderful this may be, but not grotesque, and without doubt it is entirely serious. Then, as Hephaestus takes over, [72/73] Achilles disappears and we have the fight between the elements of fire and water. We are now upon the Olympian plane; no mortal will appear until the battle of the gods is over (*Il.* 21.328–520). This, as always, is a matter between us and the poet; and at this point comes the usual comic or fantasy-relief.

The battle of the gods themselves cannot be tragic for, as Aristotle might have said, no one can kill anybody.[31] After Xanthus has been forced to plead for mercy and return within his banks, the gods draw up for battle and Zeus smiles as he sees them, in fact he laughs outright (*Il.* 21.389–390). The dramatic purpose of the battle is perhaps to emphasize the superiority of the gods on the Greek side, the side of Achilles, but the details are frankly amusing: Athena lays out Ares; Aphrodite leads him out of the battle but Athena pushes her down on top of him; Hera jeers at Artemis, holds her by the wrists and boxes her ears; Artemis then rushes up to Zeus but he refuses to take the incident seriously. There is no major battle between great gods equally matched, and when Poseidon challenges Apollo the latter refuses. We laugh with Zeus, and then the gods retire and leave the field to the much more terrible struggle between mortals.

---

[30] E.g. by E. T. Owen: *The Story of the Iliad* (Toronto 1946) 211–212.
[31] See *Poetics*, 13.1453a. 39.

One thing is clear: the poet did not try to depict a mighty battle of the gods and fail; he obviously did not try. He is indulging his usual fantasies about the gods, and amuses us before we face the tragic death of Hector. This is true of the battle itself; but there is nothing funny about the gods' descent from heaven or Achilles' fight with Xanthus.

If the frivolous and serious aspects of the gods are here kept separate, the Diomedeia, where Diomede wounds both Ares and Aphrodite, is the boldest mixture of serious and funny business in our epics. The reason is that Diomede must never rise to the same level of greatness as Achilles, but he must do the same kind of things. So he too fights the gods, but under the direct supervision of Athena who sees to it that things do not get out of hand and his encounter with the gods remains more than half comic. Before Apollo or the lightning of Zeus he gives way (*Il.* 5.440–445; 8.169).

The personal interventions of particular gods to encourage their side or on behalf of their favourites are very numerous. If the question of fairness is raised, they are all equally unfair. Commentators are inclined here to strain at the gnat while they swallow the camel, and their modern feelings lead them to object to certain details of the interference. We should always remember that the appearance of a god on behalf of a hero is a poetic symbol of that hero's greatness, so that it is *ex hypothesi* impossible for that greatness to be tarnished by [73/74] the help of the god. We dislike the way Apollo pushes Patroclus, strikes him in the back and sends his helmet flying, thus making him an easy prey for Euphorbus and Hector (*Il.* 16.694, 788);[32] yet the poet feels that Zeus is giving glory to Hector and he is compared to a lion when he delivers the final blow (*Il.* 16.800, 827). We dislike the deceit which Athena practises on Hector to make Achilles' task easier. That is because we like Patroclus and Hector, and we have modern notions of sportsmanship, but these interventions are like many others. Nobody likes Pandarus, but Athena's instigation to break the common oath is at least as objectionable (*Il.* 4.90–102) and if it be said that Pandarus is a poor lot anyway (forgetting that it is Athena who made him so), what of Rhesus who has done no harm, and Athena's conduct throughout the Doloneia, or the less deadly, but so unsporting interventions of the gods in the games (*Il.* 23.380, 392, 774, 865)? The details of these interventions vary as fancy dictates, they have no moral significance whatever; they are dramatic and poetic symbol of the greatness of particular heroes.

Some interventions are even less objectified, and the god seems part of the human personality, as when Aphrodite appears to Helen to make her look after Paris (*Il.* 4.386–420) or Athena stops Achilles

---

[32] "The poet has piled up point after point in his description of the circumstances of Patroclus' death, so that even the least imaginative reader must burn with indignation at the way it is accomplished. That is what Homer wants, for he is motivating the terrific fury and grief of Achilles" (Owen, *The Story* 163).

from drawing his sword (*Il.* 1.195). Our trouble here is that we objectify the gods more than Homer. Aphrodite is not only the goddess of love, she *is* love or passion, and she is Helen's passion, both at the same time—a synthesis which few modern readers seem able to achieve. Homer provides the answer himself, when Odysseus says to Eurycleia: "Now that you've thought of this and a god has put it in your mind" (*Od.* 19.485). Divine intervention does not exclude human activity, it is merely a poetic and imaginative way of describing the same activity.

Let us always remember that the gods are forces rather than persons. It would be very strange if we could feel about them as Homer did; the wonder is rather that we can accept so much and enjoy so much. The reason for this is probably the same reason which caused these Olympians to remain objects of worship for another thousand years, and never to lose their imaginative appeal: they are forces many of which every man knows and recognizes in his own life, forces which control a great part of life, and which no one can deny.[33] Lightning and thunder, fire, death, sexual passion, music and the arts, and those lesser spirits, Fear, Panic, Rumor, Death and the rest, are they not obviously true, and has anyone represented them more vividly than Homer? [74/75]

The picture of life represented by the gods of Homer is a true picture, even if it is incomplete. But over all these forces Zeus has been established as master. That mastery is pregnant with the problems of later religion, when men will insist that the order of Zeus must be a moral order, or refuse to believe. Then Ionian scepticism will arise, but it is as foreign to Homer as are the other implications of his anthropomorphic Olympian company. At most we find in the epic only the very first glimmerings of such an order of thought, as men have only just begun to feel the need to impress upon the gods the essentials of their own moral code, when they hope or begin to expect that these gods will punish perjurers, protect strangers seeking hospitality, and punish those who have no respect for the property of an absent laird.

It will not be till later still that the gods' conduct will be looked upon as an example to mankind. This is entirely absent from the epic. To attribute scenes which depict such divine conduct to interpolators and later poets is to miss the whole spirit of those scenes themselves, to read into Homer what belongs to later centuries, and a point of view which is quite incompatible with that full, poetic, irresponsible anthropomorphism which is one of the chief glories of the Homeric epic. [75]

---

[33] "Die Götter sind da." Wilamowitz, *Der Glaube* 17, 42. There is an interesting discussion of the meaning of some Homeric terms in Bruno Snell, *Die Entdeckung des Geistes* (Hamburg 1946) 15–36, and the Homeric "belief" in the gods, 40–41.

THE *ODYSSEY*: EPIC STYLE AND EPIC POEM

Homer's Realism: The Individual Voice

ERICH AUERBACH

READERS OF THE *Odyssey* WILL REMEMBER THE WELL-PREPARED AND touching scene in book 19, when Odysseus has at last come home, the scene in which the old housekeeper Euryclea, who had been his nurse, recognizes him by a scar on his thigh. The stranger has won Penelope's good will; at his request she tells the housekeeper to wash his feet, which, in all old stories, is the first duty of hospitality toward a tired traveler. Euryclea busies herself fetching water and mixing cold with hot, meanwhile speaking sadly of her absent master, who is probably of the same age as the guest, and who perhaps, like the guest, is even now wandering somewhere, a stranger; and she remarks how astonishingly like him the guest looks. Meanwhile Odysseus, remembering his scar, moves back out of the light; he knows that, despite his efforts to hide his identity, Euryclea will now recognize him, but he wants at least to keep Penelope in ignorance. No sooner has the old woman touched the scar than, in her joyous surprise, she lets Odysseus' foot drop into the basin; the water spills over, she is about to cry out her joy; Odysseus restrains her with whispered threats and endearments; she recovers herself and conceals her emotion. Penelope, whose attention Athena's foresight had diverted from the incident, has observed nothing.

All this is scrupulously externalized and narrated in leisurely fashion. The two women express their feelings in copious direct discourse. Feelings though they are, with only a slight admixture of the most general considerations upon human destiny, the syntactical connection between part and part is perfectly clear, no contour is blurred. There is also room and time for orderly, perfectly well-articulated, uni-

Erich Auerbach, "Odysseus' Scar," in *Mimesis, The Representation of Reality in Western Literature*, trans. Willard R. Trask (Princeton: Princeton University Press, 1953), pp. 3–23. Reprinted by permission of Princeton University Press. Copyright 1953 by Princeton University.

formly illuminated descriptions of implements, ministrations, and gestures; even in the dramatic moment of recognition, Homer does not
omit to tell the reader that it is with his right hand that Odysseus takes
the old woman by the throat to keep her from speaking, at the same
time that he draws her closer to him with his left. Clearly outlined,
brightly and uniformly illuminated, men and things stand out in a
realm where everything is visible; and not less clear—wholly expressed,
orderly even in their ardor—are the feelings and thoughts of the persons
involved. [3/4]

In my account of the incident I have so far passed over a whole
series of verses which interrupt it in the middle. There are more than
seventy of these verses—while to the incident itself some forty are
devoted before the interruption and some forty after it. The interruption, which comes just at the point when the housekeeper recognizes
the scar—that is, at the moment of crisis—describes the origin of the
scar, a hunting accident which occurred in Odysseus' boyhood, at a
boar hunt, during the time of his visit to his grandfather Autolycus.
This first affords an opportunity to inform the reader about Autolycus,
his house, the precise degree of the kinship, his character, and, no less
exhaustively than touchingly, his behavior after the birth of his grandson; then follows the visit of Odysseus, now grown to be a youth; the
exchange of greetings, the banquet with which he is welcomed, sleep
and waking, the early start for the hunt, the tracking of the beast, the
struggle, Odysseus' being wounded by the boar's tusk, his recovery, his
return to Ithaca, his parents' anxious questions—all is narrated, again
with such a complete externalization of all the elements of the story
and of their interconnections as to leave nothing in obscurity. Not until
then does the narrator return to Penelope's chamber, not until then,
the digression having run its course, does Euryclea, who had recognized the scar before the digression began, let Odysseus' foot fall
back into the basin.

The first thought of a modern reader—that this is a device to increase suspense—is, if not wholly wrong, at least not the essential explanation of this Homeric procedure. For the element of suspense is
very slight in the Homeric poems; nothing in their entire style is calculated to keep the reader or hearer breathless. The digressions are not
meant to keep the reader in suspense, but rather to relax the tension.
And this frequently occurs, as in the passage before us. The broadly
narrated, charming, and subtly fashioned story of the hunt, with all
its elegance and self-sufficiency, its wealth of idyllic pictures, seeks to
win the reader over wholly to itself as long as he is hearing it, to make
him forget what had just taken place during the foot-washing. But an
episode that will increase suspense by retarding the action must be so
constructed that it will not fill the present entirely, will not put the
crisis, whose resolution is being awaited, entirely out of the reader's
mind, and thereby destroy the mood of suspense; the crisis and the

suspense must continue, must remain vibrant in the background. But Homer—and to this we shall have to return later—knows no background. What he narrates is for the time being the only present, and fills both [4/5] the stage and the reader's mind completely. So it is with the passage before us. When the young Euryclea (vv. 401 ff.) sets the infant Odysseus on his grandfather Autolycus' lap after the banquet, the aged Euryclea, who a few lines earlier had touched the wanderer's foot, has entirely vanished from the stage and from the reader's mind.

Goethe and Schiller, who, though not referring to this particular episode, exchanged letters in April 1797 on the subject of "the retarding element" in the Homeric poems in general, put it in direct opposition to the element of suspense—the latter word is not used, but is clearly implied when the "retarding" procedure is opposed, as something proper to epic, to tragic procedure (letters of April 19, 21, and 22). The "retarding element," the "going back and forth" by means of episodes, seems to me, too, in the Homeric poems, to be opposed to any tensional and suspensive striving toward a goal, and doubtless Schiller is right in regard to Homer when he says that what he gives us is "simply the quiet existence and operation of things in accordance with their natures"; Homer's goal is "already present in every point of his progress." But both Schiller and Goethe raise Homer's procedure to the level of a law for epic poetry in general, and Schiller's words quoted above are meant to be universally binding upon the epic poet, in contradistinction from the tragic. Yet in both modern and ancient times, there are important epic works which are composed throughout with no "retarding element" in this sense but, on the contrary, with suspense throughout, and which perpetually "rob us of our emotional freedom"—which power Schiller will grant only to the tragic poet. And besides it seems to me undemonstrable and improbable that this procedure of Homeric poetry was directed by aesthetic considerations or even by an aesthetic feeling of the sort postulated by Goethe and Schiller. The effect, to be sure, is precisely that which they describe, and is, furthermore, the actual source of the conception of epic which they themselves hold, and with them all writers decisively influenced by classical antiquity. But the true cause of the impression of "retardation" appears to me to lie elsewhere—namely, in the need of the Homeric style to leave nothing which it mentions half in darkness and unexternalized.

The excursus upon the origin of Odysseus' scar is not basically different from the many passages in which a newly introduced character, or even a newly appearing object or implement, though it be in the thick of a battle, is described as to its nature and origin; or in which, upon the appearance of a god, we are told where he last was, what [5/6] he was doing there, and by what road he reached the scene; indeed, even the Homeric epithets seem to me in the final analysis to be traceable to the same need for an externalization of phenomena in terms preceptible to the senses. Here is the scar, which comes up in the course of the narrative; and Homer's feeling simply will not permit him to see it appear out of the darkness of an unilluminated past; it must be set in full light, and with it a portion of the hero's boyhood— just as, in the *Iliad*, when the first ship is already burning and the Myrmidons finally arm that they may hasten to help, there is still time not only for the wonderful simile of the wolf, not only for the order of the Myrmidon host, but also for a detailed account of the ancestry of several subordinate leaders (16, vv. 155 ff.). To be sure, the aesthetic effect thus produced was soon noticed and thereafter consciously sought; but the more original cause must have lain in the basic impulse of the Homeric style: to represent phenomena in a fully externalized form, visible and palpable in all their parts, and completely fixed in their spatial and temporal relations. Nor do psychological processes receive any other treatment: here too nothing must remain hidden and unexpressed. With the utmost fullness, with an orderliness which even passion does not disturb, Homer's personages vent their inmost hearts in speech; what they do not say to others, they speak in their own minds, so that the reader is informed of it. Much that is terrible takes place in the Homeric poems, but it seldom takes place wordlessly: Polyphemus talks to Odysseus; Odysseus talks to the suitors when he begins to kill them; Hector and Achilles talk at length, before battle and after; and no speech is so filled with anger or scorn that the particles which express logical and grammatical connections are lacking or out of place. This last observation is true, of course, not only of speeches but of the presentation in general. The separate elements of a phenomenon are most clearly placed in relation to one another; a large number of conjunctions, adverbs, particles, and other syntactical tools, all clearly circumscribed and delicately differentiated in meaning, delimit persons, things, and portions of incidents in respect to one another, and at the same time bring them together in a continuous and ever flexible connection; like the separate phenomena themselves, their relationships—their temporal, local, causal, final, consecutive, comparative, concessive, antithetical, and conditional limitations—are brought to light in perfect fullness; so that a continuous rhythmic procession of phenomena passes by, and never is there a form [6/7] left fragmentary or half-illuminated, never a lacuna, never a gap, never a glimpse of unplumbed depths.

And this procession of phenomena takes place in the foreground— that is, in a local and temporal present which is absolute. One might think that the many interpolations, the frequent moving back and forth, would create a sort of perspective in time and place; but the Homeric style never gives any such impression. The way in which any impression of perspective is avoided can be clearly observed in the procedure for introducing episodes, a syntactical construction with which every reader of Homer is familiar; it is used in the passage we are considering, but can also be found in cases when the episodes are much shorter. To the word scar (v. 393) there is first attached a relative clause ("which once long ago a boar . . ."), which enlarges into a voluminous syntactical parenthesis; into this an independent sentence unexpectedly intrudes (v. 396: "A god himself gave him . . ."), which quietly disentangles itself from syntactical subordination, until, with verse 399, an equally free syntactical treatment of the new content begins a new present which continues unchallenged until, with verse 467 ("The old woman now touched it . . ."), the scene which had been broken off is resumed. To be sure, in the case of such long episodes as the one we are considering, a purely syntactical connection with the principal theme would hardly have been possible; but a connection with it through perspective would have been all the easier had the content been arranged with that end in view; if, that is, the entire story of the scar had been presented as a recollection which awakens in Odysseus' mind at this particular moment. It would have been perfectly easy to do; the story of the scar had only to be inserted two verses earlier, at the first mention of the word scar, where the motifs "Odysseus" and "recollection" were already at hand. But any such subjectivistic-perspectivistic procedure, creating a foreground and background, resulting in the present lying open to the depths of the past, is entirely foreign to the Homeric style; the Homeric style knows only a foreground, only a uniformly illuminated, uniformly objective present. And so the excursus does not begin until two lines later, when Euryclea has discovered the scar—the possibility for a perspectivistic connection no longer exists, and the story of the wound becomes an independent and exclusive present.

The genius of the Homeric style becomes even more apparent when it is compared with an equally ancient and equally epic style from a different world of forms. I shall attempt this comparison with the account [7/8] of the sacrifice of Isaac, a homogeneous narrative produced by the so-called Elohist. The King James version translates the opening as follows (Genesis 22:1): "And it came to pass after these things, that God did tempt Abraham, and said to him, Abraham! and he said, Behold, here I am." Even this opening startles us when we come to it from Homer. Where are the two speakers? We are not told. The reader, however, knows that they are not normally to be found together in one place on earth, that one of them, God, in order to speak to Abraham, must come from somewhere, must enter the earthly realm from some unknown heights or depths. Whence does he come, whence does he call to Abraham? We are not told. He does not come, like Zeus or Poseidon, from the Aethiopians, where he has been enjoying a sacrificial feast. Nor are we told anything of his reasons for tempting Abraham so terribly. He has not, like Zeus, discussed them in set speeches with other gods gathered in council; nor have the deliberations in his own heart been presented to us; unexpected and mysterious, he enters the scene from some unknown height or depth and calls: Abraham! It will at once be said that this is to be explained by the particular concept of God which the Jews held and which was wholly different from that of the Greeks. True enough—but this constitutes no objection. For how is the Jewish concept of God to be explained? Even their earlier God of the desert was not fixed in form and content, and was alone; his lack of form, his lack of local habitation, his singleness, was in the end not only maintained but developed even further in competition with the comparatively far more manifest gods of the surrounding Near Eastern world. The concept of God held by the Jews is less a cause than a symptom of their manner of comprehending and representing things.

This becomes still clearer if we now turn to the other person in the dialogue, to Abraham. Where is he? We do not know. He says, indeed: Here I am—but the Hebrew word means only something like "behold me," and in any case is not meant to indicate the actual place where Abraham is, but a moral position in respect to God, who has called to him—Here am I awaiting thy command. Where he is actually, whether in Beersheba or elsewhere, whether indoors or in the open air, is not stated; it does not interest the narrator, the reader is not informed; and what Abraham was doing when God called to him is left in the same obscurity. To realize the difference, consider Hermes' visit to Calypso, for example, where command, journey, arrival and reception of the visitor, situation and occupation of the person visited, [8/9] are set forth in many verses; and even on occasions when gods appear suddenly and briefly, whether to help one of their favorites or to deceive or destroy some mortal whom they hate, their bodily forms, and usually the manner of their coming and going, are given in detail. Here, however, God appears without bodily form (yet he "appears"), coming from some unspecified place—we only hear his voice, and that utters nothing but a name, a name without an adjective, without a descriptive epithet for the person spoken to, such as is the rule in every Homeric address; and of Abraham too nothing is made perceptible except the words in which he answers God: *Hinne-ni*, Behold me here—with which, to be sure, a most touching gesture expressive of obedience and readiness is suggested, but it is left to the reader to visualize it. Moreover the two speakers are not on the same level: if we conceive of Abraham in the foreground, where it might be possible to picture him as prostrate or kneeling or bowing with outspread arms or gazing upward, God is not there too: Abraham's words and gestures are directed toward the depths of the picture or upward, but in any case the undetermined, dark place from which the voice comes to him is not in the foreground.

After this opening, God gives his command, and the story itself begins: everyone knows it; it unrolls with no episodes in a few independent sentences whose syntactical connection is of the most rudimentary sort. In this atmosphere it is unthinkable that an implement, a landscape through which the travelers passed, the serving-men, or the ass, should be described, that their origin or descent or material or appearance or usefulness should be set forth in terms of praise; they do not even admit an adjective: they are serving-men, ass, wood, and knife, and nothing else, without an epithet; they are there to serve the end which God has commanded; what in other respects they were, are, or will be, remains in darkness. A journey is made, because God has designated the place where the sacrifice is to be performed; but we are told nothing about the journey except that it took three days, and even that we are told in a mysterious way: Abraham and his followers rose "early in the morning" and "went unto" the place of which God had told him; on the third day he lifted up his eyes and saw the place from afar. That gesture is the only gesture, is indeed the only occurrence during the whole journey, of which we are told; and though its motivation lies in the fact that the place is elevated, its uniqueness still heightens the impression that the journey took place through a vacuum; it is as if, while he traveled on, Abraham had [9/10] looked neither to the right nor to the left, had suppressed any sign of life in his followers and himself save only their footfalls.

Thus the journey is like a silent progress through the indeterminate and the contingent, a holding of the breath, a process which has no present, which is inserted, like a blank duration, between what has passed and what lies ahead, and which yet is measured: three days! Three such days positively demand the symbolic interpretation which they later received. They began "early in the morning." But at what time on the third day did Abraham lift up his eyes and see his goal? The text says nothing on the subject. Obviously not "late in the evening," for it seems that there was still time enough to climb the mountain and make the sacrifice. So "early in the morning" is given, not as an indication of time, but for the sake of its ethical significance; it is intended to express the resolution, the promptness, the punctual obedience of the sorely tried Abraham. Bitter to him is the early morning in which he saddles his ass, calls his serving-men and his son Isaac, and sets out; but he obeys, he walks on until the third day, then lifts up his eyes and sees the place. Whence he comes, we do not know, but the goal is clearly stated: Jeruel in the land of Moriah. What place this is meant to indicate is not clear—"Moriah" especially may be a later correction of some other word. But in any case the goal was given, and in any case it is a matter of some sacred spot which was to receive a particular consecration by being connected with Abraham's sacrifice. Just as little as "early in the morning" serves as a temporal indication does "Jeruel in the land of Moriah" serve as a geographical indication; and in both cases alike, the complementary indication is not given, for we know as little of the hour at which Abraham lifted up his eyes as we do of the place from which he set forth—Jeruel is significant

not so much as the goal of an earthly journey, in its geographical relation to other places, as through its special election, through its relation
to God, who designated it as the scene of the act, and therefore it must
be named.

In the narrative itself, a third chief character appears: Isaac. While
God and Abraham, the serving-men, the ass, and the implements are
simply named, without mention of any qualities or any other sort of
definition, Isaac once receives an appositive; God says, "Take Isaac,
thine only son, whom thou lovest." But this is not a characterization of
Isaac as a person, apart from his relation to his father and apart from
the story; he may be handsome or ugly, intelligent or stupid, tall or
short, pleasant or unpleasant—we are not told. Only what we need
[10/11] to know about him as a personage in the action, here and now,
is illuminated, so that it may become apparent how terrible Abraham's
temptation is, and that God is fully aware of it. By this example of the
contrary, we see the significance of the descriptive adjectives and
digressions of the Homeric poems; with their indications of the earlier
and as it were absolute existence of the persons described, they prevent
the reader from concentrating exclusively on a present crisis; even
when the most terrible things are occurring, they prevent the establishment of an overwhelming suspense. But here, in the story of Abraham's
sacrifice, the overwhelming suspense is present; what Schiller makes
the goal of the tragic poet—to rob us of our emotional freedom, to turn
our intellectual and spiritual powers (Schiller says "our activity") in
one direction, to concentrate them there—is effected in this Biblical
narrative, which certainly deserves the epithet epic.

We find the same contrast if we compare the two uses of direct
discourse. The personages speak in the Bible story too; but their speech
does not serve, as does speech in Homer, to manifest, to externalize
thoughts—on the contrary, it serves to indicate thoughts which remain
unexpressed. God gives his command in direct discourse, but he leaves
his motives and his purpose unexpressed; Abraham, receiving the command, says nothing and does what he has been told to do. The conversation between Abraham and Isaac on the way to the place of sacrifice is only an interruption of the heavy silence and makes it all the
more burdensome. The two of them, Isaac carrying the wood and
Abraham with fire and a knife, "went together." Hesitantly, Isaac
ventures to ask about the ram, and Abraham gives the well-known
answer. Then the text repeats: "So they went both of them together."
Everything remains unexpressed.

It would be difficult, then, to imagine styles more contrasted than
those of these two equally ancient and equally epic texts. On the one
hand, externalized, uniformly illuminated phenomena, at a definite time
and in a definite place, connected together without lacunae in a perpetual foreground; thoughts and feeling completely expressed; events
taking place in leisurely fashion and with very little of suspense. On

the other hand, the externalization of only so much of the phenomena as is necessary for the purpose of the narrative, all else left in obscurity; the decisive points of the narrative alone are emphasized, what lies between is nonexistent; time and place are undefined and call for interpretation; thoughts and feeling remain unexpressed, are only suggested by the silence and the fragmentary speeches; the whole, [11/12] permeated with the most unrelieved suspense and directed toward a single goal (and to that extent far more of a unity), remains mysterious and "fraught with background."

I will discuss this term in some detail, lest it be misunderstood. I said above that the Homeric style was "of the foreground" because, despite much going back and forth, it yet causes what is momentarily being narrated to give the impression that it is the only present, pure and without perspective. A consideration of the Elohistic text teaches us that our term is capable of a broader and deeper application. It shows that even the separate personages can be represented as possessing "background"; God is always so represented in the Bible, for he is not comprehensible in his presence, as is Zeus; it is always only "something" of him that appears, he always extends into depths. But even the human beings in the Biblical stories have greater depths of time, fate, and consciousness than do the human beings in Homer; although they are nearly always caught up in an event engaging all their faculties, they are not so entirely immersed in its present that they do not remain continually conscious of what has happened to them earlier and elsewhere; their thoughts and feelings have more layers, are more entangled. Abraham's actions are explained not only by what is happening to him at the moment, nor yet only by his character (as Achilles' actions by his courage and his pride, and Odysseus' by his versatility and foresightedness), but by his previous history; he remembers, he is constantly conscious of, what God has promised him and what God has already accomplished for him—his soul is torn between desperate rebellion and hopeful expectation; his silent obedience is multilayered, has background. Such a problematic psychological situation as this is impossible for any of the Homeric heroes, whose destiny is clearly defined and who wake every morning as if it were the first day of their lives: their emotions, though strong, are simple and find expression instantly.

How fraught with background, in comparison, are characters like Saul and David! How entangled and stratified are such human relations as those between David and Absalom, between David and Joab! Any such "background" quality of the psychological situation as that which the story of Absalom's death and its sequel (II Samuel 18 and 19, by the so-called Jahvist) rather suggests than expresses, is unthinkable in Homer. Here we are confronted not merely with the psychological processes of characters whose depth of background is veritably abysmal, but with a purely geographical background too. For David

[12/13] is absent from the battlefield; but the influence of his will and his feelings continues to operate, they affect even Joab in his rebellion and disregard for the consequences of his actions; in the magnificent scene with the two messengers, both the physical and psychological background is fully manifest, though the latter is never expressed. With this, compare, for example, how Achilles, who sends Patroclus first to scout and then into battle, loses almost all "presentness" so long as he is not physically present. But the most important thing is the "multilayeredness" of the individual character; this is hardly to be met with in Homer, or at most in the form of a conscious hesitation between two possible courses of action; otherwise, in Homer, the complexity of the psychological life is shown only in the succession and alternation of emotions; whereas the Jewish writers are able to express the simultaneous existence of various layers of consciousness and the conflict between them.

The Homeric poems, then, though their intellectual, linguistic, and above all syntactical culture appears to be so much more highly developed, are yet comparatively simple in their picture of human beings; and no less so in their relation to the real life which they describe in general. Delight in physical existence is everything to them, and their highest aim is to make that delight perceptible to us. Between battles and passions, adventures and perils, they show us hunts, banquets, palaces and shepherds' cots, athletic contests and washing days—in order that we may see the heroes in their ordinary life, and seeing them so, may take pleasure in their manner of enjoying their savory present, a present which sends strong roots down into social usages, landscape, and daily life. And thus they bewitch us and ingratiate themselves to us until we live with them in the reality of their lives; so long as we are reading or hearing the poems, it does not matter whether we know that all this is only legend, "make-believe." The oft-repeated reproach that Homer is a liar takes nothing from his effectiveness, he does not need to base his story on historical reality, his reality is powerful enough in itself; it ensnares us, weaving its web around us, and that suffices him. And this "real" world into which we are lured, exists for itself, contains nothing but itself; the Homeric poems conceal nothing, they contain no teaching and no secret second meaning. Homer can be analyzed, as we have essayed to do here, but he cannot be interpreted. Later allegorizing trends have tried their arts of interpretation upon him, but to no avail. He resists any such treatment; the interpretations are forced and foreign, they do not crystallize into a unified [13/14] doctrine. The general considerations which occasionally occur (in our episode, for example, v. 360: that in misfortune men age quickly) reveal a calm acceptance of the basic facts of human existence, but with no compulsion to brood over them, still less any passionate impulse either to rebel against them or to embrace them in an ecstasy of submission.

It is all very different in the Biblical stories. Their aim is not to bewitch the senses, and if nevertheless they produce lively sensory effects, it is only because the moral, religious, and psychological phenomena which are their sole concern are made concrete in the sensible matter of life. But their religious intent involves an absolute claim to historical truth. The story of Abraham and Isaac is not better established than the story of Odysseus, Penelope, and Euryclea; both are legendary. But the Biblical narrator, the Elohist, had to believe in the objective truth of the story of Abraham's sacrifice—the existence of the sacred ordinances of life rested upon the truth of this and similar stories. He had to believe in it passionately; or else (as many rationalistic interpreters believed and perhaps still believe) he had to be a conscious liar—no harmless liar like Homer, who lied to give pleasure, but a political liar with a definite end in view, lying in the interest of a claim to absolute authority.

To me, the rationalistic interpretation seems psychologically absurd; but even if we take it into consideration, the relation of the Elohist to the truth of his story still remains a far more passionate and definite one than is Homer's relation. The Biblical narrator was obliged to write exactly what his belief in the truth of the tradition (or, from the rationalistic standpoint, his interest in the truth of it) demanded of him—in either case, his freedom in creative or representative imagination was severely limited; his activity was perforce reduced to composing an effective version of the pious tradition. What he produced, then, was not primarily oriented toward "realism" (if he succeeded in being realistic, it was merely a means, not an end); it was oriented toward truth. Woe to the man who did not believe it! One can perfectly well entertain historical doubts on the subject of the Trojan War or of Odysseus' wanderings, and still, when reading Homer, feel precisely the effects he sought to produce; but without believing in Abraham's sacrifice, it is impossible to put the narrative of it to the use for which it was written. Indeed, we must go even further. The Bible's claim to truth is not only far more urgent than Homer's, it is tyrannical—it excludes all other claims. The world of the Scripture stories is not satisfied [14/15] with claiming to be a historically true reality—it insists that it is the only real world, is destined for autocracy. All other scenes, issues, and ordinances have no right to appear independently of it, and it is promised that all of them, the history of all mankind, will be given their due place within its frame, will be subordinated to it. The Scripture stories do not, like Homer's, court our favor, they do not flatter us that they may please us and enchant us—they seek to subject us, and if we refuse to be subjected we are rebels.

Let no one object that this goes too far, that not the stories, but the religious doctrine, raises the claim to absolute authority; because the stories are not, like Homer's, simply narrated "reality." Doctrine and promise are incarnate in them and inseparable from them; for that very reason they are fraught with "background" and mysterious, containing a second, concealed meaning. In the story of Isaac, it is not only God's intervention at the beginning and the end, but even the factual and psychological elements which come between, that are mysterious, merely touched upon, fraught with background; and therefore they require subtle investigation and interpretation, they demand them. Since so much in the story is dark and incomplete, and since the reader knows that God is a hidden God, his effort to interpret it constantly finds something new to feed upon. Doctrine and the search for enlightenment are inextricably connected with the physical side of the narrative—the latter being more than simple "reality"; indeed they are in constant danger of losing their own reality, as very soon happened when interpretation reached such proportions that the real vanished.

If the text of the Biblical narrative, then, is so greatly in need of interpretation on the basis of its own content, its claim to absolute authority forces it still further in the same direction. Far from seeking, like Homer, merely to make us forget our own reality for a few hours, it seeks to overcome our reality: we are to fit our own life into its world, feel ourselves to be elements in its structure of universal history. This becomes increasingly difficult the further our historical environment is removed from that of the Biblical books; and if these nevertheless maintain their claim to absolute authority, it is inevitable that they themselves be adapted through interpretative transformation. This was for a long time comparatively easy; as late as the European Middle Ages it was possible to represent Biblical events as ordinary phenomena of contemporary life, the methods of interpretation themselves forming the basis for such a treatment. But when, through too great a change in environment and through the awakening of a critical [15/16] consciousness, this becomes impossible, the Biblical claim to absolute authority is jeopardized; the method of interpretation is scorned and rejected, the Biblical stories become ancient legends, and the doctrine they had contained, now dissevered from them, becomes a disembodied image.

As a result of this claim to absolute authority, the method of interpretation spread to traditions other than the Jewish. The Homeric poems present a definite complex of events whose boundaries in space and time are clearly delimited; before it, beside it, and after it, other complexes of events, which do not depend upon it, can be conceived without conflict and without difficulty. The Old Testament, on the other hand, presents universal history: it begins with the beginning of time, with the creation of the world, and will end with the Last Days, the fulfilling of the Covenant, with which the world will come to an end. Everything else that happens in the world can only be conceived as an element in this sequence; into it everything that is known about the world, or at least everything that touches upon the history of the Jews, must be fitted as an ingredient of the divine plan; and as this too became possible only by interpreting the new material as it poured in, the need for interpretation reaches out beyond the original Jewish-Israelitish realm of reality—for example to Assyrian, Babylonian, Persian, and Roman history; interpretation in a determined direction becomes a general method of comprehending reality; the new and strange world which now comes into view and which, in the form in which it presents itself, proves to be wholly unutilizable within the Jewish religious frame, must be so interpreted that it can find a place there. But this process nearly always also reacts upon the frame, which requires enlarging and modifying. The most striking piece of interpretation of this sort occurred in the first century of the Christian era, in consequence of Paul's mission to the Gentiles: Paul and the Church Fathers reinterpreted the entire Jewish tradition as a succession of figures prognosticating the appearance of Christ, and assigned the Roman Empire its proper place in the divine plan of salvation. Thus while, on the one hand, the reality of the Old Testament presents itself as complete truth with a claim to sole authority, on the other hand that very claim forces it to a constant interpretative change in its own content; for millennia it undergoes an incessant and active development with the life of man in Europe.

The claim of the Old Testament stories to represent universal history, their insistent relation—a relation constantly redefined by conflicts [16/17]—to a single and hidden God, who yet shows himself and who guides universal history by promise and exaction, gives these stories an entirely different perspective from any the Homeric poems can possess. As a composition, the Old Testament is incomparably less unified than the Homeric poems, it is more obviously pieced together—but the various components all belong to one concept of universal history and its interpretation. If certain elements survived which did not immediately fit in, interpretation took care of them; and so the reader is at every moment aware of the universal religio-historical perspective which gives the individual stories their general meaning and purpose. The greater the separateness and horizontal disconnection of the stories and groups of stories in relation to one another, compared with the *Iliad* and the *Odyssey*, the stronger is their general vertical connection, which holds them all together and which is entirely lacking in Homer. Each of the great figures of the Old Testament, from Adam to the prophets, embodies a moment of this vertical connection. God chose and formed these men to the end of embodying his essence and will—yet choice and formation do not coincide, for the latter proceeds gradually, historically, during the earthly life of him upon whom the choice has fallen. How the process is accomplished, what terrible trials such a formation inflicts, can be seen from our story of Abraham's sacrifice. Herein lies the reason why the great figures of the Old Testament are so much more fully developed, so much more fraught with their own biographical past, so much more distinct as individuals, than are the Homeric heroes. Achilles and Odysseus are splendidly described in many well-ordered words, epithets cling to them, their emotions are constantly displayed in their words and deeds—but they have no development, and their life-histories are clearly set forth once and for all. So little are the Homeric heroes presented as developing or having developed, that most of them—Nestor, Agamemnon, Achilles—appear to be of an age fixed from the very first. Even Odysseus, in whose case the long lapse of time and the many events which occurred offer so much opportunity for biographical development, shows almost nothing of it. Odysseus on his return is exactly the same as he was when he left Ithaca two decades earlier. But what a road, what a fate, lie between the Jacob who cheated his father out of his blessing and the old man whose favorite son has been torn to pieces by a wild beast!—between David the harp player, persecuted by his lord's jealousy, and the old king, surrounded by violent intrigues, whom Abishag the Shunnamite warmed in his bed, and he knew her [17/18] not! The old man, of whom we know how he has become what he is, is more of an individual than the young man; for it is only during the course of an eventful life that men are differentiated into full individuality; and it is this history of a personality which the Old Testament presents to us as the formation undergone by those whom God has chosen to be examples. Fraught with their development, sometimes even aged to the verge of dissolution, they show a distinct stamp of individuality entirely foreign to the Homeric heroes. Time can touch the latter only outwardly, and even that change is brought to our observation as little as possible; whereas the stern hand of God is ever upon the Old Testament figures; he has not only made them once and for all and chosen them, but he continues to work upon them, bends them and kneads them, and, without destroying them in essence, produces from them forms which their youth gave no grounds for anticipating. The objection that the biographical element of the Old Testament often springs from the combination of several legendary personages does not apply; for this combination is a part of the development of the text. And how much wider is the pendulum swing of their lives than that of the Homeric heroes! For they are bearers of the divine will, and yet they are fallible, subject to misfortune and humiliation—and in the midst of misfortune and in their humiliation their acts and words reveal the transcendent majesty of God. There is hardly one of them who does not, like Adam, undergo the deepest humiliation—and hardly one who is not deemed worthy of God's personal intervention and personal inspiration. Humiliation and elevation go far deeper and far higher than in Homer, and they belong basically together. The poor beggar Odysseus is only masquerading, but Adam is really cast down, Jacob really a refugee, Joseph really in the pit and then a slave to be bought and sold. But their greatness, rising out of humiliation, is almost superhuman and an image of God's greatness.

The reader clearly feels how the extent of the pendulum's swing is connected with the intensity of the personal history—precisely the most extreme circumstances, in which we are immeasurably forsaken and in despair, or immeasurably joyous and exalted, give us, if we survive them, a personal stamp which is recognized as the product of a rich existence, a rich development. And very often, indeed generally, this element of development gives the Old Testament stories a historical character, even when the subject is purely legendary and traditional.

Homer remains within the legendary with all his material, whereas [18/19] the material of the Old Testament comes closer and closer to history as the narrative proceeds; in the stories of David the historical report predominates. Here too, much that is legendary still remains, as for example the story of David and Goliath; but much—and the most essential—consists in things which the narrators knew from their own experience or from firsthand testimony. Now the difference between legend and history is in most cases easily perceived by a reasonably experienced reader. It is a difficult matter, requiring careful historical and philological training, to distinguish the true from the synthetic or the biased in a historical presentation; but it is easy to separate the historical from the legendary in general. Their structure is different. Even where the legendary does not immediately betray itself by elements of the miraculous, by the repetition of well-known standard motives, typical patterns and themes, through neglect of clear details of time and place, and the like, it is generally quickly recognizable by its composition. It runs far too smoothly. All cross-currents, all friction, all that is casual, secondary to the main events and themes, everything unresolved, truncated, and uncertain, which confuses the clear progress of the action and the simple orientation of the actors, has disappeared. The historical event which we witness, or learn from the testimony of those who witnessed it, runs much more variously, contradictorily, and confusedly; not until it has produced results in a definite domain are we able, with their help, to classify it to a certain extent; and how often the order to which we think we have attained becomes doubtful again, how often we ask ourselves if the data before us have not led us to a far too simple classification of the original events! Legend arranges its material in a simple and straightforward way; it detaches it from its contemporary historical context, so that the latter will not confuse it; it knows only clearly outlined men who act from few and simple motives and the continuity of whose feelings and actions remains uninterrupted. In the legends of martyrs, for example, a stiff-necked and fanatical persecutor stands over against an equally stiff-necked and fanatical victim; and a situation so complicated—that is to say, so real and historical—as that in which the "persecutor" Pliny finds himself in his celebrated letter to Trajan on the subject of the Christians, is unfit for legend. And that is still a comparatively simple case. Let the reader think of the history which we are ourselves witnessing; anyone who, for example, evaluates the behavior of individual men and groups of men at the time of the rise of National Socialism in Germany, or the behavior of individual peoples [19/20] and states before and during the last war, will feel how difficult it is to represent historical themes in general, and how unfit they are for legend; the historical comprises a great number of contradictory motives in each individual, a hesitation and ambiguous groping on the part of groups; only seldom (as in the last war) does a more or less plain situation, comparatively simple to describe, arise, and even such a situation is subject to division below the surface, is indeed almost constantly in danger of losing its simplicity; and the motives of all the interested parties are so complex that the slogans of propaganda can be composed only through the crudest simplification—with the result that friend and foe alike can often employ the same ones. To write history is so difficult that most historians are forced to make concessions to the technique of legend.

It is clear that a large part of the life of David as given in the Bible contains history and not legend. In Absalom's rebellion, for example, or in the scenes from David's last days, the contradictions and crossing of motives both in individuals and in the general action have become so concrete that it is impossible to doubt the historicity of the information conveyed. Now the men who composed the historical parts are often the same who edited the older legends too; their peculiar religious concept of man in history, which we have attempted to describe above, in no way led them to a legendary simplification of events; and so it is only natural that, in the legendary passages of the Old Testament, historical structure is frequently discernible—of course, not in the sense that the traditions are examined as to their credibility according to the methods of scientific criticism; but simply to the extent that the tendency to a smoothing down and harmonizing of events, to a simplification of motives, to a static definition of characters which avoids conflict, vacillation, and development, such as are natural to legendary structure, does not predominate in the Old Testament world of legend. Abraham, Jacob, or even Moses produces a more concrete, direct, and historical impression than the figures of the Homeric world —not because they are better described in terms of sense (the contrary is the case) but because the confused, contradictory multiplicity of events, the psychological and factual cross-purposes, which true history reveals, have not disappeared in the representation but still remain clearly perceptible. In the stories of David, the legendary, which only later scientific criticism makes recognizable as such, imperceptibly passes into the historical; and even in the legendary, the problem of the classification and interpretation of human history is already passionately [20/21] apprehended—a problem which later shatters the framework of historical composition and completely overruns it with prophecy; thus the Old Testament, in so far as it is concerned with human events, ranges through all three domains: legend, historical reporting, and interpretative historical theology.

Connected with the matters just discussed is the fact that the Greek text seems more limited and more static in respect to the circle of personages involved in the action and to their political activity. In the recognition scene with which we began, there appears, aside from Odysseus and Penelope, the housekeeper Euryclea, a slave whom Odysseus' father Laertes had bought long before. She, like the swineherd Eumaeus, has spent her life in the service of Laertes' family; like Eumaeus, she is closely connected with their fate, she loves them and shares their interests and feelings. But she has no life of her own, no feelings of her own; she has only the life and feelings of her master. Eumaeus too, though he still remembers that he was born a freeman and indeed of a noble house (he was stolen as a boy), has, not only in fact but also in his own feeling, no longer a life of his own, he is entirely involved in the life of his masters. Yet these two characters are the only ones whom Homer brings to life who do not belong to the ruling class. Thus we become conscious of the fact that in the Homeric poems life is enacted only among the ruling class—others appear only in the role of servants to that class. The ruling class is still so strongly patriarchal, and still itself so involved in the daily activities of domestic life, that one is sometimes likely to forget their rank. But they are unmistakably a sort of feudal aristocracy, whose men divide their lives between war, hunting, marketplace councils, and feasting, while the women supervise the maids in the house. As a social picture, this world is completely stable; wars take place only between different groups of the ruling class; nothing ever pushes up from below. In the early stories of the Old Testament the patriarchal condition is dominant too, but since the people involved are individual nomadic or half-nomadic tribal leaders, the social picture gives a much less stable impression; class distinctions are not felt. As soon as the people completely emerges—that is, after the exodus from Egypt—its activity is always discernible, it is often in ferment, it frequently intervenes in events not only as a whole but also in separate groups and through the medium of separate individuals who come forward; the origins of prophecy seem to lie in the irrepressible politico-religious spontaneity of the people. We receive the impression that the movement emerging [21/22] from the depths of the people of Israel-Judah must have been of a wholly different nature from those even of the later ancient democracies—of a different nature and far more elemental.

With the more profound historicity and the more profound social activity of the Old Testament text, there is connected yet another important distinction from Homer: namely, that a different conception of the elevated style and of the sublime is to be found here. Homer, of course, is not afraid to let the realism of daily life enter into the sublime and tragic; our episode of the scar is an example, we see how the quietly depicted, domestic scene of the foot-washing is incorporated into the pathetic and sublime action of Odysseus' homecoming. From the rule of the separation of styles which was later almost universally accepted and which specified that the realistic depiction of daily life was incompatible with the sublime and had a place only in comedy or, carefully stylized, in idyl—from any such rule Homer is still far removed. And yet he is closer to it than is the Old Testament. For the great and sublime events in the Homeric poems take place far more exclusively and unmistakably among the members of a ruling class; and these are far more untouched in their heroic elevation than are the Old Testament figures, who can fall much lower in dignity (consider, for example, Adam, Noah, David, Job); and finally, domestic realism, the representation of daily life, remains in Homer in the peaceful realm of the idyllic, whereas, from the very first, in the Old Testament stories, the sublime, tragic, and problematic take shape precisely in the domestic and commonplace: scenes such as those between Cain and Abel, between Noah and his sons, between Abraham, Sarah, and Hagar, between Rebekah, Jacob, and Esau, and so on, are inconceivable in the Homeric style. The entirely different ways of developing conflicts are enough to account for this. In the Old Testament stories the peace of daily life in the house, in the fields, and among the flocks, is undermined by jealousy over election and the promise of a blessing, and complications arise which would be utterly incomprehensible to the Homeric heroes. The latter must have palpable and clearly expressible reasons for their conflicts and enmities, and these work themselves out in free battles; whereas, with the former, the perpetually smouldering jealousy and the connection between the domestic and the spiritual, between the paternal blessing and the divine blessing, lead to daily life being permeated with the stuff of conflict, often with poison. The sublime influence of God here reaches so deeply into the everyday that the two realms of the sublime [22/23] and the everyday are not only actually unseparated but basically inseparable.

We have compared these two texts, and, with them, the two kinds of style they embody, in order to reach a starting point for an investigation into the literary representation of reality in European culture. The two styles, in their opposition, represent basic types: on the one hand, fully externalized description, uniform illumination, uninterrupted connection, free expression, all events in the foreground, displaying unmistakable meanings, few elements of historical development and of psychological perspective; on the other hand, certain parts brought into high relief, others left obscure, abruptness, suggestive influence of the unexpressed, "background" quality, multiplicity of meanings and the need for interpretation, universal-historical claims, development of the concept of the historically becoming, and preoccupation with the problematic.

Homer's realism is, of course, not to be equated with classical-antique realism in general; for the separation of styles, which did not develop until later, permitted no such leisurely and externalized description of everyday happenings; in tragedy especially there was no room for it; furthermore, Greek culture very soon encountered the phenomena of historical becoming and of the "multilayeredness" of the human problem, and dealt with them in its fashion; in Roman realism, finally, new and native concepts are added. We shall go into these later changes in the antique representation of reality when the occasion arises; on the whole, despite them, the basic tendencies of the Homeric style, which we have attempted to work out, remained effective and determinant down into late antiquity.

Since we are using the two styles, the Homeric and the Old Testament, as starting points, we have taken them as finished products, as they appear in the texts; we have disregarded everything that pertains to their origins, and thus have left untouched the question whether their peculiarities were theirs from the beginning or are to be referred wholly or in part to foreign influences. Within the limits of our purpose, a consideration of this question is not necessary; for it is in their full development, which they reached in early times, that the two styles exercised their determining influence upon the representation of reality in European literature. [23]

Homeric Epic: The Traditional Voice

DENYS PAGE

To THE QUESTIONS HOW, WHEN, AND WHERE THE *Iliad* AND *Odyssey* WERE composed we can give none but vague answers, inspired partly by common sense and partly by our own judgment of their form and contents. There is not, and so far as we know never has been, any reliable historical record of these matters. The fact that tradition attached to both poems a single name, Homer, would be instructive if we knew what it meant. Taken literally, that tradition is certainly misleading: whether one man composed (substantially) either poem may be eternally disputed; that the same man did not compose both I take to be beyond question. The attribution of both *Iliad* and *Odyssey* (and incidentally a number of other Epic poems) to Homer may, for all we know, mean no more than that a poet of this name was pre-eminent among those through whose hands the traditional poems passed to-

From Denys Page, "The Method, Time, and Place of the Composition of the *Odyssey*," in *The Homeric Odyssey* (Oxford: The Clarendon Press, 1955), pp. 137–145. Reprinted by permission of The Clarendon Press, Oxford.

wards the end of a long period of development: we should still not know in what form the poems existed before him, or how much of their final shape and substance was his work.

It is proper to dismiss from the mind at the outset the prejudice, for which there is no confirmation in historical records, that the burden of proof rests upon those who deny unity of authorship, whether for *Iliad* or for *Odyssey*. Nothing was ever certainly known about Homer (at least since the sixth century B.C.) except the name, and except the tradition which linked the name to the making of Epic poems in general, the *Iliad* and *Odyssey* in particular. When he lived, and where he lived, and precisely what he did, nobody ever knew in historical times: already in the fifth and fourth centuries B.C. widely different guesses were being made. Homer was a name without a history, though soon enough it acquired a fable. [137/138]

I see no reason to doubt that a person, indeed a great poet, of that name existed and was remembered from the obscure past: but I think it certain that both the Wrath of Achilles and the Return of Odysseus were the subject of Epic poetry for (at least) several centuries; and that the two poems which we possess are not, in any ordinary sense of the word, original compositions, substantially the work of any one person. They are the final state of a long and continuous process of development. Suppose, if you will, that Homer was the name of the poet who created that final form: it is surely obvious that we, who do not possess for comparison any earlier form, have no hope of discovering what that process of development may have been, or what precisely its last great developer may have done—unless it should happen that the contents of the poems themselves give us some insight into their pre-Homeric form.

Now while I believe that the answers to our questions belong to the region of guesswork, not knowledge, I hold with equal firmness the opinion that such guesswork must be based on certain securely established foundations. I shall try, in this chapter, to summarize what I believe these foundations to be. What follows will be brief, dogmatic, and disappointing. In the vast desert of uncertainty, what green oases of comfort have been, or may still be, found?

I. If it is our desire to discover how the *Odyssey* was composed, to look into the minds and methods of Greek Epic poets in the centuries before the dawn of history, to understand and evaluate their achievement, it is absolutely necessary first to recognize how great a gulf divides two kinds of poetry—that which is composed and remembered in the mind, *without* the aid of writing, and that which is composed *with* the aid of writing. That the Homeric poems were composed and carried in the mind, and recited by word of mouth, and that this was the only method of their composition, and this for a long time the only mode of their publication to the audiences for which they were designed—the proof of these things is the outstanding achievement of an American [138/139] scholar, Milman Parry,[1] whose premature death extinguished the brightest light that has been shed on the Greek Epic in our time.

In societies where the art of writing is unknown, the poet makes his verses out of metrical formulas—fixed groups of words, traditional phrases descriptive of particular ideas and readily adaptable to similar ideas; the stock of such formulas, gradually accumulated over a long period of time, supplies the poet at need with a whole group of lines, or a single line, or a part of a line, all ready-made. He cannot stop to meditate while he recites; he cannot read over—let alone change—what he composed a few hundred lines ago; he cannot plan in advance except in very broad outline. But whatever he wants to say, within the limits of certain traditional themes, may (and often must) be expressed in phrases long ago designed for that purpose, and immediately suggested to him by his practised memory. He may or may not be a good poet: he must be a good craftsman. There is a stock-in-trade, the vast number of traditional formulas, to be learnt only by long apprenticeship; and there is a technique, the craft of using and adapting formulas and systems of formulas, to be acquired only by long experience.

The Homeric Epic differs from all other Greek poetry, and from all poetry with which we (most of us) are familiar today, in just this respect: its elements are phrases, not words. It is largely composed of traditional formulas, fixed word-patterns, almost infinitely adaptable to the ideas suggested to the poet's imagination within the limits of his theme; and supplying lines, or parts of lines, more or less ready-made. In the *Iliad* and *Odyssey* this technique may be seen at a very advanced state of development, refined and thrifty, purified of superfluities, so that (in general) one formula cannot take the place of another, in the same part of the verse, without altering the meaning of what is being said. If the poet wishes to begin his verse with the thought 'But when they arrived . . .', he has one way, and one only, of expressing this, αὐτὰρ ῥ᾽ ἵκοντο, 'denying himself all other ways of expressing the idea'.[2] The creation of the vast number of formulas, adaptable to almost all possible emergencies, must have been the [139/140] work of many generations of poets; and from the refinement, thrift, and economy of the Homeric stock of phrases we are obliged to infer that we are at or near the culmination of a very long process.

Now the *Odyssey*, no less than the *Iliad*, is composed in this way:

[1] The Homeric writings of Milman Parry are conveniently listed by A. B. Lord, *AJA* 52 (1948) 43 f.; cf. also Wade-Gery in *The Poet of the Iliad* (1952) 81. Much that I might have added here will be found in the first chapter of Rhys Carpenter's *Folk Tale, Fiction, and Saga, & c.* (Sather Classical Lectures XX), 1946, and in the second chapter of M. I. Finley's *World of Odysseus* (1954).

[2] Parry, *Harv. Stud.* 41 (1930) 89: the examples on p. 88 are very impressive and instructive.

it reveals from start to finish the memory-technique of verse-making, the practice of composing from memory without the aid of writing. Whether the art of writing was known to its composers we may never know: what we do know, because we see it with our own eyes, is that the art of writing, if it was familiar, made little or no difference to the technique employed in the actual verse-making; that is still the formula-technique, the building of verses out of traditional phrases learnt by one generation from another and supplied to the poet by his practised memory at the moment required.

There is no longer any doubt about the fact; but one may well wonder whether it does not suggest some further questions of exceptional difficulty. Is not the complexity of the structure of the *Odyssey*—its blend of three stories into one; its blend of episodes within one story—beyond the limit of what is possible for a man who has nothing but his memory to assist him? And would not a poem thus composed be continually changing? Would it not differ from one recitation to another, and would it not become unrecognizably transformed in the course of a generation or two? Modern analogies confirm what common sense suggests—that 'the oral poem even in the mouth of the same singer is ever in a state of change; and it is the same when his poetry is sung by others'.[3]

These are difficult questions; I do no more than indicate the region in which their answer may be found. It is possible, or even likely, that the art of writing was practised (though not in general use) at the time when the first continuous *Odyssey* was composed. Now though that art played little or no part in the making of the poem, it might nevertheless be used to record the poem when made (or rather while making).[4] If this were so, the boundaries of the poet's powers would be greatly extended: he could then build, as nobody before such a time could build, a structure of [140/141] considerable size and some complexity, if each development was preserved in writing; and his admirers or apprentices would be able to reproduce their master's voice much more faithfully than before, not because they could learn it from the written record—that was merely the architect's plan, not his structure—but because the version which they heard from the master was more or less unvarying. This does not imply that the master himself (and others after him) would cease to expand or otherwise alter his poem in the course of time: the written record is nothing more than an aid to memory, a tool of the trade. The text of a poem was still the spoken, not the written, word; the whole conception of a static poem in a standard text is entirely foreign to the memory-technique of verse-making and to the manner of its transmission from one generation to another.

---

[3] Ibid. 43 (1932) 15.

[4] See Wade-Gery, op. ct. 9 ff.: but I cannot find any reason (let alone evidence) for the supposition that the alphabet was '*invented* [my italics] as a notation for Greek verse'.

This conception of an oral poetry, composed in the mind and designed for preservation by memory alone, has—or rather ought to have—revolutionized our understanding of the *Iliad* and *Odyssey*. It should be obvious that many of the principles of criticism applicable to a Virgil or a Milton have no place here. Virgil and Milton may be expected to choose a particular word or phrase because it most accurately represents their thought in a particular context. However much they may owe to the past, they are seldom limited by tradition to a particular mode of expression; they are free to form an individual style. In the Homeric poems, whatever the context and whoever the person may be, the same act, thought, or emotion is likely to be described in the same words; not because those words are particularly suitable to that person or context, but because those are the words which tradition supplies ready-made to the poet for the description of that act, thought, or emotion. His style is traditional and typical, not individual. He does not, as a rule, select or invent: he uses what his memory offers him, already adapted or readily adaptable to the part of his verse which he has to fill. It should be obvious too that the memory-technique of verse-composition and the employment of a traditional stock of phrases naturally impose severe limitations on the structure of the story [141/142] and the characterization of the persons. It is very improbable that a poet who depends on nothing but his memory both for the making and for the preservation of his verses will so construct his plot that the true significance of an earlier part will emerge only in the light of a later part, and vice versa; except in very broad and simple conceptions integral to the main structure of his story. Delicate and subtle preparations *now* for what will follow in five hundred lines' time; veiled and indirect allusions *now* to what happened five hundred lines ago—such artifice lies beyond his power, even supposing that it lay within the bounds of his imagination. References backwards and forwards (over more than a short space) will be more or less explicit, and limited to the broad outlines of the story.

As with the plot, so with the characters. In poetry of this kind the characters will be—as indeed they are—envisaged in fairly broad outline. Their thoughts will be (for the most part) expressed in language which is traditional and typical, not specially designed for a given person in a given place; and the thoughts themselves (apart from their expression) will often be traditional and typical, not individual. Subtlety of soul, complexity of character, true portrayal of personality—for these we must wait until the practice of the art of writing affords the poet the necessary leisure and the necessary means for reflection, for planning the future in some detail, and for correcting the past.

Thus in answering the question how the *Odyssey* was composed we must start from the established position that this poem was composed in the mind, and destined for preservation by the memory alone, by a poet or poets highly skilled in the use of a traditional language which had been gradually developed over a very long period of time.

Do not therefore suppose that little or no room is left for the exercise of an individual's poetic talent. A man may be either the master or the slave of the rules by which he lives; the conventions of an art have never yet confined genius and mediocrity in equal chains. The meeting of Hector and Andromache, the embassy to Achilles, the Doloneia, the ransom of Hector's body, the stories of Nausicaa and of Polyphemus (to [142/143] give only a few examples) prove that those who worked within the limits prescribed by the Greek Epic tradition could attain the highest point of excellence in the poetic art. Only we have wholly misunderstood the nature of their achievement unless we recognize that they do, and must, work within those limits. They are not free (except to a very limited extent) to frame their own phraseology; they are not free (except, again, to a very limited extent) to invent new characters or to depict traditional characters in a mode contrary to tradition; they are narrowly limited in their choice of theme, in what their persons say and do; and there are some aspects of life and manners which they may not reflect at all. 'Homer' has often been highly praised for doing what had been done before him, and what he could have done in no other way. Intricacy of design and subtleties of thought wholly alien to the oral technique of composition have often been sought (and found) in him. The road is open (since Milman Parry found it for us) to a juster understanding of the distinction between the traditional and the non-traditional elements in the *Iliad* and *Odyssey*.

So much for the first of our fundamental facts. And here, with the utmost brevity, is the second.

The study of the language of Homer (and particularly its spelling) in our manuscripts proves beyond question that our manuscripts are the ultimate posterity of an *Athenian* parentage. The fact is certain: the detail of the genealogy is at many points conjectural. It appears probable that at Athens, in the sixth century B.C., there was made, and thereafter copied and circulated, a more or less standard text of the two poems; a descendant (or descendants) of this survived into the age of Alexandrian scholarship, when it was re-edited especially by Aristarchus, whose text became the standard for all succeeding ages. Fragments of the *Iliad* and *Odyssey* written on papyrus from the first century B.C. onwards for half a millennium have taught us that our Homer is Aristarchus' Homer, the direct descendant of his standard text; and that the poems have suffered no alterations of any importance since his time. Unfortunately we are unable to make the further comparison between the text of Aristarchus in the first [143/144] century and the text of the Athenians in the sixth century B.C.: the former we know, the latter we do not know; evidence concerning its form and substance is meagre, mostly indirect, and often of doubtful reliability. For the *Iliad*, what can be done has been done by Professor Bolling; for the *Odyssey*, I must provisionally confine myself to the negative position that there is very little evidence to suggest that the text of Aristarchus differed substantially from the Athenian text of the sixth century B.C.; though we must reckon with a considerable number of minor additions and alterations.

The evidence of our own manuscripts proves the existence of a standard Athenian text of Homer; and history assures us that there is only one era in which this could have been made—the sixth century B.C., whether early, in the time of Solon, or later, in the time of Peisistratus or his sons. Now it happens that it was common knowledge, recorded for us from the fourth century onwards, that the recitation of the whole of Homer, 'exclusively and consecutively', was instituted at Athens for the festival of the Panathenaea in the sixth century; it was common knowledge too that the Athenians in that century had been able in some way to affect the text of Homer, inserting additional lines to which appeal might thereafter be made, as if their text, and no other, was generally acknowledged to be the standard. We are pleased to welcome this external evidence, though we did not really need it: the history of our own manuscripts had already proved essentially the same conclusion. As Professor Rhys Carpenter says, 'If antiquity had neglected to record for us the Peisistratean recension of Homer, we should have had to invent it for ourselves as a hypothesis essential to the facts.'

It thus appears certain enough that the creative phase of the Greek Epic, when poems composed in the mind were preserved in the memory, ended in what might be called an editorial phase, when the finally developed memory-poems were committed to writing in a particular form, and forever thereafter preserved in that form. It follows that in the study of the *Odyssey* we must make proper allowance for the possibilities that the editorial phase may have been the first full and continuous text ever made in writing; [144/145] and that the form in which it survived thereafter may have been very much affected by the conditions—unknown but by no means unimaginable—under which the Athenian text-makers performed their task. In short, our minds must be open to the fact that the text of our *Odyssey* may owe something, or even much, to two sources in particular—the persons who preserved the poems by memory for (at least) several generations, and the person (or persons) who made that standard written text at Athens in the sixth century B.C. which is the ultimate written source of our text today. . . . [145]

THE *ODYSSEY:*
THEME AND STRUCTURE

Revenge

FRANK W. JONES

THE *Odyssey* HAS FOUR MAIN THEMES: THE WANDERINGS OF ODYSSEUS, his return home, the crimes of the suitors, and his vengeance upon them. If the poet, writing for a public of hearers, had in his mind from the start the construction of the poem as we know it, then one of his hardest technical problems faced him at its threshold. The tale of the revenge itself was not to be begun until fully half the recitation was over, and yet the whole poem aspired to that consummation. How could this dominant theme be so impressed upon the audience that their concentration on it would not be diluted during the lengthy narratives of the voyages and encounters of Telemachus and his father? The poet's solution of this problem is visible if we analyze closely his handling of the Revenge theme in the Ithacan scenes comprised in the exposition (Books 1, 2). Here, during a development extending over almost 700 lines, or about one-twentieth of the poem, the theme is given unforgettable verbal stature. I shall summarize, then comment on, the nine principal passages[1] in which this is achieved.

The theme is announced as the curtain rises on Scene I, after the Prologue in Heaven. Telemachus is discovered: watching the suitors gamble and carouse, he "fancies his father's sudden arrival from somewhere, somehow . . ., and the scatter there would be, through the palace" (1.113 ff.).[2] Then his thoughts become words, addressed to the stranger whose appearance interrupts the [195/196] daydream: "If they but saw him returning to Ithaca . . ., they would pray for fleet-footedness, not wealth" (163 ff). In the ensuing conversation, the stranger (Athene, as Mentes) takes up this vision of vengeance and enriches it with details: what a swift doom would befall the suitors if Odysseus

---

[1] That is, statements giving positive force to the thought and plan of Odysseus' vengeance, not those which comment on it from other standpoints (e.g., the example of Orestes, 1.298ff.; the suitors' incredulity, 2.243ff.). These keynote passages total 65 lines.

[2] I take these and some other phrases from T. E. Lawrence's translation of the *Odyssey* (1935).

Frank W. Jones, "The Formulation of the Revenge Motif in the *Odyssey*," *Transactions and Proceedings of the American Philological Association*, LXXII (1941), 195–202. Reprinted by permission of the author and the publisher.

were to appear now . . ., with helmet, shield and spears, as "Mentes" once saw him long ago! (255 ff.). And soon the mood of vengeance moves from wish to plan. "Mentes," having given Telemachus instructions for the voyage to Pylos and Sparta, bids him consider, on returning, "how he may kill the suitors within his halls, either by fair fight or by stratagem" . . . : for he is of an age to put away childish things (293 ff.). So, when Athene goes, Telemachus faces the suitors "like a peer of the gods" and re-phrases her parting words as his first warning to them: he will call upon the ever-living gods for vengeance, that the suitors may "perish within the house, unavenged" . . . (380). On the following day, during the assembly, he repeats this threat (2.143 ff.) in a more intense context of longer and more ominous appeals to divine wrath . . . (66 f.). In immediate response to this heightened fervor, Zeus sends an omen of fighting eagles. The seer Halitherses, interpreting it, makes the first concrete statement of imminent vengeance (160 ff.): Odysseus is already close, "bearing the seeds of murder and doom" for all his foes . . . The assembly disperses; and Athene, appearing again (as Mentor) in answer to a second prayer of Telemachus, reiterates the certainty and nearness of revenge (281 ff.): "They do not apprehend the death and dark doom . . . hovering over them, to overwhelm them all in a day." Heartened, Telemachus utters a third and final warning to the suitors (314 ff.): this time no appeal to deity, but a bare assertion of individual intent, most mature in tone for the temperamental youth who that very morning dashed his sceptre to the ground in tears: "Now that *I* am grown, and finding out things from what others tell me, and *my* mettle is mounting within me, *I* shall try how *I* may visit evil dooms upon you" . . . This declaration of war sums up the central drives of the exposition: the development of Telemachus' character, the help of the gods (Athene being the "others" from whom he learns), and the theme of Revenge. [196/197] Swiftly the crisp words become action: in an hour or two Odysseus' son is bound for Pylos.

These key passages fall into three groups of three each: a triad of triads[3]—the most elaborate construction of this type in the poem,

---

[3] The principle of triadic structure—definitively expounded, for Homeric and other epic, by Drerup and Stürmer in *Homerische Poetik*, 1 and 3 (1921; see Indices *s.v. Dreizahl*)—can be illustrated from most narrative and dramatic poetry, e.g.:

> When went there by an age, since the great flood,
> But it was fam'd with more than with *one man?*
> When could they say till now, that talk'd of Rome,
> That her wide walls encompass'd *but one man?*
> Now is it Rome indeed and room enough,
> When there is in it *but one only man.*

(Shakespeare, *Julius Caesar*, I, 2). This is triadic heightening at its simplest: addition to a repeated *phrase;* but the principle is the same in the more complex repetition of *ideas,* with or without that of phrase, in the Homeric passages under discussion.

exerting great mnemonic force by evenly distributed stress on the three vital components of the theme of Vengeance: its agent, the absent Odysseus; its object, the suitors' hybris; and its instrument, Telemachus and the contrivances of Athene in general. The first triad expresses hope for revenge, in three visualizations, mounting in scope and intensity, of Odysseus' return and the effect it would have on the suitors. The second definitely announces vengeance, by three assertions that the suitors will be slain for their wrongdoing. And the third drives the point home by crystallizing the theme in three powerful phrases of almost identical length, in the same metrical position, all sounding the dread word *doom* like a battle-cry—the last and most menacing being given to Telemachus. The demarcations of these triads, and the order of their assignment to the characters, correspond to the entries of new subjects and motivations. First, after the council of the gods, which has emphasized Odysseus' present plight, his past glory and future fulfilment are suggested by the figure of his son and the things on which he broods: a mood of retrospection and hope is expressed by Telemachus, and then intensified by Athene. This leads her to state her plan,[4] which changes the boy's mood to a purposeful one: and his ensuing words to the suitors, with their reiteration in the next scene, balance the two sighs of longing which have introduced him. The highest dramatic level of the exposition is reached with the omen from Zeus, a symbol of fulfilment vouchsafed to the hero's son at the crisis of the [197/198] emotions Athene's plan has roused in him. On this final level, the theme of Vengeance finds a new mouthpiece, Halitherses, whose message of imminent doom is again uttered, in the two concluding scenes, by Athene and Telemachus. Thus the total context of decisive events, not the formal factor of scene-change,[5] determines the grouping of the nine passages and their symmetrical order of appearance (Telemachus, Telemachus, Athene; Athene, Telemachus, Telemachus; Halitherses, Athene, Telemachus).

The integration of the three triads with one another and with the total context emerges in all its richness when they are examined separately.[6]

The first triad intensifies three themes concurrently: Hybris, Nostos and Revenge. Each visualization of the vengeance makes the suitors' guilt appear more grave, Odysseus' return more specific, and his vengeance more crushing. At first the Hybris theme is only implied: Telemachus dreams of his father "recovering *his* honor and property"; then he speaks of the suitors' desire for "gold and fine clothes"; and finally, after Athene has broached the subject of their wooing (1.226) and Telemachus has explained the matter (245 ff.), this cardinal point

---

[4] The change of tone is clearly marked (1.267ff.). . . .

[5] Always a subsidiary element in Homer: cf. S. E. Bassett, *The Poetry of Homer* (1938) 33ff., on Homeric use of this and the time element.

[6] Henceforth in this paper the term "Hybris" is used for the theme of the suitors' guilt; "Nostos" and "Revenge" for those of Odysseus' return and vengeance.

of their guilt appears in the phrase *bitterly married*. In harmony with this heightening of the Hybris theme, Odysseus' return is first envisaged vaguely as "from somewhere," then "home to Ithaca," and finally "at the outer gate of the house"; and his revenge is first suggested by the single word "scatter," then made more vivid by portraying the suitors' terror on seeing him, and finally bodied forth in detail by Athene's vision of him "with helmet, shield and two spears, laying hands on the shameless suitors." The last of the visualizations is especially masterly in that it subjects the content and phrasing of the theme to an expansion and a contraction both supremely dramatic in effect. The description of Odysseus at Ephyra, an apparent digression, really strengthens the themes of Nostos and Revenge by associated ideas and presages.[7] Its evocation of the Ithaca that was adds overtones to the note of longing for the master's return, and its picture of him as a bowman in quest of poison for his arrow-tips patently foreshadows the killing of the [198/199] suitors.[8] And hard on this "digression" follows a phrase which fuses the Revenge and Hybris themes into two words: "swift-doomed and bitterly married"—the shadow of retribution swooping over the thought of the suitors' wooing almost as soon as it is uttered.

Athene renders Telemachus active in her plan for the return and vengeance. The second triad concentrates on the Revenge theme, reinforcing it with detail and widening its frame of reference. Complementing their visualizations of the vengeance, which concentrated on the avenger, Athene and Telemachus color the picture of his victims: adjective grows into verb: the suitors, scattering, terrified, swift-doomed, will be utterly destroyed . . . , in the heart of the palace at whose gate the avenger appears, and without hope of counter-retribution. This last touch comes from Telemachus when he turns on the suitors to voice Athene's plan as a threat: the added detail fits the heightening of emotional tone. On his repetition of the threat next day, the invocation of divine wrath effects a further heightening; it also leads into the omen scene, and foreshadows Telemachus' parting hint (2.314–316) that the manhood-fostering gods are on his side. Beyond these specific heightenings, the second triad manifests a gradual enrichment in general significance. Beginning on the personal, individual plane with Athene's announcement of plan ("*You* shall kill them in *your* house"), it passes to the social implications of the act ("They shall be unavenged"), and thence to its meaning as an expression of divine Nemesis.[9]

---

[7] Telemachus' later informants, Nestor and Menelaus, also use recollections of Odysseus' prowess in this connection (3.218ff.; 4.341ff.).

[8] An implication driven home by the suitors' comments on Telemachus' announcement of intended departure: some of them sarcastically suppose he is going to Ephyra for poison to put into their wine (2.325 ff.).

[9] Thus approaching the level on which the poem begins: cf. Zeus's remarks on the moral order, 1.32 ff.

After this extension of the Revenge theme, the total context calls for some corresponding development in those of Nostos and Hybris; for the central figure of the poem is still the absent Odysseus, and his son's part in the vengeance will plainly bring on some further conflicts with the disrespectful suitors as long as he stays in Ithaca. Accordingly, the third triad, after an initial expansion of the Nostos and Hybris themes, culminates that of Revenge by showing its explosion as active conflict between the characters, in such a way that the theme of Hybris becomes indelibly tinged with implications of vengeance—a presage of the distant final outcome. This is achieved [199/200] not only by masterly narration, but by a concentration and intensification of phrasing which may be said to raise the Revenge theme to its third power. First, the themes of Nostos, Hybris and Revenge are chanted in unison, as it were, in the speech of Halitherses interpreting the omen. Not only is the avenger alive, he cries, but the twenty years' wanderings are nearly ended, and doom from the hero is so close that the suitors had best desist from their offences at once. Both the Nostos and Hybris themes are here carried a point beyond their previous stages. To the place-details of the return in the first triad are added those of time (the twentieth year) and circumstance (the hero will not be recognized); and the Hybris is further dramatized by the seer's suggestion that it is not too late to mend, that doom may yet be averted. But his words begin and end with the warning note sounded in the phrase "He bears the seeds of murder and doom." The suitors, of course, deride the prophecy, incredulous that one man could overcome so many foes (2.246 ff.); and Athene comments on this foolish ignorance: they are *senseless* (282), their hybris has blinded them to what is coming: *death and dark doom,* a phrase still stronger than Halitherses' *murder and doom.* So the goddess and the suitors themselves expose the fatal nature of their error: their very hybris makes revenge more sure. As in the first and second triads, so in the key-phrases of the first two passages in the final triad, the emphasis falls first on the doer, then on the sufferer of the doom (*murder—death,* active—passive). In the third passage, Telemachus' cry, "I will visit evil dooms upon you," is the triumph of the active element: it proclaims the fulfilment of the *doom* which is taking shape in his father (φυτεύει). This effect is attained simply by isolating the essential word, *doom,* and reinforcing it with the adjective *evil,* with its implications of a ghastly death for the suitors. It is notable, too, that Telemachus' last words bring the thought of vengeance back to the frame of reference in which the second triad began. After Halitherses has seen in the omen of Zeus the revenge to come, and Athene has stressed its relation to the suitors, Telemachus stands forth as its personal, individual agent. This reversal of the foregoing order of meanings narrows the connotation of the theme to the very razor-edge of drama.

It is now possible to appreciate the role of Homer's use and [200/201] choice of words in this great crescendo of action, character, and mood. His phrasing distils the special essence of each triad into single, climactic lines: "punch-lines," to borrow a useful term from Broadway. The first triad, imagining the physical clash between hero and villains, is typified in the line: "Then would they all be swift-doomed and bitterly married" (1.266). The second, developing the moral that the vengeance is the suitors' deserved punishment, is summarized in the twice-spoken threat: "May they perish within the house, unavenged" (1.380, 2.145); and the third, infusing the Revenge theme with utmost dramatic force, makes its point in the three closely related lines: "Being near, he bears the seeds of murder and doom for them" (2.165), "They know nothing of their death and dark doom" (283), "I shall try how I may visit evil dooms upon you" (316). The proportion 1 : 2 : 3, then, represents not only the qualitative increase in power throughout the texture of the exposition, but the numerical increase in summary or formulaic lines concentrating that power into a few words. This procedure shapes the Revenge theme into what may well be called a motif, on the analogy of the *Leitmotiv* in Wagnerian opera;[10] and the whole gradual, symmetrically heightened formulation[11] of this Revenge motif burns it once for all into the hearer's mind, so that henceforth any occurrence of it or associated motifs will set up in him the sound, vibration, rhythm of those ominous phrases expressing the *idées-fixes*: *vengeance, murder, death, doom*.

The passages I have analyzed exemplify an important aspect of Homeric formula-technique, exhaustive study of which is only beginning.[12] It is plain throughout the *Iliad* and *Odyssey* that the [201/202]

---

[10] The analogy of musical with Homeric composition is generally treated by G. M. Calhoun in "Homeric Repetitions," *Univ. Cal. Pub. Class. Phil.* 12.1 (1938) 5ff., 10, 21ff. Specifically, the *Leitmotiv* of Wagner (or the *idée-fixe* of Berlioz) is analogous to Homeric formula because it is also employed as a simple mnemonic device to further the unity-in-multiplicity of a complex work of art. The parallel of Wagner is particularly striking in that *Der Ring des Nibelungen* takes about as long to perform as the *Odyssey* probably did to recite (cf. Drerup, *op. cit.* 1.428ff.). Wagner, incidentally, was a lifelong devotee of Homer: in his schooldays he even made a verse translation of the first twelve books of the *Odyssey*, and it has been suggested that he used a line from this in *Tannhäuser* (*Wagner-Jahrbuch* 1913.332).

[11] The symmetry is manifest even in so small a point as the number of lines used to pursue the theme. In each triad it is given at least one terse utterance of exactly three lines or eighteen feet (1.115–117, 163–165, 378–380; 2.143–145, 164–167).

[12] See e.g., M. Parry, "Studies in the Epic Technique of Oral Verse-Making," *HSPh* 41 (1930) 73ff.; 43 (1932) 1ff.; G. M. Calhoun, *op. cit.*, and "The Art of Formula in Homer—ΕΠΕΑ ΠΤΕΡΟΕΝΤΑ," *CPh* 30 (1935) 215 ff., and Parry's reply, "About Winged Words," *CPh* 32 (1937) 59ff.; J. T. Sheppard, "Zeus-Loved Achilles," *JHS* 55 (1935) 113ff., and "Great-Hearted Odysseus," *JHS* 56 (1936) 36ff. Parry recognized the presence of variation in the use of formula: "Perhaps the change of an old formula, or the making of a new one on the pattern of the old, or the fusing of old formulas, or a new way of putting them together" (*HSPh* 43 [1932] 9); but he was little inclined to credit such variation to high creative

poet or poets worked with "ready-made" epithets and phrases. . . .
But the artistic function of such phrases can be discerned only by relating their occurrences to the context. In this case it is abundantly clear
that the choice and variation of formulaic phrases was guided by a
superb sense of structure, not by mathematical formalism, or a
simplisme of superfluous repetition, or merely the exigencies of metre.
The phrases "He bears the seeds of murder and doom" and "I will visit
evil dooms upon you"—in the original, metrically equivalent and easily
interchangeable—occur where they do because the second speaker is
Telemachus hurling threats at his foes, not Halitherses intoning a
prophecy: *evil* fortifies *doom, visit* is a harsher verb than *bear the
seeds*. Nor is it simply the epic Rule of Three which decrees that there
shall be one "punch line" in the first triad, a repeated one in the second,
and three in the third. These six lines suit the word to the action in the
six leading scenes of the exposition: Telemachus and Mentes, Telemachus confronting the suitors in the palace, then in the assembly, the
Omen, Telemachus and Mentor, Telemachus' farewell. This, given the
prime poetic gift which can create such evocative "formulas," is the
patterning and organizing procedure which makes of narrated matter
a shapely poem. No amount of structural analysis can reach the central
creative secret; but it is good to discern, even partially, the articulation
of the wonderful organism which it brings to life. [202]

---

effort. As against this, cf. Sheppard, "Zeus-Loved Achilles," 114. I agree with
Calhoun that the poet or poets of the *Iliad* and *Odyssey* "composed in lines or
groups of lines as freely as does the modern poet in words."

Guilt and Free Will

EDWARD F. D'ARMS AND KARL K. HULLEY

INGENIOUSLY INTERTWINED IN CERTAIN INSTANCES WITH A *Leitmotiv*
serving in its turn for other significant purposes, there recurs repeatedly
throughout the *Odyssey* an idea which is maintained with marked consistency. The first statement of this idea occurs in the scene on Mt.
Olympus with which the action of the *Odyssey* begins, when Zeus,
who has been thinking of Aegisthus and his death at the hands of
Orestes, addresses the initial speech of the poem to the assembled gods.
This situation in itself is enough to convince most moderns who are

Edward F. D'Arms and Karl K. Hulley, "The *Oresteia*-Story in the *Odyssey*,"
Transactions and Proceedings of the American Philological Association, LXXVII
(1946), 207–213. Reprinted by permission of the authors and the publisher.

reading the *Odyssey* for the first time that the gods will control all the actions of the epic.[1] But let us see. The speech of Zeus reads as follows:

"Lo, how men blame the gods! From us, they say, comes evil. But through their own perversity, and more than is their due, they meet with sorrow; even as now Aegisthus, pressing beyond his due, married the lawful wife of the son of Atreus and slew her husband on his coming home. Yet he well knew his own impending ruin; for we ourselves forewarned him, dispatching Hermes, our clear-sighted Speedy-comer, and told him not to slay the man nor woo the wife. 'For vengeance follows from Orestes, son of Atreus, when he comes of age and longs for his own land.' This Hermes said, but though he sought Aegisthus' good, he did not change his purpose. And now Aegisthus makes atonement for it all."[2]

Here, at the very beginning of the *Odyssey*, linked to the *Leitmotiv* which will be discussed later, appears an idea which is corroborated many, many times in the course of the epic: Men bring their own sorrows upon themselves. Along with this idea is the negative form of it: Men blame the gods for their troubles.[3] Although no attempt will be made to present documentary evidence [207/208] for every appearance of this idea in the *Odyssey*, a few of the most striking examples may be mentioned.

I

Athene, immediately after the conference of the gods, visits Telemachus, assuming the form of Mentes for the purpose. She persuades him to tell the story of his situation. In the course of his recital, Telemachus states that once his house was fortunate, "but the hard-purposed gods then changed their minds" (1.234) and kept Odysseus away from home. He continues (1.243 f.), "Yet now I do not grieve and mourn for him alone. The gods have brought me other sore distress," by which he means the suitors. Athene does not reply directly but indicates clearly that Telemachus might do something about the situation if he tried. In fact, most of the first four books of the *Odyssey* might be called "The Education of Telemachus," for throughout it is Athene's avowed purpose to inspire Telemachus to assume the responsibility for acting.[4] For example, in Book III Telemachus has reached the home of Nestor. The story of Orestes is told in some detail, and Nestor exhorts Telemachus (3.199 f.) that he too should be brave and win fame for the future. Telemachus replies:

[1] On the rôle of the gods in Homer, see George M. Calhoun, "Homer's Gods: Prolgomena," *TAPhA* 68 (1937) 11–25.

[2] *Od.* 1.32 ff. All translations are quoted from the rendering of George Herbert Palmer, revised edition (Cambridge, 1920).

[3] It is interesting to compare the attitude of Priam, who, though courteously absolving Helen from all blame for the Trojan war, places none of it on any of the Trojans (*Il.* 3.164 f.).

[4] See the discussion of W. J. Woodhouse, *The Composition of Homer's Odyssey* (Oxford, 1930) 208 ff.

"O Nestor, son of Neleus, great glory of the Achaeans, stoutly that son took vengeance, and the Achaeans shall spread his fame afar, that future times may know. Oh, that to me, as well, the gods would give the power to pay the suitors for their grievous wrongs, for they with insult work me outrage! But no such boon the gods bestowed on me and my father. Now, therefore, all must simply be endured."[5]

Nestor, like Athene previously, prods Telemachus by asking (3.214 f.), "Do you willingly submit, or are the people of your land averse to you, led by some voice of God?" The development of Telemachus' manhood can be traced in detail, as he gradually gathers confidence, assumes control of many matters in his own home, joins with Odysseus in planning the destruction of the suitors, takes a worthy part in their slaughter when the time comes, and finally stands with Laertes and Odysseus against the numerous relatives of the slain suitors in Book xxiv. In brief, we may say that he learns [208/209] that the gods are not averse, but that if he will act himself he can improve his situation.[6]

In the story of Odysseus and his comrades, there are many examples of mortals causing their destruction by their own perversity, even though they frequently blame the gods. After the successful raid on the Ciconians, Odysseus ordered his men to withdraw; but they foolishly disobeyed, and as a result one hundred and twenty of them were slain. Yet Odysseus himself says (9.52 f.), "And now an evil fate from Zeus beset our luckless men, causing us many sorrows." Six of Odysseus' men perished in the cave of the Cyclops, not as the result of Fate or the will of the gods, but rather, as Eurylochus says (10.437), "by his <Odysseus'> folly." After leaving the island of Aeolus with all the winds shut up in a leather bag except the one that would bring them home, Odysseus' men, without any intervention of the gods, opened the bag while he slept. The adverse winds rushed out; the men, already in sight of Ithaca, were driven back to Aeolus' island and thence wandered on their fatal journey from which none of them returned. Yet, when they arrived at Aeolus' home a second time, he refused to help them, on the grounds that Odysseus and his men were hated and accursed by the gods. Actually, as Odysseus himself says (10.27), "By our folly we were lost."

The most important episode in deciding the fate of Odysseus' companions is that which involves the cattle of the Sun. Three times a prophecy referring to the loss of his companions appears: when the Cyclops, Polyphemus, invokes a curse on Odysseus and his men, which Poseidon grants (9.530 ff.);[7] when Teiresias warns Odysseus in the lower world (11.104 ff.); and when Circe again tells Odysseus after his return from Hades (12.127 ff.). In the last two instances the prophecy is essentially the same; in both it is stated that *if* Odysseus' comrades

---

[5] *Od.* 3.202 ff.
[6] Cf. Calhoun, *op. cit.* (see note 1) 16.
[7] Polyphemus, of course, makes no reference to the cattle of the Sun.

kill the cattle of the Sun then dire consequences will follow. In no place is it stated or implied that his comrades must kill the cattle. Furthermore, when the actual slaughter takes place, Eurylochus knows full well the consequences of his act, but deliberately chooses to run the risk of death by shipwreck rather than die of starvation (12.340 ff.). Hence the statement of the introduction of the *Odyssey* (1.6 ff.) is true, "Yet even so, despite his zeal, he did not save his men; for through their own perversity they [209/210] perished, having recklessly devoured the kine of the exalted Sun, who therefore took away the day of their return."

After Odysseus and his assistants have slain the suitors, Eurycleia, the old nurse, appears and is about to exult over the deliverance of Penelope and the household from the unwelcome guests. Odysseus, however, says to her:

"Woman, be glad within; but hush, and make no cry. It is not right to glory in the slain. The gods' doom and their reckless deeds destroyed them; for they respected nobody on earth, bad man or good, who came among them. So through their own perversity they met a dismal doom."[8]

And finally, lest this appear an *ex parte* statement, there is the pronouncement of the seer Halitherses, made to the relatives of the dead suitors when they are debating vengeance:

"Hearken now, men of Ithaca, to what I say. By your own fault, my friends, these deeds are done; because you paid no heed to me nor yet to Mentor, the shepherd of the people, in hindering your sons from foolish crime. They wrought a monstrous deed in wanton willfulness, when they destroyed the goods and wronged the wife of one who was their prince, saying that he would come no more. Let then the past be ended, and listen to what I say: do not set forth, or some may find a self-sought ill."[9]

Other examples may be found in the *Odyssey*, but this part of our exposition will be concluded with the brief mention of Elpenor, Odysseus' companion who fell from the roof of Circe's house, where he was sleeping off the effects of drink. When Odysseus met Elpenor's unburied shade in Hades, Elpenor stated the cause of his death thus (11.61): "Heaven's cruel doom destroyed me, and excess of wine." Even after death, it would appear, man is unwilling to accept the responsibility for his acts, but prefers to blame the gods.

II

The Oresteia-motif appears about a dozen times in the *Odyssey* in more or less complete form. Its most important occurrences are as follows: It is the subject of Zeus's reflections at the opening of the

[8] *Od.* 22.411 ff.
[9] *Od.* 24.454 ff.

Odyssey, as we have already seen. It occurs twice, at some length, in Book III (193 ff.; 253 ff.), when Telemachus is visiting Nestor. It appears again in great detail in Book IV (512 ff.) in the [210/211] course of Menelaus' account of events to Telemachus. In Book XI (382 ff.), almost one hundred lines are used to recount Odysseus' conversation with Agamemnon in Hades, and most of this conversation deals with Agamemnon's murder at the hands of Aegisthus and Clytemnestra. There is a brief reference to the story in Book XIII (383 ff.), shortly after Odysseus has reached Ithaca, and finally, in the νέκυια δευτέρα [second scene in the Underworld] with which Book XXIV opens, Agamemnon appears again in the lower world, discusses with Achilles their respective fates, and meets the souls of the dead suitors as they arrive. To this last-mentioned scene in particular, objection has been made since the time of Aristarchus, who athetized the passage, as he did apparently everything else subsequent to line 296 of Book XXIII.[10] What, then, is the reason for the repetition of the motif, what purpose does it serve, what is the significance of its final appearance?

As already suggested above, the first use of the motif is to state the theme of man's responsibility for his own troubles, and we have seen how this theme is repeated, with crescendo effects, throughout the *Odyssey.* Secondly, it serves for purposes of comparison.[11] This function is obvious in several instances, less obvious in others. For example, as mentioned above, the first four books of the *Odyssey* are largely occupied with the education of Telemachus. Here Telemachus is frequently compared, directly or indirectly, with Orestes. Each appears, at that stage of the poem, to have a parent to avenge and a patrimony to win. Orestes has comported himself gallantly and has won not only his kingdom but undying fame as well. Telemachus is urged by Athene,[12] by Nestor, and by Menelaus to do the same.

Again, in the final use of the motif in Book XXIV, Agamemnon concludes his lengthy conversations with Achilles and Amphimedon [211/ 212] with a glorious tribute to Penelope, whose fame as the constant wife shall be everlasting, and also with an equally fervent curse on Clytemnestra, the treacherous wife, whose name shall be a disgrace to

---

10 Modern scholars differ in their views; e.g., Rose (*A Handbook of Greek Literature* [New York, 1934]) omits the scene completely in his outline of the plot of the *Odyssey,* but is obviously hesitant in including it among the passages he would regard as interpolations (see his page 46, note 77); moreover, about the conclusion as a whole, he argues (page 30, note 30) that "A modern would have ended at Book XXIII; Homer could not leave his hero with an unsettled blood-feud hanging over him." Cf. Woodhouse, *op cit.* (see note 4) 116, 205 f., 246 f.; Walter Allen, Jr., "The Theme of the Suitors in the *Odyssey,*" *TAPhA* 70 (1939) 104–124 (esp. 121 ff.). Mackail ("The Epilogue of the *Odyssey*": *Greek Poetry and Life* [Oxford, 1936]) agrees with those who definitely regard it as an addition.

11 Cf. Woodhouse, *op. cit.* 140 f., 246 f.

12 Cf. Woodhouse, *op. cit.* 246 f.; F. W. Jones, "The Formulation of the Revenge Motif in the *Odyssey,*" *TAPhA* 72 (1941) 195–202.

womankind forever. And the comparison of the two is direct and pointed, as Agamemnon deliberately emphasizes the utter difference in their character.[13]

A less elaborate, but no less significant, comparison is introduced between Agamemnon and Odysseus. When Athene appears to Odysseus after his arrival in Ithaca, she informs him of the suitors, their plot against Telemachus, and their general insolence. Odysseus replies (13.383 ff.), "Certainly here at home I too had met the evil fate of Agamemnon, son of Atreus, had not you, goddess, duly told me all." Here, obviously, the comparison has nothing to do with Penelope and Clytemnestra or with Telemachus and Orestes, for Odysseus is simply voicing the similarity of what might have been his fate to that of Agamemnon.[14]

Yet this last example brings out a point which might be inferred from other passages, but which seems not to be explicitly recognized as part of the structure of the plot. Briefly, it is this: Just as Penelope is the "opposite number" of Clytemnestra, and Telemachus of Orestes, and Odysseus of Agamemnon, so the suitors must correspond to Aegisthus. And, just as Aegisthus was warned what would happen to him, so the suitors have been warned by Telemachus (1.372 ff.; 2.138 ff.), by Halitherses (2.161 ff.), by Theoclymenus (20.350 ff.), and by the omens themselves (2.146 ff.). But just as Aegisthus persisted in his course, despite the warning from Hermes, so the suitors have persisted in their impious conduct. Consequently, since we have seen that men bring their own troubles upon themselves by their own perversity, the suitors deserve their fate at the hands of Odysseus. We have already noticed the pronouncements of Odysseus and of Halitherses that the suitors have brought their fate upon themselves. Thus it can be seen that the introduction of the Oresteia-motif is an important part of the justification of the plot. [212/213]

A third possible reason for the introduction of this recurring motif is that it has the effect of ennobling Penelope and Telemachus, and even to some extent the suitors. That is to say, all four of the characters in the Agamemnon story were well known. Not only was Agamemnon the commander-in-chief of the Greek forces at Troy; as Thucydides points out (1.9.1), he was also the mightiest king of his day in the Greek world. Furthermore, he was a descendant of the house of Pelops, so famous in Greek legend and literature. Aegisthus was famous for the same reason, since he represented the other branch of the family. Clytemnestra, as the sister of Helen, was famous in her own right, as

---

[13] Mackail, who in his discussion of the scene says (*op. cit.* 4) that "Its 'purpose' is to sum up . . . the 'moral' of the whole story . . . and it winds up on the key-motif of the whole *Odyssey* . . . the contrast of Penelope and Clytemnestra," holds (*op. cit.* 7) that "a 'moralization' is no more required at the conclusion of the *Odyssey* than it is required at the conclusion of the *Iliad*." Cf., however, Woodhouse, *op. cit.* 205 f., 232 f., 246 f.

[14] Cf. Woodhouse, *op. cit.* 140 f., 246 f.

well as for being the wife of Agamemnon and the mother of Iphigenia, Orestes, and Electra. And throughout the *Odyssey*, Orestes is represented as being a worthy son of a great house, the ruling family in Argos and Mycenae, the richest and most powerful of Greek cities in that age. Compared with Argos, Ithaca was insignificant, "the provinces" as opposed to the capital of the Greek world. Odysseus himself was well known, but only because of his adventures at Troy with the other great heroes of Greece. It is interesting to observe that there are no extant works of the classical period of Greek literature or earlier which have Penelope or Telemachus as their subject. In other words, Homer has dared to take a comparatively obscure family and setting, and to make them of epic proportions. One way in which he succeeded is by the constant use of the comparison of Odysseus and his family with Agamemnon and his family.

In conclusion, one other possible use of this *Leitmotiv* may be noted briefly. According to the account of Menelaus and later of Agamemnon himself, Aegisthus accomplished the murder of Agamemnon and his followers by inviting them to a feast and slaughtering them there as "at some rich, powerful man's wedding, or banquet, or gay festival" (11.414 f.; cf. 4.534 ff.). Since this was exactly the way in which Odysseus slew the suitors, at a feast on the festival of Apollo, it may be that Homer intentionally used the similarity of setting to heighten the contrast in the outcome of the action.[213]

The *Odyssey* as Comedy

WALTER MORRIS HART

MATTHEW ARNOLD'S PRAISE OF SOPHOCLES AS ONE WHO "SAW LIFE steadily and saw it whole" is perhaps even more applicable to Homer. For he, like Sophocles, was concerned with both gods and men, and on the human side went far beyond Sophocles, approaching even something like Shakespeare's cloudless, boundless view. Epic tradition required him to write of the heroic past, of kings and heroes, but he manifests his love for the humble present and for lowly people. His view of them all is not without that sympathy and reverence which, in Chesterton's opinion, are of supreme importance to true humor.[1]

[1] G. K. Chesterton, essay on Bret Harte, in *Varied Types* (New York, 1903), pp. 179 ff.

Walter Morris Hart, "High Comedy in the *Odyssey*," *University of California Publications in Classical Philology*, XII (1943), 263–278. Reprinted by permission of the publisher.

Looking at life steadily did not prevent him from shifting his point of view, seeing it now as tragedy, now as comedy. The *Iliad* is a tragedy; but even in the *Iliad* there are flashes—often, indeed, more than flashes—of the comic.

The *Odyssey* is romance, but it is rich in comedy; its comic scenes are developed by Homer with especial and loving elaboration.[2]

The comic in the two poems is remarkable for its variety, for its range from low to high. It is well to approach it with Shakespeare's comedies in mind. Even in the lightest of these there are serious subplots, as, in the *Comedy of Errors,* the story of old Aegeon, condemned as a Syracusan to die in Ephesus, or, in *The Merry Wives of Windsor,* the romantic love affair of Anne Page and Fenton. In the romantic comedies there are comic subplots, and the main plots involve the characters in comic situations. These main plots are often little Odysseys, concerned with adventures by land and sea, largely in Homer's Mediterranean world: Sicily (on whose eastern shore one may still see the small islands which are the rocks that Polyphemus flung after the ship of the escaping Odysseus), Illyria, the eastern shore of the Adriatic, Epidamnum (not far from Ithaca, the island home of Odysseus), Verona, Venice, Rome, Athens, the famous "sea coast of Bohemia." There are possibilities of tragic outcome, averted to achieve a happy ending: threat of death, with actual death for minor characters, even for those who, like Antigonus the savior of Perdita, have the reader's sympathy. There is separation [263/264] of wives and husbands, brothers and sisters. There are disguises, impersonations, mistaken identities, with subsequent recognitions and reunions.

There is a wide range of the comic from low to high in both main plots and subplots: in the main plots from matters like the discomfiture of Falstaff, in *The Merry Wives of Windsor,* carried in a basket with dirty linen and thrown into the Thames like a barrow of butcher's offal, to matters like Portia's outwitting of Shylock in *The Merchant of Venice:* in the subplots, from the practical jokes on Malvolio, in *Twelfth Night,* to the play of character and wit in the affair of Benedick and Beatrice in *Much Ado about Nothing.*

The *Odyssey* is, obviously, not comedy in the sense of drama: it is not "adapted to be acted upon a stage"; "the story" is not "wholly related by means of dialogue and action."[3] But it is not purely epic; the narrative is not continuous, for as Aristotle said: "Homer . . . knows the right proportion of epic narrative; when to narrate, and when to let the characters speak for themselves. . . . With little prelude [he] leaves the stage to his personages, men and women, all with

---

[2] Indebtedness to *The Composition of Homer's Odyssey,* by W. J. Woodhouse, Oxford, 1930, is gratefully acknowledged.

The translations used are those of Lang, Leaf, and Myers, for the *Iliad;* and T. E. Shaw, and Butcher and Lang, for the *Odyssey.*

[3] *Oxford English Dictionary,* s.v. "Drama."

characters of their own."⁴ The "right proportion," Aristotle implies, is much dialogue and little narrative; Homer brings epic close to drama; the casual reference to the stage is significant—Homer "leaves the stage to his personages." Those personages have characters of their own, which appear in what they say, rather than in what the poet says about them. Character is implied also by gesture, attitude, surroundings, as on the stage.

The scenes to which I wish now to invite attention approximate the drama in form; in them Homer leaves the stage to his personages and allows them to speak for themselves.

I shall recall first a few instances of low comedy, in part to illustrate Homer's range and variety, in part to bring out by contrast the quality of the comedy which I venture to characterize as "high."

I begin with the Polyphemus episode. This is not high comedy. We are invited to laugh chiefly at the pain suffered by the Cyclops; also at his incredible stupidity. Exaggeration, too, plays its part—the mere size of Polyphemus, the horrid details of his Gargantuan meals. It is easy to find amusement also in the mental sufferings of Odysseus, who, since it is he who is telling the story, cannot very well have been eaten, first or last.

Aftertimes found this story comic: two Greek comedies, now lost, dealt with it; Euripides wrote, and Shelley translated, a Satyr play based upon it; Lucian, in his *Dialogues of the Sea Gods,* could see it from the comic point of view; and so could Alfred Noyes in his *Forty Singing* [264/265] *Seamen,* who roar out the chorus: "Since Ulysses bunged his eye up with a pine-torch in the dark" (in the *Odyssey,* the torch is green olive wood; Noyes requires a monosyllabic stake).

As part of the entertainment of Odysseus at the court of the Phaeacians, the minstrel Demodocus sings not only of the Trojan war and the great deeds of the heroes, but also a purely comic tale concerning certain scandalous deeds of Ares and Aphrodite. "The Lady Goddesses," says Demodocus, "remained at home, all of them, quite out of countenance . . . but unquenchable was the laughter that arose from the blessed gods as they studied the tricky device of Hephaestus." The other gods whispered to one another, but Apollo loudly asked, "Hermes . . . would you not choose even the bondage of those rough chains if so you might sleep . . . by golden Aphrodite?" And to him the gods' messenger replied, "If there were chains without end, thrice as many as are here, and all you Gods and all the Goddesses to look on, yet would I be happy beside the Golden One." At his saying more laughter arose among the Immortals.

"This," Homer adds, "was the song the famous minstrel sang; and Odysseus listened and was glad at heart, and likewise did the Phaeacians."

⁴ *Poetics* 1460 A 5, as translated by W. P. Ker, *Epic and Romance* (London 1897), p. 17.

Mere farce, with the lightest possible touch on the characters of those concerned, this story closely resembles the thirteenth-century French *fabliaux*, those medieval drummers' tales, which Chaucer retold in English verse and Boccaccio in Italian prose. Many of these were of Oriental origin and it is not inconceivable that Homer heard this one in Smyrna, whither commercial travelers of his day had brought it from regions farther south and east. "When the veil is over women's faces," said George Meredith, "you cannot have society, without which the senses are barbarous and the Comic Spirit is driven to the gutters of grossness to slake its thirst." It is significant that Gods and Goddesses cannot laugh in concert.

My final instance of the lower kind of comedy springs from the ironic situation resulting from Odysseus' presence disguised as a beggar in his own home, a situation that persists through the latter half of the *Odyssey*, wherein Odysseus is not recognized by the other persons of the epic. There are, in consequence, opportunities for ironic incident and dialogue, and of these Homer makes effective use.

One such incident is the encounter of the disguised Odysseus with the tramp Irus, who had come on purpose to pick a quarrel. The Wooers of Penelope sprang up, laughing, and pressed round the scarecrow tramps.

The appearance of Odysseus, stripped for the fight, struck terror to the heart of Irus. The workmen had to hold him and push him forward, the flesh of his limbs quaking in panic. Odysseus was puzzling himself whether it were better to strike the other so starkly that life would leave [265/266] him when he fell, or to tap him gently and just stretch him out. On the whole, the gentle way seemed right. So Odysseus only hooked him to the neck under the ear and crushed the bones inward, so that blood gushed purple from his lips and with a shriek he fell in the dust, biting the ground and drumming with his feet. The suitors flung up their hands and died of laughing; but Odysseus took him by the leg and dragged him out and propped him against the fence, saying "Sit there and play bogy to the dogs and pigs . . ." The suitors still laughed merrily.

Four hundred years after Homer, Aristophanes amused Athenian audiences by the sight of physical suffering. The Roman Plautus followed his example. From him Shakespeare borrowed a play and delighted the groundlings with Dromio, expecting thanks for bringing a rope's end and, mistaken for his brother, getting a beating with it instead. In both instances there is something more than the mere beating; there is the matter of the mistaken identity. Irus had unwittingly taken on one of the greatest of the Greek heroes, the very greatest of crafty fighters. Only Telemachus and we know that this ragged beggar is Odysseus. And we, moreover, have had a glimpse of Odysseus' mind: we know that, lest he be recognized as Odysseus, he has chosen the gentle way, merely crushing the bones inward. We feel superior; and there is a bit of thinking in our laughter; it is not the completely thoughtless mirth of the suitors.

Shakespeare's *Twelfth Night* furnishes a closer parallel than the *Comedy of Errors*. There practical jokers arrange a duel between two unwilling combatants. We know, however, that Viola is a girl in disguise and recognize in her fear a becoming feminine timidity, as, in that of Sir Andrew Aguecheek, the baseless terror of the male coward. The pain, it is true, turns out to be wholly mental; there is nothing of the Homeric brutality in the outcome. The ironic situation, however, is the same. Our amusement is heightened by our knowledge that neither combatant has any real reason to fear the other. Not profound thought, obviously, but thinking of a sort, is necessary for our appreciation. To this extent our laughter is thoughtful laughter.

We may enter the regions of higher comedy by way of a portrait of a character seen from the comic point of view, the portrait of Nestor.

Nestor is not a conspicuously amusing figure. Indeed, had not Shakespeare intervened with his portrait of Polonius, it would not, perhaps, occur to us to find him comic. However, once we have been made aware, it is difficult to believe that Homer did not smile as he wrote his long speeches. Like Polonius, Nestor is a highly self-satisfied, loquacious, and reminiscent, and yet a wise and kind, old man. He appears first near the beginning of the *Iliad*, attempting to make peace between Agamemnon and Achilles. "He made harangue to them and said: 'Verily all the Trojans would be glad were they to hear all this tale of strife between [266/267] you twain. Of old days held I converse with better men even than you, and never did they make light of me . . . I played my part in fight; and with mine enemies could none of men that are now on earth do battle. And all laid to heart my counsels and hearkened to my voice.'"

In the *Odyssey*, Telemachus, who has set out to learn tidings of his father from Menelaus at Sparta, stops, on his way, at Pylos, home of Nestor. As in the *Iliad*, Nestor speaks of his own past greatness. "Never a man," he tells Telemachus, "could match with Odysseus in wisdom, for he outdid the rest in all manner of craft; . . . and Odysseus and I," he adds, "were always of one mind." He could tell Telemachus nothing of the fate of his father, but he insisted upon detaining the impatient youth for the long ceremony of a sacrifice to Athene. However, he supplied chariot and horses for the journey to Sparta and sent his son Peisistratus to act as guide.

The two youths became good friends. On the return, after Telemachus had lingered far too long at Sparta and was now eager to be in Ithaca once more, he beseeched Peisistratus: "Do not drive me past my ship, . . . but set me down beside her, that the old man's sense of hospitality may not have power to keep me chafing in his house. I would speed homeward."

The son of Nestor pondered if this was a thing he could properly accept and perform. Reflection showed it to be best. So he turned his team out of the way to the water's edge and transferred to the ship all the noble gifts of Menelaus. . . . Then he said urgently to Telemachus: "Now get aboard and have your crew mustered before my reaching home warns the old man. My heart and head assure me that his wilfulness will take no excuse. He will himself come here and hail you; refusing, as I say, to go back alone. This will fling him in a rage."

Thus youth, as youth will, conspires against age. But it is a defensive and justifiable conspiracy, implying no lack of respect for the old man and his kindly, if too insistent and selfish, hospitality. Telemachus appears in a better light than Hamlet: he has nothing to say like "These tedious old fools!"

Homer, it is to be noted, has said nothing. He has left the stage to his personages to speak for themselves. We come to know Nestor through his own words and through the words of the two young men and their action in relation to him.

"There never will be civilization where comedy is not possible," I quote George Meredith once more, "and that comes of some degree of social equality of the sexes." Such equality is clearly indicated in both *Iliad* and *Odyssey*, and notably in the three great scenes which are now to engage our attention: Telemachus and Helen; Odysseus and Nausicaa; and Odysseus and Athene. In the first of these, Telemachus and Helen, there is, beside social equality, marked feminine superiority in intelligence [267/268] and in awareness of mutual relations. It is this awareness that enlivens the scene with the quality of comic irony.

Telemachus and Peisistratus were well received by Menelaus. He waved them to his bounty, saying, "Take of our food and be glad: so that after you have eaten we may enquire of you who you are . . ." When their longings for food and drink had been put away Telemachus leaned his head across near the son of Nestor and whispered in his ear, that the others might not catch his words, "See what a blaze of polished copper and gold and amber and silver and ivory goes through this echoing hall. Surely the mansions of Olympian Zeus must be like this one, one great glory within of things wonderful beyond all telling."

Menelaus had overheard his whisper. He opened his mouth to them with thrilling words: "Dear children, with Zeus no mortal man can vie. His houses and his treasures are from everlasting to everlasting. On earth—well, there may be a man as rich as myself, or there may not: but it was only after terrible suffering and eight years of adventure in foreign parts that I won home from overseas with this my wealth."

Menelaus goes on, one thing leading naturally to another, to speak of the lands that he has seen, of his brother Agamemnon slain on his return, of other companions slain before Troy or lost on the homeward voyage.

"Yet above and beyond all my company do I especially grieve for one. No man of the Achaeans deserved so greatly or labored so greatly as great Odysseus labored and endured . . . Without doubt *they* mourn him too, old Laertes and self-possessed Penelope, and Telemachus, who was no more than a child newly-born, left behind by his father in the house."

Thus they reveal themselves: Telemachus, the country boy, young and inexperienced, overheard in his naïve whispering; Menelaus, vain and self-satisfied, saved for our appreciation by his admiration for Odysseus.

And now Helen, like a vision of Artemis of the golden distaff, came out from her high-coffered, incense-laden room, with her women; of whom Adraste carried the graceful reclining-chair for her mistress, while Alcippe had her soft woolen carpet, and Phylo a silver basket mounted on a carriage with gold-rimmed wheels. It was heaped full of the smoothest yarn and across it . . . lay the distaff with wool of a wood-violet blue. The queen sat down in her long chair which had a stool to support her feet.

Homer shows no less skill in his dramatic use of stage properties and stage business than in his use of dialogue. His method just here foreshadows the famous characterizing line in one of Chaucer's *Canterbury Tales* in which it is said of a certain Friar that, "from the bench he drove away the cat . . . and sat himself softly down."[5] [268/269]

Helen, womanlike, sees at once the resemblance of Telemachus to Odysseus. "Surely," she says, "this must be Telemachus, that son he left behind him a mere infant in the house, when for the sake of this worthless self of mine all·you Achaeans came up breathing savage war against the town of Troy."

"Indeed," says Menelaus, "now I can see the likeness which you limn."

Peisistratus speaks for Telemachus, who is, he says, slow-spoken, and states that he is the son of that man, the one and only. All four have a desire to weep.

But into the wine they were drinking Helen cast a drug which melted sorrow and made men forgetful of their pains. Then she recalled a story of Odysseus, how he had entered Troy disguised as a slave,—she alone knew him,—and he slew many Trojans.

"My heart laughed," she says, "for now my desire had shifted to get back home, and deplored too late the infatuation engendered by Aphrodite to lead me away from my own dear country, abandoning child and marriage-ties and a lord not poor in wit or looks."

Menelaus is not displeased by this flattery, and he too remembers a tale about Odysseus, but in this one it is Helen who plays the chief part. He remembers how when they lay hidden in the wooden horse

[5] *The Somnour's Tale,* v. 1775.

she had circled about it calling by name upon the leaders of the Greeks, upon each in the voice of his absent wife. They raged furiously to leap up and call her, but with main strength Odysseus held them back.

Thus Menelaus unconsciously reveals Helen—her quick intuition, her skill as actress and impersonator, her gay irresponsibility: she did not tell the Trojans the truth about the wooden horse, yet by her little joke exposed the Greeks to death. Had it succeeded, Troy would not have fallen. That drug which she cast into the wine was, surely, her tact and the personal charm which led all men to forget their sorrows. What better way to hearten the son than to tell tales of the prowess of the father? Homer calls it a drug, not, I am sure, because of his masculine ignorance, but rather to rationalize for the benefit of his hearers.

Menelaus urged Telemachus to tarry for eleven days or even for twelve. Telemachus could not stay so long, he said; yet he lingered, not for twelve days but for thirty; so effective, obviously, was Helen's drug. At last Athene put him in mind of his return and he begged Menelaus to speed him thence. Menelaus made the famous answer: "Cherish the stranger in the house and speed him so soon as he has the mind," which Pope translated: "Welcome the coming, speed the parting guest."

As a farewell gift Menelaus gave Telemachus a double cup and a silver mixing bowl; Helen, a garment of her own needleworking that glittered like a star. "This," she said, "is to be my gift, dear child, a keepsake from Helen's hand for your bride to wear on the day of expectation, your wedding day; till then lay it up with your mother in your house." [269/270]

Thus the experienced woman speaks to the very young man; "dear child," she calls him. And, "let your mother keep the robe, lest you give it on impulse to the first pretty girl you meet. For I see that you are susceptible; the way you look at me shows that. I have often seen that look." Telemachus, of course, does not read her meaning quite so precisely; but he must feel vaguely that he has been put in his place. He does not fail to report to his mother that he has seen "Argive Helen, for whose sake the Greeks and Trojans bore much travail by the gods' designs."

Throughout the scene, Helen must be aware of more than Menelaus and Telemachus hear in her words. In speaking of her "worthless self" she is indulging in an irony akin to the Socratic, a dissimulation not, as with him, of ignorance, but of worthlessness. It was not her way to think of herself as worthless. Her view would be that of the old men of Troy, who commented as she passed: "Small blame is it that Trojans and . . . Achaeans should for such a woman long time suffer hardships; marvelously like is she to the immortal goddesses to look upon." And in this scene at Sparta she blames Aphrodite for her infatuation; she herself was not responsible.

Equality of the sexes is again fundamental in the second of the great comedy scenes. This is symmetrical with the first, for now the naïve young girl falls in love with the mature, worldly-wise, and already married man: Nausicaa with Odysseus. The implications are now clear.

Odysseus, after his long and tempestuous voyage, after the wreck of his raft and his two days' wandering in the swell of the sea, swam ashore at last in the land of the Phaeacians. He crept beneath twin olive trees, where Athene shed sleep upon his eyes.

To Nausicaa, beautiful daughter of Alcinous, king of that land, Athene appeared in a dream, suggesting that she go a-washing and reminding her that her marriage day was near at hand. She begged of her father mules and wagon that she might take the goodly raiment to the river mouth. She was ashamed to speak of glad marriage, but he saw all and grudged her nothing. When she and her maidens had finished treading down the garments in the trenches and had spread them out along the shore, they fell to playing at ball. The princess, by chance, cast the ball into the river, whereat they all raised a piercing cry. Odysseus awoke and crept out from under the coppice. The girls fled in terror; only Nausicaa stood firm. To her he spoke a sweet and cunning word:

"I supplicate thee, O queen, whether thou art a goddess or a mortal! Have pity on me. . . . Direct me to the city . . . Give me an old garment to cast about me . . . And may the gods grant thee all thy heart's desire: a husband and a home and a mind at one with his may they give—a good gift, for there is nothing higher and nobler than when man and wife are of one heart and mind in a house, a grief to their foes, and to their friends great joy, but their own hearts know it best." [270/271]

Doubtless Odysseus, as he speaks these beautiful words concerning wedded life, is thinking of Penelope. But doubtless also in thus praying the gods to provide for the princess a husband and a home he is seeking tactfully to convey to her the idea that he is not a candidate for her hand—much as Helen indirectly warns Telemachus. Nausicaa, however, does not seem to understand the warning. She gave him the raiment he desired, and when he was clad in it Athene made him greater and more mighty to behold, and the princess marveled at him and said to her fair-tressed maidens:

"Erewhile this man seemed to me uncomely, but now he is like the gods. Would that such an one might be called my husband, that it might please him here to abide." Then she called on Odysseus: "Up now stranger, that I may convey thee to the house of my father. But when we set foot within the city, do thou linger in the fair grove of Athene. I would avoid the ungracious speech of the people, lest some one of the baser sort might meet me and say: 'Who is this that goes with Nausicaa, this tall and goodly stranger? Where found she him?

Her husband he will be . . . for verily she holds in no regard the Phaeacians here in this country, the many men and noble who are her wooers.' "

Thus she flatters Odysseus, informs him that she is much sought in marriage, naïvely speaks of him as a possible husband. So Desdemona, when Othello had told her the story of his life, bade him, if he had a friend that loved her, he should but teach him to tell such a tale and that would win her. "Upon this hint" Othello spoke. Odysseus could not "speak." But he had foreseen the hint; he had asked the gods to grant Nausicaa a husband and a home.

The delicate irony of the scene is comparable, too, with Viola's wooing of the unconscious Orsino, or Rosalind's of the unconscious Orlando. And it suggests that charming story of the Princess Royal, who, being perhaps of Juliet's age, informed Lord Kitchener that she had chosen him for her husband. Whether his tact equaled that of Odysseus is not known.

Odysseus, who appears only as a shipwrecked stranger, is a king at home in Ithaca; Nausicaa is a princess; there is no doubt of social equality. But that that is characteristic of Phaeacian society, that indeed the woman's position is even more important than the man's, Homer takes special pains to make clear. Nausicaa directs Odysseus, if he wishes to insure his return to his fatherland, to pass her father by and throw his hands about her mother's knees. The King himself had expressly decreed: "So long as I am to have lordship and life amongst you . . . be it understood that the word of the Queen holds good." And Athene, too, tells Odysseus that Arete is worshiped by the people and that "she will resolve the disputes of those for whom she has countenance, even when the affair is an affair of men." [271/272]

Odysseus and Nausicaa part at the city gates. Odysseus is received with generous hospitality: there are games in his honor, and feasting; the minstrel sings; gifts are prepared; yet the hero has not yet made himself known. He is bathed and anointed and dressed in a rich robe and tunic. "And he went out from the bath-house to join the men at their wine-drinking. On the way, by a pillar of the massy roof, stood Nausicaa in her god-given beauty, admiring Odysseus with all her eyes: and she spoke to him winged words:[6] 'Farewell, Stranger, and when in your native land think of me, sometimes; for it is chiefly to me that you owe . . . your life.' Odysseus answered her saying, 'Nausicaa, . . . if Zeus . . . the Thunderer wills that I reach home, . . . then and there will I pay vows to you as to a Divine One; forever and ever throughout all my days. For you gave me life, Maiden.' "

---

[6] Here I refer to the Butcher and Lang translation. *Winged words,* as Professor Calhoun has shown, are not merely words that fly from one to the other, but words spoken with unusual emotion or intensity. "The Art of Formula in Homer," *Classical Philology,* XXX, 215 ff. Shaw's "words came and she addressed him directly" is clearly not so good.

Nausicaa, then, knows that he is not for her; this is a last farewell. She does not know that he is the great Odysseus; he has not yet told the tale of his wanderings. She in her ignorance and innocence has been directing the experienced man of the world, the lover of Circe and Calypso, the husband of Penelope, with whom never a man could match in wisdom, Odysseus of many devices. Only we and the hero can be aware of the irony.

The motif of the married hero rescued by the maiden who desires him for her husband doubtless existed independently before Homer's day. It is to be found in many a folktale and not infrequently in the literature of art. In all the versions there is an implication of regret that the maiden cannot have her way, and some of the more primitive permit the hero to have two wives. Musäus, a reteller of folktales in the gaily cynical eighteenth-century manner, provides the Pope's dispensation for the bigamous marriage, but doubts, he says, whether this is a favor to the hero or a punishment for his sins.[7] In our own time, in Kipling's *Without Benefit of Clergy*, the hero has, it is true, no wife, but is prevented from marriage by other reasons. The death of the heroine is the only possible way out. But neither marriage nor death would be a proper ending for the episode in the *Odyssey*. Homer's solution, which is no solution, unsatisfactory as it may seem, is the only possible conclusion.

Equality of the sexes is clearly implied in the household at Sparta; in the land of the Phaeacians it is expressly emphasized; yet in neither case are the individuals precisely on the same level: Helen, the daughter of a God, is in wisdom, in insight, in humorous comprehension of a situation, superior to Menelaus and to Telemachus; and while there is little [272/273] to choose between King Alcinous and Queen Arete, Odysseus, most experienced of men, is naturally superior in understanding to the naïve Nausicaa. In these instances only the woman or the man is aware; woman and man cannot laugh in concert.

It is only in the relations of Athene and Odysseus that this ideal of high comedy is achieved. Only a goddess can meet Odysseus on equal terms; only an Odysseus can so meet Athene. If the accident of birth gives her a certain superiority, it is no more than is needful for her part. The exercise of her divine powers serves only to heighten the effect of the hero's easy familiarity with her. Homer's three high-comedy scenes form a pattern not unlike that in the "Marriage Act" of Chaucer's *Canterbury Tales*: in the *Wife of Bath's Tale*, the husband leaves an important decision to his wife and is thereupon made happy; in *The Clerk's Tale*, Patient Griselda is wholly governed by her husband's will and after much suffering finds content; in *The Franklin's Tale*, Dorigen and Arveragus agree to obey one another and achieve a perfect union.

---

[7] J. K. A. Musäus, *Melcchsala*, in *Volksmärchen der Deutschen*, 1782–1786.

The relation of Odysseus and Athene culminates in a delightful comedy scene in the thirteenth book of the *Odyssey*, but in both *Odyssey* and *Iliad* there is evidence that they have long been interested in one another. He has been the object of her especial care.[8] And with good reason, for of all the heroes he most resembles her. She is inaccessible to love; he is not amatory;[9] and in their relation there is no passion.[10] She [273/274] is Goddess of Power, in her chief aspect armed and warlike;[11] Odysseus' valor is worthy of his patroness.[12]

Athene is Goddess of Wisdom; but her wisdom, in Homer, is of a practical, humane, shrewdly human sort, and not without humor. She has even at times a certain playfulness, a puckish quality that would scarcely be at home in the solemn clubs that bear her name in Boston

---

[8] In the *Iliad*, Diomedes declares that Pallas Athene loves him (X, 245); Aias, that she from of old like a mother stands by Odysseus' side (XXIII, 782 f.); she chooses him as best fitted to recall the retreating Greeks (II, 169). In the *Odyssey*, Nestor tells Telemachus that Athene had singled out his father with loving care; never had Nestor seen such open affection on the part of the gods as was there displayed by Pallas, who would stand openly by his side (III, 221 f.).

Invisibly, or openly in her own person, or in the character of another, the Goddess aids and comforts her favorite. She speaks for him in assemblies of the Gods; fights for him in battle; saves him from drowning; sheds upon his eyelids restoring sleep; conceals him, at need, in a mist, or transforms him into a beggar, or gilds his head and shoulders with nobility; insures for him a hospitable reception by strangers; encourages him by her praise; judges him to be more worthy than Aias to receive the arms of Achilles; yet is careful not to show her favor when it might offend Poseidon. She is mindful also of his wife and son.

[9] Odysseus is involved in no quarrel about women, prefers no woman before his wedded wife. He is selected to return Chryseis to her father, Chryses. He becomes the lover of Circe only on the urgent advice of Hermes, to win ultimate escape. In the matter of Calypso he had no choice; and even to the Goddess herself he ventures to say: "I do most surely know how far short of you discreet Penelope falls in stature and in comeliness. For she is human; and you are changeless, immortal, and ever young. Yet even so I choose—yea, all my days are consumed in longing—to travel home and see the day of my arrival dawn." And doubtless Odysseus is thinking of Penelope when he tells Nausicaa of the happiness of married life. He is speaking to a young girl, and his words are appropriate to the occasion; but there is no reason to doubt his sincerity.

[10] Homer speaks often of Athene's "heart's friendliness" toward Odysseus, of "the love she bore him." But it is abundantly clear that her affection was of a purely spiritual character. Athene was no Circe or Calypso. Her relation with Odysseus was not that of Aphrodite with Anchises; it was, more nearly, a communion of soul with soul.

[11] As represented in the familiar statues, with helm and spear and shield, or as described in *Iliad*, V, 732 ff. She fights even with Ares, smiting him on the neck with a huge stone (XXI, 400 ff.). With her spear she would daunt the bravest warriors (*Odyssey*, I, 100). She joins Odysseus in his great last battle with the suitors, proving his force and fervor by her words: "How are your strength and manhood fallen, O Odysseus, since . . . you battled with the Trojans, . . . and slaughtered them by heaps in the deadly struggle. . . . Hither, dear heart; stand by me and watch my work" (XXII, 226 ff.).

[12] Odysseus was not named among those most worthy to meet Hector in single combat; and he held himself inferior to Achilles with the spear. Yet when left by the wounded Diomedes, standing alone among the Trojans, he kills or wounds or puts to flight all who venture to attack him (*Iliad*, XI, 401 ff.).

and in London. She is not the immobile and austere figure designed by Phidias to adorn his Parthenon; she is rather, one imagines, to be visualized as the light and graceful Athene Victory of the little temple on the Acropolis: the Goddess, it seems, in swift movement, has paused for an instant, her garments still a-flutter, and bends to fasten a sandal that has come untied.

However, it is not possible to visualize Athene as in herself she really is. The Goddess eludes us, as a goddess should. For she is not content with the varieties of her own character; she delights to impersonate others, to assume the appearance appropriate to the part, to invent a story to go with the character, to enjoy the ironic situations which inevitably arise.[13]

If in Athene power and wisdom are blended, so they are in Odysseus. He is shrewd, reflective, not likely to act from anger or on any impulse. He is likely to consider two possible courses of action before committing himself to either.[14] Even as he hesitates to follow the first prompting of [274/275] his own mind, he hesitates to believe what others tell him. His skepticism is thoroughly characteristic; it manifests itself in distrust even of the Gods themselves.[15]

Odysseus, doubtless, would suspect his fellow men, conscious always that his own words were often false. He is preëminently an inventor of tales. He is in this way a self-conscious artist. He thinks highly of the professionals.[16]

[13] In *Odyssey*, I, she appears to Telemachus as Mentes, and at length almost deceives the reader, so convincing is the corroborative detail of her story—the voyage and its purpose, the sparkling iron ore, the copper, the position of the ship, the grumbling of the impatient crew. Later, she impersonates Mentor; then Telemachus, mustering his crew. Again as Mentor (III) she accompanies Telemachus to Pylos, hears Nestor speak of her loving care for Odysseus, and declines his invitation to spend the night in his house. She must, she says, lie by the ship to hearten the crew and in the morning push on to the estimable Cauconians, who have long owed her no small sum. At Scheria she appears to Nausicaa in the guise of a playmate (VI, 22). She met Odysseus at the entrance of the town in the likeness of a young girl bearing a water jar (VII, 20). In the character of the King's herald she summoned the Phaeacians to the council (VIII, 8), and later encouraged Odysseus in the weight-throwing contest (VIII, 193 ff.).

[14] As, when left alone among his enemies, whether to flee or stand and be taken (*Iliad*, XI, 401 ff.); after landing in Scheria, whether to remain for the night down by the river or climb the slope to the dark wood (*Odyssey*, V, 465 ff.); when awakened by the cries of the maidens, whether to clasp Nausicaa's knees in entreaty or stand off and cajole her with honeyed words (VI, 142 f.); whether to kill Irus with a single blow or to tap him gently (XVIII, 90); whether or not to explore the island of Circe (X, 151).

[15] "Surely," he tells Calypso, "something not at all to my advantage lies behind this your command that on a raft I launch out over the sea" (V, 173). He fears that Ino's command to abandon the raft may be some new snare (V, 356).

[16] "It is right," he says, "that bards should receive honor and reverence from every man alive, inasmuch as the Muse cherishes the whole guild of singers and teaches to each one his rules of song" (VIII, 479 ff.). He lauds Demodocus above all mortal men, praising his history of the mishaps of the Achaeans as accurate, complete, realistic, convincing (VIII, 486 ff.).

He himself dislikes to tell the same story twice. "It goes against my grain," he says, "to repeat a tale already plainly told" (XII, 452 f.).

Odysseus has not Athene's power of transformation; only she can make of him now a ragged beggar, now a hero, tall and strong, with hyacinthine locks. Yet, like the Goddess, he is a skilled impersonator, and like her he delights to invent stories appropriate to the occasion on which he tells them and to the characters that he assumes. Indeed, in the number and elaboration of these tales he far outdoes Athene herself. Many are told after his arrival in Ithaca.[17] He had not yet told these false tales in the semblance of truth when Athene calls him a "plausible, various, cozening wretch" who delights in "crooked and shifty words" and in "speaking in character" (XIII, 291 ff.). "It was thanks to me," she says, "that you were welcomed by the entire society of the Phaeacians." The implication seems to be that the long tale of adventure with which he charmed Alcinous and his court was also a piece of fiction. There are no other earlier tales.

Arete and Alcinous have had their doubts, but in the end choose to believe the story, partly because of Odysseus' appearance, partly because of the excellent form of the narrative. "We will not be persuaded that you are a pretender or a thief, like those many vagrant liars our dark earth breeds to flourish and strut behind so thick a mask of falsehood that none can pierce it to read their worth" (XI, 363). Yet Athene, who knows Odysseus best, seems to say that he had, precisely, been strutting behind a mask of falsehood at the Phaeacian court, a mask that she herself had constructed for him. We also, then, may take her view and add the Phaeacian story (IX–XII) to the list of his achievements in fiction. [275/276]

Odysseus, with the gifts of the Phaeacians, was put ashore in his sleep on the island of Ithaca. When he awoke he was ignorant of his whereabouts, and so he lamented, not knowing what to do with his wealth or with himself. Athene drew nigh, seeming a young man, some shepherd lad, but gentle and dainty like the sons of kings when they tend sheep. She had gathered her fine mantle scarflike round her shoulders and carried a throwing-spear; on her lovely feet were sandals. Odysseus went forward with a swift greeting, asking in what land he was. A well-known land, she answered: "Stranger, the name *Ithaca* is rumored abroad, even to Troy, which is said to be so far from our Achaean coasts."

Her word made his heart leap. Yet he swallowed back the words that were on his lips to make play with his instinctive cunning. He had heard of Ithaca, he said, even in his home in Crete, whence he had fled, having killed a man . . .

As he was running on, the Goddess broke into a smile and petted

---

[17] He has a tale (XIV) of his own adventures for Eumaeus (and overcomes with difficulty the swineherd's skepticism); a similar but shorter tale for Antinous (XVII); another for Penelope (XIX); another for Laertes (XXIV).

him with her hand. She waxed tall; she turned womanly: she was beauty's mistress, dowered with every accomplishment of taste. She spoke to him winged words: "Any man, or even any God, who would keep pace with your all-around craftiness must needs be a canny dealer and sharp-practised. O plausible, various, cozening wretch, can you not even in your native place let be these crooked and shifty words which so delight the recesses of your mind? Enough of such speaking in character between us two past-masters of these tricks of trade—you the cunningest mortal to wheedle or blandish, and me, famed above other gods for knavish wiles. And yet you failed to recognize in me the daughter of Zeus, Pallas Athene, your stand-by and protection throughout your toils!"

Fluently Odysseus answered: "Your powers let you assume all forms, Goddess, and so hardly may the knowingest man identify you. Yet well I know of your partiality towards me . . . But surely I am not in clear-shining Ithaca?"

Said Athene: "Your mind harps on that, and I cannot leave on tenterhooks one so civil, witty, and shrewd. Any other returned wanderer would have dashed home to see his children and his wife. Only you choose to be sceptical . . ."

She showed him the familiar landmarks, aided him to conceal his treasure in a cave, plotted with him the doom of the extravagant wooers, told him to wait at the house of the swineherd Eumaeus—"until I have recalled Telemachus, who went to the house of Menelaus, trying to find out if you were still alive."

He said to the Goddess: "Why did you not tell him so much, out of your all-knowing heart? Must he, too, painfully roam the barren seas . . . ?" The grey-eyed one replied: "Take it not so much to heart . . . He suffers no hardship." [276/277]

In this scene, Odysseus and Athene manifest themselves clearly, fully, and engagingly to one another and to the reader. Their relation, we are reminded, had been of long standing. It had become intimate and informal: on his part, appreciation of her powers, gratitude, respect without awe: he now does not hesitate to express doubt of her veracity and to reproach her for sending Telemachus on a futile errand. This, however, she takes in good part, for she admires her hero, finding in him qualities like her own. Her affection shines through the scolding which is also praise: "O plausible, various, cozening wretch . . . !"

Odysseus manifests his characteristic propensity to dramatize a part for himself and to tell a tale. It must be a new tale; he has said that he hates to repeat himself. And this one must be improvised on the spur of the moment. But on this occasion, ironically enough, he has an auditor who knows the truth, who cannot help smiling at his inventive fluency.

And Athene, manifestly, had delighted in her impersonation of the gentle and dainty shepherd lad, a very Florizel, Prince of Bohemia, complete with sandals and throwing-spear. The same delight in play-acting—which leads her to construct, as a dramatist might, the plot for action against the suitors—is evident in her transformation or make-up of Odysseus at the end of the scene, with the complete costume and all the properties of the ragged beggar, realistic and convincing. Odysseus willingly accepts the part and plays it well.

In the dialogue one may venture to see a foreshadowing of the merry war between Benedick and Beatrice in *Much Ado about Nothing,* wherein skirmishes of wit conceal and yet express mutual interest and affection. The resemblance to Odysseus and Athene is not close. What is remarkable is that Homer had so early, under social conditions so different, discovered the possibilities of high comedy in such a pair of evenly matched and lively intelligences.

The Goddess's impersonation of the gentle shepherd may, furthermore, suggest the male disguises of Rosalind and Viola, or, better, of Portia, who, if she lacks the divine power, yet has the human cleverness to save the life of her husband's friend. If she lacks the omnipotence of a Goddess, she is yet the mistress in her own right of a great estate, who commands the obedience of all those about her. If not able to transform herself, she can yet impersonate with complete success the young and learned doctor of Rome, Balthazar, a Daniel come to judgment. Like Athene, she delights in the success of the deception: her gay and teasing triumph over her discomfited husband makes the delightfully ironic closing scene of the play.

For thus Homer does seem to foreshadow Shakespeare. The greatest of epic poets and the greatest of dramatic poets are interested in the same kinds of characters, plots, motifs, situations, human relations. Both like to leave the stage to their personages, allowing them to speak for themselves. [277/278]

In comedy, Homer foreshadows Shakespeare's range and variety, and awakens the most thoughtful laughter when women have social equality with men.

Both delight in the appearances which contrast with reality and in pointing up ironic situations by ironic dialogue. The works of both say more than they seem to, as Voltaire remarked of his *Zadig.*

Consideration of the comic seems to deepen one's impression of the essential humanity of Homer, his tolerance, his kindliness.

If the High Comedy in the *Odyssey* leads us to think of Shakespeare, it leads us to think also of life itself, of the ways of people whom we know: the screams of Nausicaa and her girl friends when their ball is thrown wild and falls in the river; Helen, as with women of all time, being first to see in Telemachus the resemblance to his father; Athene's very human delight in Odysseus' failure to recognize her in the handsome shepherd lad.

Merely to name these three—Nausicaa, Helen, Athene—is to set them forth as individual women, each with a character in her own right. I recall George Meredith's dicta: "When the veil is over women's faces, you cannot have society, without which the Comic Spirit is driven to the gutters of grossness to slake its thirst"; and, "There never will be civilization where comedy is not possible, and that comes of some degree of social equality of the sexes." Today it is well to place Hitler's words beside Meredith's. "Hitler said: 'The program of our national socialist women's movement has only one point. That point is called the child.'[18] That has meant [Deuel explains] the almost total banishment of women from public office, their withdrawal from professions in favor of cannon-foddering and such 'womanly' vocations as domestic service."

From Homer to Hitler; from the beginning of that common culture which has drawn the peoples of the West together, to what threatens to be its end! [278]

[18] Wallace R. Deuel, *People Under Hitler;* review in *Time*, March 9, 1942, p. 84.

THE *ODYSSEY:*
THREE CONTEMPORARY
INTERPRETATIONS

The Epic of Success

L. A. POST

. . . IT WILL HELP US TO GET THE RANGE OF OUR MATERIAL IF FOR ONCE we disregard chronological order and study the *Odyssey* before the *Iliad.* The *Odyssey* is not only a sequel but a complement to the *Iliad.* In both poems the poet considers it his function to stimulate the passion for glory and to hold up ideals of glorious conduct for emulation by later ages. In the *Iliad* he glorifies a warrior, Achilles, and shows how he gloried not only in military prowess and in adherence to the precepts of honesty and honor, but in passionate loyalty to his friend Patroclus even after death. In the *Odyssey* it is a woman who is glorified because of her loyal love for a husband who has been twenty years absent and may be supposed to be dead. The theme of loyalty and courage as the true glory is the same in both, but the shifting of attention from one sex to the other produces great changes in environment and in the pattern of action. There is another great difference in that [12/13] the glory of Achilles is displayed in contempt for death. The soldier must compete for honor without hope of other reward than glory itself. His dead friend cannot be restored to him, and the *Iliad* has, as Aristotle says, a tragic plot. He calls the plot of the *Odyssey* in contrast ethical and complex. It is complex because it has recognition scenes and because the tables are suddenly turned for the suitors when Odysseus is recognized.

The ethical plot is a plot that was common in Greek tragedies and popular in the theater, but Aristotle distinguishes tragedy proper with its unhappy ending from the kind of story in which all turns out well in the end. He calls this kind of plot—the success story, the pattern of trouble and deliverance or misunderstanding and clarification—ethical, I suppose, because it is the success of good characters only that is insured, while bad characters are in some way punished. The effect

From L. A. Post, "The Pattern of Success: Homer's *Odyssey*," in *From Homer to Menander* (Berkeley: University of California Press, 1951), pp. 12–26. Reprinted by permission of the publisher.

might thus be supposed to be highly moral. At any rate, Aristotle distinguishes the plots proper to comedy and tragedy, though Greek tragedies often have happy endings and differ in practice from comedy only in their treatment of character. Unfortunately this has led to a certain ambiguity in the meaning of the word comedy ever since his time. Such comedies as Dante's *Divine Comedy* and Shakespeare's *Winter's Tale* are not particularly comic, but they end happily and thus satisfy Aristotle's criterion. When a tale is actually treated in a comic spirit, it is quite possible to have a success story that ends happily for bad characters, like the Punch and Judy show. The immorality is part of the comedy. Aristotle notes the inferiority of comic characters, but implies that the characters who win out in the success story of tragedy are not inferior. But he knows a tragedy, the *Orestes* of Euripides, in which one character at least is inferior. He means, no doubt, that the general effect is comic. You obviously may have a burlesque of a tragic story or may present with tragic seriousness a story of success in which success is preceded by tragic dangers and decisions. Longinus lays down the rule that sublimity is as closely connected with suffering or emotion as pleasure with *êthos*.[1] [13/14]

Now *êthos* is a very elusive word in Greek. It means good character, character of any kind, and normal life. The *Odyssey* is pleasurable as the *Iliad* is sublime. The later poem gives us scenes from common life; it depicts character in unemotional scenes; and it affords a model of normal morality. The *Odyssey* makes up by extension in time and space what it lacks in intensity.

Once we admit that the success story should be moral, we are committed to an interest in correct sentiments rather than in noble fury, in the usages of polite society rather than in the rude conflicts of men in a state of nature. Homer goes further, however, by depicting more than one kind of life. The Cyclopes have no state at all, and there are many peoples with strange ways that a wanderer might be tempted to adopt, notably the Lotus-eaters and the Phaeacians. In describing the latter, Homer seems to be as insistent as Plato was, later, on the danger to morals involved in isolation and control of the sea. It is here that the climax of temptation comes for Odysseus. It is characteristic of Homer to make his good woman more tempting than any bad woman could be. Nausicaä is an unmarried Andromache, and like Andromache she tempts the hero in Book 6 of his poem. As Andromache tempts Hector to forget honor and refrain from battle, so Nausicaä tempts Odysseus to forget his wife and refrain from further perils by sea and land. The bad women who tempt Odysseus are the nymphs Circe and Calypso. When he resists, their power yields to the behest of the gods, who are alert to further the cause of morality.

[1] See note 2 to chap. viii for references to fuller discussion of the ethical plot. For the *Orestes* see *Poetics* 25.31:61ᵇ 21. See also *On the Sublime* 29.2.

Odysseus risks not only his life but his virtue more than once in the course of his travels. Homer would never have suggested such a sentiment as "Be good, sweet maid, and let who will be clever." It is only the clever Odysseus who succeeds in being good and so returning to his wife. Odysseus' cleverness may indeed strike us sometimes as being inconsistent with plain honesty, but Homer justifies him by giving him a god in his own image to guide him. Athena directs not only his actions but those also of his wife Penelope and his son Telemachus. She tells all parties what she thinks is good for them, and encourages Telemachus to find out for himself [14/15] what news of his father he can. As she explains, a young man needs to see the world and meet difficulties for himself. In fact, Homer is rather fond of pointing out alternatives to make the rightness of a decision conspicuously clear. The *Odyssey* is a guide to ancient etiquette, a comedy of manners in which manners are not at odds with morals.[2]

It divides easily into parts A, B, C, and D. In D, Books 13–24, we are in Ithaca and all the gods are united in support of Odysseus and his family against the usurping suitors. In A, Books 1–4, and B, Books 5–8, the gods support Odysseus, but have to reckon with Poseidon, who cherishes a private pique because Odysseus blinded his son, the Cyclops Polyphemus. Athena helps Telemachus in Ithaca and on his travels without fear of Poseidon's anger. During the simultaneous adventures of Odysseus in Phaeacia, she helps him, but only in disguise. After all, Poseidon was her uncle and Poseidon was Odysseus' enemy until he reached Ithaca. Poseidon's last fling was to turn to stone the ship of the Phaeacians which conducted Odysseus at last to his homeland.

The gods in council took no interest in Odysseus during the first ten years of his wanderings. The moral intent of Homer is plain here too. By putting the council so late, he can permit Odysseus to wander unfriended on the fringes of the world where nymphs and monsters take the place of gods. In Books 9–12, which I call part C, we hear little or nothing of the gods except what an uninspired mortal might deduce for himself. This account of adventures that occurred many years before the opening of the *Odyssey* is put into the mouth of Odysseus himself, perhaps because Homer wished in this part of his epic to omit divine machinery. The reason why can be discovered from one or two passages where it is revealed that all the gods were angry with all the Achaeans after the sack of Troy because of the violation of temples. They were angry with Odysseus also, naturally, since he was one of the offending Achaeans. If the gods had been brought into part C, it would have appeared at once that they were against Odys-

---

[2] See Plato, *Laws* 4.704d–707d, and for Athena, *Od.* 13.416–428. Odysseus considered (6.141–144) whether he should clasp Nausicaä's knees or address her from a distance. Penelope considered (23.85–87) whether she should embrace Odysseus at once or question him first. Caution prevailed in both cases.

seus because the hero had been bad. Since it is Odysseus himself who [15/16] relates the tale of these years of wandering, we are not surprised that the attitude of the gods is left undefined. Thus Odysseus can arrive in Ithaca with no disqualification for the part that he is to play as leader of society and friend of religion. In this work Homer is dealing in black and white. He, no more than the gods, will sponsor Odysseus in part C; the hero must perforce speak for himself. The late date of the council of the gods also enables Homer to cite the history of Clytemnestra, who was unfaithful and slew her husband, in contrast to the loyalty of Penelope. The example of Orestes, who avenged his father Agamemnon, is also held up for imitation by Telemachus, who is bound to take the part of his father. This moral contrast between the good woman Penelope and the bad woman Clytemnestra, between the wise Odysseus and the foolish Agamemnon, is strongly emphasized at the beginning, middle, and end of the *Odyssey*.[3]

In a success story, criticism of life centers on a particular obstacle. Some individual or group or perhaps society as a whole stands in the way of welfare and happiness for the hero and his friends. The possibility is not faced, as in tragedy, that the universe may be hostile to man, or that man may have to compromise with destiny. At most, in comedy a man may need to find new resources or a new attitude in himself before he can win happiness. In the *Odyssey* a united family is the goal, and the gods at the start make a reunion of the family their goal too. Odysseus, who has been many years with Calypso on her island, has nothing new to learn about life. He must merely display his qualities of craft and courage and restraint. Penelope has a more important role, for she must create a new pattern by being more loyal to her husband than current custom demands. Telemachus, who is just coming of age, must develop into a man. Since the goal is clear-cut, Homer need not show us much psychological conflict. Decisions will be concerned with means rather than ends. In Penelope's choice of an ideal we know her decisions rather than her doubts, but the doubts and the inner triumph are sufficiently indicated from time to time. As a woman, she is more passive than active, so that the men and [16/17] their adventures seem more interesting at first; but she is made the emotional center of the action as she remains in the women's apartment of the palace of Odysseus at Ithaca and refuses to leave, though suitors, relatives, and even her son would prefer it. The crisis arrives when her son comes of age, so that it is no longer her duty to watch over him and protect his interests. She has no excuse for refusing to marry again except her woman's intuition, which persists in believing that her husband may be alive.

[3] Agamemnon and Orestes are introduced in Book 1 and in Book 11 especially. Clytemnestra is mentioned by name in Books 3 and 11 and is cited as a model of evil in women in contrast to Penelope in *Od.* 24.192–202. Orestes is brought in as an example to Telemachus, Agamemnon as a warning to Odysseus, and Clytemnestra as a foil to Penelope.

After the council of the gods, Athena goes to Ithaca to send Telemachus in search of his father, while Hermes goes to Calypso to order the release of Odysseus. At Ithaca we see the troubles of Penelope and Telemachus that are caused by the many suitors who feast daily and threaten the estate with ruin. Telemachus might order his mother to go home to her parents and take the suitors with her, but conscience forbids him to lay constraint upon a free woman. Penelope must make her own decision; he can hold out for another year. Not only the gods but the state is brought into the picture when Telemachus warns the suitors in public assembly that their violation of the rights of Odysseus as well as his own will be punished. The rest of Books 1–4 tells the story of his adventures at Pylos and Sparta as he seeks news of his father. The suitors plan to slay him on his return, thus deepening the blackness of their guilt.[4]

In Books 5–8 we see the simultaneous adventures of Odysseus on his way home and note how he pines always for his rocky homeland where men are men and for his own wife who has grown old waiting for him. This sentiment motivates his action throughout. The old theme of the shipwrecked sailor rescued by the princess may have been taken by Homer from folklore, but the moral tone which he infuses by making Nausicaä so obviously attractive as a wife and Phaeacia so luxurious as a residence is all his own. Odysseus may not accept the offer of Nausicaä's hand even out of gratitude. Homer in the end waxes satirical at the expense of the Phaeacians, who are not great athletes, but good sailors, dancers, and listeners to immoral stories about the gods. [17/18]

In the third group of four books it is Odysseus' life that is threatened rather than his virtue, though he is given the chance to remain under the spell of Circe's beauty. His voyage to the land of ghosts permits Homer to recall again the wickedness of Clytemnestra and to inform Odysseus of the virtues of his wife, but the episodic nature of the adventures related by Odysseus is plain enough. The episodes are carefully planned in their arrangement and interesting in themselves, but here if anywhere Homer was using stories that had long been current. His hero emerges from every ordeal undaunted, but in this part of the story the force of circumstance outweighs the moral forces. Character is less than adventure. Homer, being as tricky as his hero, draws a veil over his relation to the gods at this time, but his adventures are clearly those of a man who is viewed by them with indifference, to say the least.

In the second half of the poem, which recounts the recognitions of Odysseus by friend and foe in Ithaca and the slaughter of the suitors, Athena is busily at work. With her help a few righteous fight against many wicked and triumph. Homer uses her to effect the mutual rec-

---

[4] Penelope's right to stay on in her husband's house as long as his death is not certain, or until she chooses to leave of her own accord, is recognized by Telemachus (2.130–145). It would be sin to coerce her.

ognition of Odysseus and Telemachus, which must not be allowed to
compete with the great recognition of husband and wife after the
slaying. Father and son are the nucleus of an intrigue against the
suitors which requires the coöperation of Penelope for its success. She
must propose the competition for her hand among the suitors that will
enable Odysseus to get in position unexpectedly with his bow and
shoot them down helpless and trapped. Yet her part in the intrigue is
carried out without any recognition on her part that her missing husband is at hand. Athena is as useful in enabling Odysseus to remain
unrecognized by his wife as in insuring his recognition by his son. Such
a difference in technique, when observed, leaves no doubt that the
author of the *Odyssey* was a great original genius, no matter how
much material he may have taken from others. The fact that he used
the methods of oral composition and no doubt composed for oral
delivery makes no difference. The use of a pen or a typewriter [18/19]
does not suddenly make the user a master of planned storytelling, nor
does the absence of these instruments prevent the inspired artist from
producing a great work. To argue that, because most or even all
modern oral poets are comparatively unoriginal, there can have been
no Homer, is like arguing that, since there is no Shakespeare in the
twentieth century, there was none in the sixteenth either.[5]

Athena is also useful in relieving Penelope and to some extent
Odysseus of any criticism when their part in the tale is to cheat and
deceive. Penelope's success in getting presents from the suitors by
arraying herself in all her charms is due to a suggestion of Athena and
receives the approval of Odysseus. It is an odd feature of the story that
it should seem to be dangerous to Odysseus to be recognized by his
wife, and that Athena should help him with his disguise and should
make Penelope unobserving when he is recognized by the nurse
Eurycleia who bathes him in his wife's presence. But it adds to our
liking for the warmhearted and yearning Penelope that she should be
unable to conceal her joy if she had once recognized her husband.

[5] The brilliant studies of Milman Parry in the technique of oral poetry enable
us to appreciate the methods of Homer; but to conclude that, because the technique of modern Yugoslav epic is comparable to that of the Homeric poems, therefore no Homeric poet existed who was very different in capacity and achievement
from modern oral poets, is a non sequitur. On this point see the review by Albert
Bates Lord of Samuel Eliot Bassett, *The Poetry of Homer* (Sather Lectures; Univ.
of California Press, 1938), in *AJPh* 68 (1947) 219–222, and Lord's article,
"Homer, Parry, and Huso," *AJA* 52 (1948) 34–44. This last gives a complete
bibliography of Milman Parry at the end. I see no reason to distinguish, as Lord
does, between Homer the Poet and Homer the Oral Poet. Rhys Carpenter admires
the work of Parry and at the same time speaks of Homer as the direct spiritual
ancestor of Attic tragedy: *op cit.* [*Folk Tale, Fiction and Saga in the Homeric
Epics*], pp. 6, 78–85, 166 f. Most of Homer's material was no doubt traditional,
but the design that is impressed upon it by Homer is as original as the design of
Sophocles' *Electra*. The fact that Aeschylus certainly, and Euripides probably, had
used the same material before merely throws into relief the great originality of
Sophocles.

Homer and his audience liked their women sincere and simple, incapable of carrying on an intrigue. The scenes between Penelope and Odysseus in disguise, in which he keeps his role of beggar while she pours out her heart, thus add another to Homer's scenes of temptation by good women. Odysseus must be hard and cruel until the suitors are out of the way. All his wit and self-control are taxed.[6]

The pains that Homer takes to denigrate the suitors are obvious. They are attacking the sanctity of the royal prerogative, of the family, and of private property, and the gods are unanimously against them. God, nature, and man will be in harmony as soon as a few wicked individuals are forced to cease from troubling. There are no bounds to the insolence of the suitors. They plan the murder of a host, make love to a woman in the home of her husband, disregard the rights of suppliants and beggars, and disregard the warning of a seer. They force their attentions upon a woman against her will. When Homer compares the case of [19/20] Odysseus with that of Agamemnon, the suitors play the part of Aegisthus, who slew him after seducing his wife. So, too, the suitors hope to slay Odysseus. The latter is wise, however, where Agamemnon was foolish. He has no Chryseïs whom he prefers to his wife, and he brings home no captive concubine like Cassandra. He trusts no women if he can help it and walks into no traps. This comparison and the attitude of the gods reinforce the blackening of the suitors.

There is more than morality in the *Odyssey*, however, if we investigate Homer's purpose in making Penelope the emotional center of the epic. The moral code of Homer enjoined respect for the gods and for suppliants, who were under their protection. Hosts and guests had mutual claims under the protection of Zeus. There was a standard procedure in city government which law-abiding citizens respected. Free and responsible married women were not to be coerced. Mere morality could hardly confer glory, however, in Homer. He is romantic enough to celebrate love—in the *Iliad* a love passing the love of women, and in the *Odyssey* a woman's love. Penelope is represented as a creative personality who, when all men doubt and disapprove, wins a personal success and glory by gambling against odds on the hope of regaining her husband. In Oriental fiction women die to prove their loyalty to a dead husband, as Evadne does in Euripides' *Suppliants* and as Anthea does in the *Cyropaedeia* of Xenophon. In the Confucian code of China a widow shows her loyalty by remaining unwed. There are many monuments to the virtue of such women in China. The Greeks were more practical; they did not expect such exaggerated loyalty to a dead husband, nor do women in Greek literature die in defense of their virtue. Penelope does not renounce the hope of marriage, once her son has come of age and her husband is known to be

[6] See *Od.* 19 for the meeting of Odysseus and Penelope.

dead. In fact Odysseus himself enjoined her to marry again after his death. Hence she does not dismiss the suitors by refusing to marry. She seeks always to gain time on one pretext or another and to get certain news of Odysseus. Her willingness to believe any rumor is marked. This is an amiable weakness, a woman's [20/21] whim, in the opinion of others. Penelope is isolated, but to her the love of her husband is a sacrament that she keeps inviolate in spite of reason or statistical odds. Thus Homer raises the standard of living for husband and wife and stamps with approval the assertion of a noble ideal by an individual. He is at pains to emphasize Penelope's disregard of public opinion and of prudential considerations, and to show her love as an emotional influence in her life. She acts wisely, as women are wise, for she does not underestimate the worth of sentiment, without which women are weaker than men. She acts with great propriety, never visiting the men's part of the palace except when she is veiled and attended by two handmaids. She does not, like the Spartan Helen, eat with the men. Yet the springs of feeling gush warm and melting when she is at last alone with the husband of her youth.[7]

Homer's interest in the ideal family relationship is easily forgotten when attention is focused on Odysseus. His desire to return home might seem to depend little on his personal affection for Penelope, though he states when necessary his loyalty to her above all other women or nymphs. He paints a glowing picture of married love for Nausicaä, and by so doing enlists her womanly pride and her romantic impulses as a maiden in his favor; but this may be the subtlety of a man in dire need. He convinces her by his understanding of the ideal marriage that he is personally a superior man, thus disarming her doubts of him and melting her suspicion. Later in Ithaca when Odysseus has the opportunity to spy upon his wife's behavior, she passes every test. She has the same passion for glory that inspires Homer's warriors, but holds that a woman's glory is to be loyal to her husband. The function of Athena in enabling Penelope to assist her husband's plot while apparently not recognizing him has been mentioned. It is clear that Homer has reasons for postponing the recognition by Penelope. Son is loyal to father as a matter of course, and men may be expected to plot together against foes. Penelope had nothing to lose materially by a change of husbands. Even her son had been warned in a dream not to trust his mother to look after his interests [21/22] when the time should come for her to marry again. Such suspicion seems

---

[7] I have described the Greek attitude toward women and their behavior in an article, "Woman's Place in Menander's Athens," *TAPhA* 71 (1940) 420–459. The continuity of the Greek traditional ideal of feminine propriety is remarkable. There is very little difference between Homer and Menander if we allow for the lower level of the characters of the latter. Women have their sphere of life quite as separate and quite as circumscribed in Homer as later. For an account of monuments to Chinese widows see M. Huc, *A Journey through the Chinese Empire* (New York, 1855), pp. 46 f.

unworthy of Penelope, but is is precisely the vulgarity of these sus-
picions that makes her actual conduct seem surprising in its nobility.
Thus Athena constantly interprets to Odysseus and Penelope their
mutual roles, while father and son speak freely together.[8]
But after the slaughter of the suitors, in which Athena has assisted,
the goddess tactfully withdraws and lets husband and wife come together with no help from her except removal of his disguise and a
general brightening up. Homer uses his gods with much discretion.
When he has a great scene in readiness, they set the stage and let the
actors show their motives. If Penelope had recognized Odysseus earlier,
the slaughter of the suitors must have become the most interesting
point of the story. When Euripides puts recognition before escape, as
in his *Helen, Electra,* and *Iphigeneia among the Taurians,* the women
are bemeaned, and psychological interest gives way to melodramatic
adventure. Homer keeps Penelope and her emotional drama at the
center of interest, first, by postponing her salvation, and secondly, by
bringing Athena and the miraculous as well as Hades back into the
episodes that follow in Book 24. Only where she is concerned do we
get a full-blooded psychological episode; in it there is even a suggestion
of tragedy. Here we find sentiment intensified to the point of passion.
When Odysseus encountered Nausicaä, nothing infringed upon the
delicate play of feeling on both sides. It was a disappointment when
Nausicaä had to take leave of Odysseus, but her disappointment is
much less tragic than Penelope's thought of what she had missed as the
years of their separation dragged by. There were other fish in the sea
for Nausicaä.

Penelope has dreamed so long that when Eurycleia awakes her
with the words, "Odysseus is here," she cannot at first adjust herself
to the reality. She is cold, then hot, but masters her excitement before
she joins the victorious Odysseus and Telemachus. Even when Odysseus had bathed and rid himself of blood and grime, even after he has
tactfully disposed of Telemachus, who is inclined [22/23] to hurry
things, she still gazes at the stranger in silence, trying to find a place
for him among her memories and dreams of a far younger man. There
is a similar scene in a Chinese drama written about two thousand years
later, in which the wife remains coy through a protracted scene before
she welcomes a long-absent husband. Here the motive is propriety, and
the Chinese play apparently is chiefly concerned to show the success
of the lady in concealing her feelings entirely in the interest of
etiquette. There is, no doubt, some emphasis on propriety in Homer
too, but he succeeds in making us feel the desperate need of Penelope
to control her emotion and to yield only when she can do so without
reserve. Here if anywhere we have an aesthetic of forces arranged in a
psychological pattern that produces naturally a deep sympathy. There

[8] See *Od.* 6.180–185, 18.255, 19.128, 15.16–23.

is a resolution of profound emotional stresses. The theme of wedded love is triumphant, and wedded love is made to seem the greatest of earthly bonds, as of course for a Greek woman it was.[9]

The courtesy of Odysseus in waiting patiently for his wife is underlined, for it was a tenet of Hellenism from Homer to Menander that free women must not be coerced in love. The slave woman was subject to her master, not so the wife or daughter. But at long last Odysseus shows feeling and speaks the bitter words, "Let my bed be made apart." His burst of feeling gives Penelope her cue. Yes, the marriage bed shall be brought out and made up for the stranger. With the mention of the marriage bed the years of absence fall away for both and revive the memory of union. The bed is symbolic; it was fixed in place by one leg, fashioned of an olive tree by Odysseus, but left rooted in the ground. It is not merely Odysseus' knowledge of the secret that assures Penelope of his identity; his righteous indignation discloses a passion that she recognizes. It is not subtlety but genuine feeling that rings in his voice as he denounces the man who has violated the ineradicable marriage bed, instrument and symbol of wedlock. About that bed are entwined the tender memories of early married love. Now Penelope sees in Odysseus, not the old veteran, but the stalwart youth whom she had sent to the war twenty years before. The emotions [23/24] of the past well up, yet Penelope's sense of loss is keen. With a shock it comes to her that the best of marriage is gone, the joy of growing up and growing old together; but she does not dwell on this sentiment, opening rather her heart to the joy that remains. Odysseus says nothing of love or disappointment, for such expression is not the man's part in a Greek tale. His actions are eloquent enough and Homer speaks for him.

Experiment will soon show that the scene could not have been so powerful if Homer had put it anywhere else in his pattern of action. He indeed created a pattern for comedy, for later comedy always dealt with family ties and usually with mutual love of man and woman. In New Comedy the happy ending always involves a reunion of husband and wife, parent and child, brother-sister and sister-brother, or two passionate lovers. The suitors in the *Odyssey* could suppose that husband and wife had conspired against them. In fact, Homer leaves the possibility open that the wise Penelope really knew her husband from the start and only refrained from greeting him because that would have interfered with his plans. It would also have detracted from the beauty of their reunion. Homer so valued that great moment that of set purpose he sacrificed his last book to it. He had to point the moral and give the world of men its due, but he does not let what happens in that world seem very important in comparison with the happiness

---

[9] For the Chinese play see the summary of *Mu Yang Chüan, The Shepherd's Pen*, in L. C. Arlington and Harold Acton, *Famous Chinese Plays* (Peiping, 1937).

of a woman. As Bentley remarked, the *Iliad* was written for men, the *Odyssey* for women.[10]

Homer in the *Iliad* lets us gently down from the exaltation of a world of heroes to the considerations of daily life. When Achilles and Priam weep together, we are recalled from the romance to the reality of war. In the *Odyssey* the mood of the whole is not elevated above that of the twenty-fourth book of the *Iliad*. It is not the romance but the reality of love that is celebrated. The only decline that is possible is a decline from the devotion of intimate family life to the concerns of men apart from women—the mood of assembly and market place and battlefield. Homer glorifies this world in the *Iliad;* to do so in the *Odyssey* would be worse than to [24/25] make his ending flat, as it is. He gives us a moral and political solution and makes it final and authoritative by using Athena as *deus ex machina,* just as she is used in the political tragedies of Athens. For the first and only time she restrains, instead of inciting, Odysseus to action. She puts a stop to his pursuit of the kin of the suitors after he has won a battle with the help of his father Laertes and his son Telemachus, as well as his loyal supporters in the community. Here Athena appears for the first time among many as the representative of political unity in Greek literature. Possibly this scene inspired the pageant of the tyrant Peisistratus when he calmed the fears of his fleeing opponents by sending before him in a chariot a woman dressed and armed as Athena. She was declared to be Athena, introducing Peisistratus as her representative, urging the Athenians to receive him without misgiving. Presumably the Athenians recognized the theatrical aspect of this piece of propaganda, but it was effective propaganda nevertheless. The sentiments with which we view a patriotic pageant are not necessarily false or misleading. Certainly the Athenians approved of such representations of Athena in their theater, if we may judge by the number of her appearances in extant drama. Thus Homer lays down a pattern not only for comedy, but for political tragedies that recount legendary history for purposes of propaganda—for example *Eumenides, Ion, Andromache,* and others. In *Ion* and *Andromache,* Euripides interwove the reunited family with his political plot. Only in New Comedy are these strands at last separated. So long did it take to throw off the clogging influence of Homer, who inserted the family within the framework of the state in the dull though statesmanlike ending of the *Odyssey.*[11]

[10] I owe the suggestion that Penelope may have recognized Odysseus from the first to A. M. Harmon of Yale University, who presented it in a presidential address delivered before the American Philological Association at Ann Arbor, Michigan, in 1939. The same idea is differently developed by P. W. Harsh, "Penelope and Odysseus in *Odyssey* XIX," *AJPh* 71 (1950) 1–21.

[11] Herodotus (1.60) tells the story how Phya, an unusually tall woman, represented Athena and was declared to be the goddess in person bringing Peisistratus back to Athens, when he made his triumphant return from exile. We need not suppose, as Herodotus does, that the Athenians really identified Phya

Still, Homer understands perfectly the use of a *deus ex machina*. The god must not be brought in to settle the main problem, but only to prevent the sudden development of a new threat. Athena intervenes only when the victory is won. To motivate this intervention Odysseus must act rashly and out of character. There is a *nodus vindice dignus*, but the knot is rather arbitrarily provided by the poet. The preceding battle bears no resemblance to the gory [25/26] struggles of the *Iliad*. It is enlivened only by the miraculous rejuvenation of the aged Laertes. Actually the miracle belittles the battle. At any rate, it all ends with an era of good-will in which king and state, along with morality, are supported by the goddess, who counsels moderation. It is too early for her to recommend democracy.[12]

Before the end, however, Homer had tied two other loose ends. A meeting between Agamemnon in Hades and the ghosts of the suitors is introduced, evidently to point once more the moral contrast between Penelope and Clytemnestra and to assert the power of poetry. Bards will sing of the two women and perpetuate their glory and shame. Thus they will bring glory or shame upon all women. The poet's didactic purpose is evident: to teach by examples the difference between virtue and vice in wives.

The ensuing recognition scene between Odysseus and his father Laertes is almost episodic, yet it serves to emphasize the importance of the male line and to mark the clan as intermediate between family and state. In the means of recognition, recalling to his father an incident that occurred when he was a small boy, Odysseus awakens his father's memory and to some extent paves the way for his rejuvenation in battle. But there is nothing here to detain us further. The glory has departed with Penelope. Homer displayed a world at war in the *Iliad;* in the *Odyssey* he makes a beginning of reconstruction after the war. It is full of the gracious light of a benign and civilizing influence. Its hero is sometimes too little concerned about means, but his general aims are represented as noble and good, to live on in peace and prosperity while he rules wisely and well and gives gods and suppliants

---

with the goddess. She symbolized Peisistratus' policy of pacification and unity, and served to advertise his good intentions.

[12] Horace (*Ars Poetica* 191 f.) forbids the employment of a god from the machine unless there is a problem that justifies the interference. It is even more important to note that the problem that brings in the god is normally not the main theme, but a new difficulty that the poet introduces for the purpose. In Greek practice, gods may symbolize some human institution or virtue and so be brought on to point a moral. They often vindicate history or predict the future, which for spectators is, of course, the past. Sometimes they establish rituals, as in *Iphigeneia in Tauris*, where the poet carefully provides a misadventure for his characters in order to justify the appearance of Athena. The late *Rhesus* might be thought to violate the canon of Horace, but the need to mourn the dead or to vindicate the dying, as Artemis does in the *Hippolytus*, should satisfy a candid critic. The Greek stage had no curtain, and either a funeral procession or an epiphany provides the play with a well-defined ending and removes the actors from the stage.

their due. It would be an anachronism to denounce Homer as a fascist because he accepts monarchy and even slavery. He idealizes his picture of the best institutions that he knew, not to recommend them in preference to some modern alternative, for such alternatives did not then exist. He was only concerned to make men behave with due consideration of themselves and others within the frame of society as he saw it. He was an educator, not a reformer. [26]

The Epic of Suffering and Fulfillment

GEORGE E. DIMOCK, JR.

> "There is no way to stand firm on both feet and escape trouble."
>
> *Odyssey* 5.413–4

IN A WAY, THE WHOLE PROBLEM OF THE *Odyssey* IS FOR ODYSSEUS TO establish his identity. "After all, who knows who his father is?" says Telemachus in the first book. "My son, if he really ever existed," says Laertes in the last. To establish his identity Odysseus must live up to his name.

This is not a new idea. A nameless ancient commentator has puzzled eitors by glossing *hēbēsas* in line 410 of the nineteenth book with *odyssamenos*. *Hēbēsas* means "when he has grown up," a meaning with which *odyssamenos* has nothing to do; but as we shall see, the scholiast means that for Odysseus to grow up, to achieve his full stature, will be for him to "odysseus"—to live up to the meaning of his name, whatever that may be.

"To odysseus" (*odyssasthai* in Greek) is usually said to mean "be wroth against," "hate," and to be connected with Latin *odisse*. Historically speaking, this may be true. For the *Odyssey's* poetical purposes, however, the verb denotes a more general sort of hostility, which Homer is at pains to define. In the fifth book the nymph Ino explains it as "planting evils," without specifying what sort of hostility is in the mind of the planter. It is true that Poseidon, who happens to be the planter in this case, is angry; but Zeus, who also odysseuses Odysseus, is not. In the nineteenth book Odysseus' grandfather Autolycus indicates that it is not a question of anger; asked to name the baby, he replies,

"I have odysseused many in my time, up and down the wide world, men and women both; therefore let his name be Odysseus."

George E. Dimock, Jr., "The Name of Odysseus." Reprinted by permission from *The Hudson Review*, Vol. IX, No. 1 (Spring 1956), 52–70. Copyright © 1956 by The Hudson Review, Inc.

Now, all we know from the *Odyssey* about Autolycus' career is that he was the foremost liar and thief of his day. Most naturally, by "odysseusing many" he means that he has been the bane of many people's existence. The secret of his palpable success would seem to be that he has never given a sucker an even break, and he [52/53] wants his grandson to be like him. In the career of Autolycus, and in the attitude which it implies, we are much closer to the *polytropon* "crafty" of the *Odyssey's* first line, than to the *mēnin* "wrath" of the *Iliad's*. So let us think no more of "wrath," which implies provocation and mental perturbation, but rather of a hand and mind against every man, by nature, or as a matter of policy. Autolycus' own name does not suggest "Lone Wolf" for nothing. These considerations, and others, lead me to think that in the *Odyssey odyssasthai* means essentially "to cause pain (*odynē*), and to be willing to do so." We need not draw the line between subjective and objective here, any more than we need do so in the case of the word "suffer." Where did Odysseus "suffer" the "woes" of the *Odyssey's* fourth line: "on the high seas," or "in his heart"? Just as "suffer" brings to mind both the external and internal aspects of being a victim, so "odysseus" implies subjectively and objectively what it is to persecute. For what it is worth, the seven-odd instances of the verb outside the *Odyssey* show nothing inconsistent with this meaning.

Autolycus, then, we discover in the nineteenth book, intended Odysseus to be a causer of pain. He has been one all along, of course. Perhaps the most prominent fact about him is that more than any other man he was responsible for taking Troy; and what it means to sack a city, we know from the simile at the end of book eight. Odysseus

wept as a woman weeps when she throws her arms around the body of her beloved husband, fallen in battle before his city and his comrades, fighting to save his town and his children from disaster. She has found him gasping in the throes of death; she clings to him and lifts her voice in lamentation. But the enemy come up and belabor her back and shoulders with spears, as they lead her off into slavery and a life of miserable toil, with her cheeks wasted by her pitiful grief.[1]

Less than a hundred lines later, at the beginning of his tale, Odysseus will say,

The same wind as wafted me from Ilium brought me to Ismarus, the city of the Cicones; I sacked the place and killed the men; their wives, together with much booty, we took out of the city and divided up.[53/54]

As has been well observed, the Sack of Ismarus is the Sack of Troy in its predatory essentials, with the glamor stripped off. This attitude Odysseus will maintain to the end. "The cattle which the suitors have

---

[1] This quotation is from E. V. Rieu's excellent translation. So, in whole or in part, are many of the passages which follow.

consumed," he says in the twenty-third book, "I will for the most part make up by raiding on my own; the Achaeans will give others." Perhaps worse than this, Odysseus' going to Troy caused Telemachus grievous mental suffering, wasted Penelope's nights in tears, and reduced Laertes, his father, to misery and squalor; his absence killed his mother, Antikleia.

So conceived, Odysseus is not an attractive character. In fact the poem implies a good deal of criticism of the Autolycan attitude. As Mr. H. N. Porter once pointed out to me, one of the first things we hear about the hero is his predilection for poisoned arrows. Athene, disguised as Mentes, tells Telemachus,

He was on his way from Ephyre, where he had stayed with Ilus Mermerides—he went there in his fast ship to get a mortal poison to smear his bronze-tipped arrows with. Ilus wouldn't give it to him in fear of the eternal gods. But my father [Zeus?] gave him some. He was terribly fond of him.

Much better, one would think, for Autolycus to have adopted Eurycleia's suggestion of Polyaretus as a name for the baby: "He's our 'Answer to Prayer' (*polyarētos*)," she remarked as she put the child on his grandfather's lap. But Autolycus preferred a name that most would regard as ill-omened.

For in spite of the fact that Odysseus is so obviously a causer of pain, the name which Autolycus wished on him strikes one as ironical. Up to the nineteenth book, Odysseus has been referred to as odysseused rather than odysseusing: "Why do you odysseus him so, Zeus?" Athene asks, before the poem is well under way; Ino and Odysseus both say that Poseidon is odysseusing him; finally, as we read the Autolycus passage, we are aware that Odysseus has just told Penelope that Zeus and the Sun-god odysseused her husband. In the *Odyssey's* proem itself, the hero seems essentially the sufferer: he is the *polytropos* man, the Autolycan rogue who treats the world as his enemy, but who sacks Troy only to be driven far astray thereafter, and take a beating. In the process, we are told, he is to win his *psychē*, which means loosely his life, and more properly the image of life after the liver is gone—in [54/55] other words something very like identity—but the whole business seems unpleasant, to say the least.

To understand the satisfaction involved in injuring and suffering and the connection between them, we must return to the nineteenth book and the scholiast's note. The giving of the name is coupled with the adventure in which Odysseus first lives up to it. *Hēbēsas* is in fact *odyssamenos*. "When he has grown up," the hero, as though undergoing an initiation, wins Autolycus' favor and recognition by going on a boar hunt; as causer of pain he kills the boar; as sufferer he is slashed by it, thus acquiring the scar important in identifying him later. The pain given and received results in joy:

Autolycus and the sons of Autolycus
Efficiently healed him and loaded him with presents;
Rejoicing they dispatched him rejoicing to his beloved
Ithaca. His father and his good mother
Rejoiced at his return, and asked for each particular
Of how he got his scar.

The suffering results from the doing, and is inseparable from it in the recognition and satisfaction produced by this exploit. Not simply "how he killed the boar" but "how he got his scar," is for Odysseus' parents the measure of their son.

To be Odysseus, then, is to adopt the attitude of the hunter of dangerous game: to deliberately expose one's self, but thereafter to take every advantage that the exposed position admits; the immediate purpose is injury, but the ultimate purpose is recognition and the sense of a great exploit. Odysseus killed a boar to win his name; he went to Troy to enlarge it; in order to keep it, he will presently kill 108 suitors in as cold blood as he can manage.

In the adventure with the Cyclops, Odysseus inflicts pain in order to identify himself, and in so doing challenges the hostility of the universe. Polyphemus' pain is obvious. Even Euripides could not have dwelt more explicitly than Homer on the boring of the red-hot stake into the great eyeball, the sizzling of the eye's fluid, and the crackling of its roots. By virtue of this deed of horror, Odysseus, until now *Outis* "nobody" as far as Polyphemus is concerned, puts himself in a position where he can tell the monster who he is, can cry his name aloud to the Cyclops' face. This cry of definance is thought to be foolish of the wily Odysseus, no less [55/56] by his crew than by the critics, but it is in reality, like the boar hunt, a case of deliberate self-exposure for the purpose of being somebody rather than nobody.

To blind the son of Poseidon, and then to defy him, is both to challenge nature to do her worst, and to demonstrate her ultimate impotence to crush human identity. It is challenging nature in the sense that the sailor does, every time he goes to sea. The hero's colonizing eye as he approaches the Cyclopes' island, the remark that they have no ships or shipwrights, the shipbuilding technique employed in blinding Polyphemus and the mention of axe, adze and auger, the tools which enabled Odysseus to leave Kalypso and set sail on his raft, all this sounds very much as though Odysseus' crime against Poseidon were the crime of all those who go down to the sea in ships. But Poseidon will not get his revenge. In the *Odyssey* navigation is a practical possibility; the elements are conquered. So to blind Polyphemus is to convict savage nature of impotence and blindness. She is indiscriminate in her blows. Her most hostile efforts, like the rocks thrown by Polyphemus, are as likely to wash the hero to safety as they are to drive him into danger. Thus the power of the elements does not render Odysseus' identity meaningless. Rather he makes sense, and the elements do not. This, I think, is the significance of the general assumption in the *Odyssey* that Poseidon will give Odysseus his belly-ful of trouble before he reaches his home, but will not kill him.

Polyphemus and Poseidon, however, are more than the hostility of inanimate nature. There is no "inanimate nature" in Homer any-way. They prefigure all the overt savagery which the universe presents, human and divine. This savagery is as able to breach the conventions, hospitality and the rest, among the civilized suitors in Ithaca, or the hypercivilized Phaeacians (remember Euryalus), as it is among the cannibal Laestrygons, or among the Cyclopes. If Poseidon and Polyphemus are the hostile aspects of this world, it is not foolish for Odysseus to cry his name in defiance of them, and so be subject to Polyphemus' rock-slinging and his curse; or rather, the foolishness or good sense of the action is not the point. To pass from the darkness of the cave into the light, to pass from being "nobody" to having a name, is to be born. But to be born is to cast one's name in the teeth of a hostile universe; it is to incur the enmity of Poseidon. In such a world, what better name could [56/57] be found than Odysseus, "Trouble"? ("Trouble" is perhaps as good a translation of Odysseus' name as any. When a character in a western movie says, "Just call me Trouble, stranger,'" we take him to be a hostile type who makes trouble for other people, and so presumably for himself also.)

That braving Polyphemus is being born is not my metaphor; it is Homer's. In the nineteenth book Odysseus hints to Penelope that her husband has undergone a birth somewhere overseas:

He put in at Amnisus, where the cave of Eileithuia is, in a difficult harbor; he barely escaped the gales.

Eileithuia is goddess of childbirth. But in the nineteenth book this is merely a way of reminding us of the Polyphemus adventure and pos-sibly of Kalypso as well. In the ninth book, as Polyphemus is in the act of rolling the stone from the mouth of the cave, we are told of his anguish for the second time. We already know how his eye hurts, but this time we hear that he is "travailing in pain"; *ōdinōn odynēsi* are the words used. Whether or not we hear in them the name of Odysseus, we should not fail to reflect that *ōdinō* means essentially "to be in labor of childbirth." We are born for trouble, the adventure of the Cyclops implies, yet to stay in the womb is to remain nobody. There is security of a sort in being nobody, but as the Cyclops promises, Nobody will be devoured in the end, though last of all.

For there are more insidious threats to identity in the *Odyssey* than those which Polyphemus represents, the dangers and sufferings consequent upon taking on the world as one's enemy. Trouble is dif-ficult and dangerous, but it can lead to identity. Security, on the other hand, is inevitable oblivion. The narrative proper of the *Odyssey* begins as follows:

By now all the others, as many as had escaped sheer destruction, were at home. Odysseus, alone of all, wanting his home and his wife, a queenly nymph held prisoner, Kalypso, divine goddess, in her hollow cave, begging him to be her husband.

This is the state of affairs which the fifth book will develop. He wants home and a wife. He has a cave and a goddess. Why do all the gods but one pity him for this? Odysseus has realized the tired soldier's or sailor's dream, an immortality of comfort and physical [57/58] satisfaction, with no troubles. But Odysseus would rather die, as Athene says. Everybody sees this paradox and understands the flaw in this paradise: such an existence has no meaning. But it adds something, I think, to see life on Ogygia in terms of identity and nonentity. Kalypso is oblivion. Her name suggests cover and concealment, or engulfing; she lives "in the midst of the sea"—the middle of nowhere, as Hermes almost remarks—and the whole struggle of the fifth book, indeed of the entire poem, is not to be engulfed by that sea. When the third great wave of book five breaks over Odysseus' head, Homer's words are: *ton de mega kyma kalypsen*—"and the great wave engulfed him." If this wave had drowned him, it would have been a "vile death," surely, as Odysseus remarks at the beginning of the storm. Much better, he says, to have died where "the spears flew thickest" at Troy; then he would have had "recognition," *kleos*. People would know about him and his death. Odysseus does not wish he were back with Kalypso. Though she offered immortality, not death—an immortality of security and satisfaction in a charming cave—it is still an immortality of oblivion, of no *kleos,* of nonentity. Leaving Kalypso is very like leaving the perfect security and satisfaction of the womb; but, as the Cyclops reminds us, the womb is after all a deadly place. In the womb one has no identity, no existence worthy of a name. Nonentity and identity are in fact the poles between which the actors in the poem move. It is a choice between Scylla and Charybdis—to face deliberately certain trouble from the jaws of the six-headed goddess, or to be engulfed entirely by the maelstrom. One must odysseus and be odysseused, or else be kalypsoed.

Odysseus did not always live up to his name. There was one occasion when oblivion seemed almost preferable to trouble. His name seemed to have lost its magic. Hence his failure with the Laestrygonians, and the necessity of winning back his identity in the Circe episode.

While we remember Polyphemus ("Much-fame") in connection with Odysseus, we are very apt to forget Antiphates ("Against-renown"), the Laestrygonian king. In the Laestrygonian affair Odysseus himself avoids the encounter, and loses his whole fleet. In this, his least creditable adventure, he never makes his identity [58/59] felt. The Laestrygonians don't know who he is, or care. Yet Odysseus survives.

With poetic rather than nautical logic, he escapes by virtue of having left his ship in an exposed position, while the rest of the fleet trusts itself to the security of the fiord and is lost.

Odysseus in the land of the Laestrygonians is not the Odysseus whom we saw with the Cyclops, though in both cases he has to do with cannibal giants. Avoiding the encounter here is perhaps as sensible as avoiding the Planctae, but there are other reasons why Odysseus is not up to it. In the interim, as we have said, his name has lost its magic. "Trouble," intended to mean success, has seemed to be failure. Aeolus has listened with interest to the tale of prowess at Troy and has sent Odysseus on his way, insuring that he will have, for once, a remarkably painless trip. But in sight of the goal, trouble strikes. Aeolus, seeing in this a sign that heaven is inveterately hostile to Odysseus, banishes him from his sight. Such trouble means to Aeolus not identity, but oblivion. Odysseus himself has nearly reached a similar conclusion. Since leaving Troy he has sacked Ismarus in characteristically ruthless fashion and rejected the passive peace of Lotos-land. By handling the situation in a manner worthy of Autolycus, he has been able to cry his name in defiance of Polyphemus. He has come within sight of his home. He has done all this only to find his achievement undone at the first relaxation of his mistrustful watchfulness. Small wonder that success on these terms should seem impossible. As the winds sped Odysseus out of sight of Ithaca, "I debated," he says, "whether to leap from my ship and end it all in the sea" (embracing thus the "vile death" of the Kalypso episode), "or whether to bear my misery and remain among the living." He adopts a sort of compromise: "I endured and I remained; *kalypsamenos* I lay in my ship," he puts it, meaning that he had wrapped his head in his cloak. This is the Odysseus who fails to confront Antiphates.

After the discouragement of the Aeolus episode, it is natural that life's difficulties should appear as insuperable as the Laestrygonians; but Odysseus will find the courage to go on. After the Laestrygonian experience his depression is shared by his men. Two days they all lie in weariness and woe on Circe's beach. But against this sea of troubles Odysseus takes arms, a spear and a [59/60] sword. As he once killed a boar, he now kills a stag. This puts heart in Odysseus' men: "dis-kalypsoed" (*ek de kalypsamenoi*) they revive. Odysseus now makes a remarkable speech:

Friends, we don't know where the darkness is, or where the dawn; where the sun that shines for mortals rises, or where it sets. Still let us quickly consider whether any resource can still be found. I for one don't think so.

The point, as Odysseus goes on to suggest, is whether they must indeed make themselves known and ask the inhabitants of the island for their route, perilous though it has proved to confront Polyphemus and Antiphates. In other words, shall they turn their backs on the comparative security of their present oblivion? Characteristically, this wider implication is stressed by a pun—a blatant pun which has been used before, in the Cyclops passage. "Whether any resource can still be found," sounds in Greek almost precisely like "Whether any of us is going to go on being nobody." "I for one don't think so," is Odysseus' comment. They have been "nobody" for some time, in fact ever since Aeolus refused to recognize their claims as human beings. This cannot go on, as the pun implies. The time has come when Odysseus must stand and be recognized.

Without taking account of the pun, critics have interpreted this passage as Odysseus at the end of his human resources, about to apply for divine aid. The moly plant, soon to be granted, becomes for them almost a symbol of grace. This is fair enough in its way. Identity in the Odyssey is in some sense a gift of the gods. But "from the gods who sit in grandeur, grace comes somehow violent."[2] Odysseus doesn't pray for grace; he exacts it, first by killing the stag and then by threatening Circe and forcing her to swear to do him no harm. Hermes, Autolycus' patron, puts him up to the threatening, but it is quite in accord with Odysseus' name and nature anyhow. We remember the oaths exacted from Helen and Kalypso. In the present instance Odysseus remains nobody, a denatured wolf or lion like Circe's other victims, until sword to throat, he makes her recognize him and speak his name. Prior to this, despite the introductory formula "he took my hand and spoke my name," Hermes had not named the hero; he only named his passive aspect, O dystēne "poor wretch." But with the gift of moly, "black at the root, but with a flower like milk," Hermes [60/61] seems to restore the magic of the name of Odysseus. However black its first effects, it will ultimately flower with balm and solace. Though she "struck [him] with her rod and named" him, Circe gives Odysseus no name at all until the hero seems "like one eager to kill her"; once having recognized him as "Odysseus polytropos" however, she uses his name every chance she gets, four times with full titles: "Zeus-sprung son of Laertes, expedient Odysseus." By choosing to live up to his name with Circe, Odysseus restored its magic; he had to in order to get anywhere, and so to be anybody, at all.

For Odysseus to choose to pursue the path of his painful identity as he did on Circe's beach, is to win power over, and recognition from, that ambiguous daughter of Sun, the life-giver, and Ocean, the all-engulfing. It is also to accept pain as the only real basis of meaning in this life or the next. This is the secret of Teiresias.

To achieve the goal of recognition and identity, and to learn the secrets of the abyss, are equally to row upon the sea of trouble. This is the meaning of the apparently witless question, "What ship brought

---

[2] Aeschylus, Agamemnon 182–3 (Lattimore's translation).

you to Ithaca, for I do not think you came on foot," and of Antikleia's first words to her son in the underworld:

My child, how did you come beneath the misty dark, alive as you are? It is hard for the living to get a sight of all this. For in between are great rivers and dreadful streams, first Ocean, which there is no way to cross on foot, if one does not have a well-built ship.

But with Aeolus the question arose, is such sea-faring endurable? To ask this question is "to enquire of Teiresias" (*Teiresiēs* in Homer); for Teiresias' name is the weariness of rowing. *"TEIReto d' andrōn thymos hyp' EIRESIĒS alegeinēs,"* Odysseus says of his crew after Aeolus denied them: *"Worn* was my men's spirit by the woeful *rowing."* To enquire of Teiresias is to ask the meaning of trouble.

This is why Odysseus is not so much interested in what the prophet has to say of the troubled future—"You seek homecoming sweet as honey, noble Odysseus; heaven will make it hard for you"— as he is in recognition, in the meaning of his own painful and pain-producing existence:

Doubtless the gods had all that in store for me. But tell me: I see here the shade of my dead mother; she sits in silence near the blood, [61/62] and has not the strength to look her son in the face or speak to him. Tell me, lord, how might she recognize the man I am?

His mother's recognition contains a blow. It was Odysseus' sweet nature, she says, that killed her. Thus it appears that even in his gentlest aspect, Odysseus gives pain. He is, after all, soft as well as hard. The predatory brooch, dog throttling fawn, pinned on him by Penelope as he left for Troy, is coupled with a second mark of identification, equally important: the shirt which gleamed on his body

like the skin of a dried onion—so gentle it was to the touch, and at the same time bright, like the sun; many were the women who admired it.

Yet Odysseus' soft side can be as painful, or as fatal, as his hardness. The love, not the hate he inspired, killed the dog Argus and wasted Penelope's nights in tears. Antikleia recognized at least part of her son's nature by dying for the love of him.

Agamemnon, dead by no sweet nature, but rather by the treacherous hand of his wife, also recognizes Odysseus; despite Penelope's virtue, he had better not, Agamemnon thinks in contrast to Antikleia, tell his wife everything. Neither of these recognitions, neither the first, evoking the hero's sweetness, nor the second, calling upon his guile, can bring Odysseus much comfort as to the value of life as Trouble. Achilles on the other hand makes it clear that it is something to be alive at all, and furthermore his concern for his son's prowess reminds us that Telemachus too, promises to become a credit to his father. Still, neither simple existence, nor existence continued through a worthy son, is of the essence. Ajax' silence, though eloquently expressive of the power of Odysseus as injurer, is discouraging; but the climax of recognition is reached when Heracles, whose "seeming" is hell's own picture of hostile ferocity, but whose reality "dwells in bliss among the immortals," equates Odysseus to himself:

> One look was enough to tell Heracles who I was, and he greeted me in mournful tones. "Zeus-sprung son of Laertes, expedient Odysseus—unhappy man! So you too are working out some such miserable doom as I was slave to when the sun shone over my head. Son of Zeus though I was, unending troubles came my way. . . . a master far beneath my rank . . . sent me down here to bring away the Hound of Hell. And under the guiding hands of Hermes and bright-eyed [62/63] Athene, I did succeed in capturing him and I dragged him out of Hades realm."

Not just Heracles, but all these people (except Ajax) explicitly recognize Odysseus; still excepting Ajax, all but Antikleia, who appropriately calls him "my child," use Odysseus' full titles. Each sees him differently, and to a greater or less degree, truly. To all of them he means, in one way or another, pain. To Antikleia he is the pain of a lost child; Agamemnon connects him with the pain and betrayal that marriage may bring; Achilles is reminded of the ultimate pain of being dead, Ajax of wounded honor. Heracles sees in him the "unending troubles" of life under the sun. For the secret of life which Odysseus has come to the realms of the dead to discover is the necessity of pain, and its value. The generations of woman ("and each proclaimed her bringing-forth") may be for good or ill, involving Zeus or Poseidon indifferently. Man's fate may seem to be Tantalus' endless craving, never satisfied; or Sisyphus' endless striving, never successful; life's basis may even be Tityus' vultures, a great gnawing in a great belly, as Odysseus several times suggests (7.216–21; 15.343–4; 17.286–9; 18.53–4). Yet Minos continues to pass his judgments, and Orion to pursue his quarry. Heracles has his heavenly, as well as his hellish aspect—and so does Odysseus, "Trouble." Ajax feels only Odysseus' hellish side, but Heracles implies that a life of pain, given and received, snatches something from Death himself. This is the secret of Teiresias, the answer to the weariness of rowing. To know himself as Trouble, and to be so known by others, is the only way for Odysseus to possess his identity.

There is no human identity in other terms than pain. To escape Kalypso, Odysseus needs a ship (4.559–60, 5.16–7), and so must accept the weariness of rowing. To see life in any other way is to live in a dream-world, as the Cyclopes do, and the Phaeacians. To avoid trouble, the Phaeacians withdrew, we are told, from their ancestral conflict with the Cyclopes. The conflict is indeed ancestral, for the Cyclopes are as savage as the Phaeacians are civilized; but both are out of touch with reality. Polyphemus thinks he can act with impunity, "for we are much mightier than the gods," but he succumbs to Trouble in the shape of a clever "weakling" and a skin of wine. The Phaeacians on the contrary trust in their piety. Nausicaa thinks that no one could possibly [63/64] come "bringing enmity, for we are dear to the gods." This she says of Odysseus, Enmity himself. To her, he is either an object of pity or a dream come true:

Doubtless she has picked up some castaway from his ship [she thinks of someone as remarking of her], a foreign man, since there is nobody like that nearby [or "those nearby are nobodies"], or else in answer to her hopes a god, long prayed-for (*polyarētos*), has come down from heaven to keep her all her days.

Eurycleia's "Polyaretus" fits Odysseus in the sense that his return to Ithaca in his hostile might is something to pray for, but he is not what Nausicaa would pray that he be. Nausicaa is victimized by her too trusting love for him, and his visit is ultimately disastrous for her people. The *Odyssey* has its dream-worlds, and, "near to the gods," Scheria is one of them. Its queen, "whose name is Prayed-for" (*Arētē d'onom' estin epōnymon*), suggests her antonym, Odysseus, who, the poem later tells us, might have been Polyaretus, but was not. "So let his name to be Trouble" (*to d'Odysseus onom' estin epōnymon*), Autolycus will say in the nineteenth book.

Odysseus no more can exist in the dream-world of Alcinous and Arete, where woman rules man and rowing is no trouble, than he can with Kalypso. In a world without trouble love must be as little serious as the affair of Ares and Aphrodite. With Nausicaa there is no scope for the relationship which Odysseus describes to her:

There is nothing nobler or more admirable than when two people who see eye to eye keep house as man and wife, *confounding their enemies* and delighting their friends, as they themselves know better than anyone.

How can love be really felt, without pain? Therefore, after arriving exhausted, naked, and unknown on Scheria, Odysseus must somehow so impress the inhabitants that they will send him on his way, neither killing him as enemy nor overmuch befriending him and settling him down with Nausicaa. This he accomplishes primarily by means of his well-advertised Tale of Woe. It is received with mingled horror and fascination. Avid for its miseries the Phaeacians certainly are. This supports our impression that their dream-world, lacking pain, is human life *manqué*. On the [64/65] other hand, after the simile of the woman led into captivity, it is easy to assume Phaeacian feelings of horror at Odysseus' brutal account of the Sack of Ismarus. The recognition accorded the tale is equivocal: "Phaeacians," Arete asks during the intermission, "what do you think of this man, his size and strength and wit?" A dubious answer is implied in Alcinous' polite comment:

O Odysseus, when we look at you we don't find you a bit like a liar and thief, [or "your *Outis* looks to us like a liar and thief"] such as the black earth produces in such far-flung numbers—thieves piling lie on lie, and where they get them all from nobody knows; your words are charming, there is good sense in them, and you tell your story as skillfully as a bard, the grim sufferings of yourself and all the Argives.

After all Odysseus has shown himself to be a pirate, and it is worth noting that Alcinous' remarks occur half-way through the story of the underworld, before the value of pain is established. But for the Phaeacians this is never established. Their rowing is without drudgery, for all their sea-faring. At the end of the tale Alcinous will tell the guest he once thought of as a son-in-law that he is sure he will never come back. One doesn't quite know whether the Phaeacians are bestowing on Odysseus more wealth than he won at Troy in recognition of his exploits, or as an invitation to leave the country; for it was Odysseus' stated willingness to stay a year that brought forth Alcinous' remarks about liars and thieves. In Odysseus the Phaeacians enjoy Trouble vicariously, but ultimately dismiss him. We may be pretty sure that, for their "painless escorting of strangers," Poseidon's threat to "surround (*amphikalypsai*) their city with mountains" will come off. Just as he turned their ship to stone, he will bar them from the sea, and therefore from any chance of future identity. The price of no trouble is oblivion.

Teiresias implies three modes of pain: first, pain administered, like the slaying of the boar and stag, or the blinding of Polyphemus. Odysseus, Teiresias predicts, will kill the suitors. Second, there is the pain of the resisted impulse. Odysseus must restrain his predatory impulses when he comes upon the cattle of the Sun. Third, to plant the oar, the symbol of the weariness of rowing, among those "who do not know the sea, nor eat their food mixed with salt, nor know of red-prowed ships, nor balanced oars, which [65/66] are a vessel's wings" is to introduce the idea of trouble to those who, like the Phaeacians, are not sufficiently aware of it. In establishing his identity, Odysseus must use these three modes of pain.

It is sufficiently clear how administering pain by killing the suitors and threatening their kinsmen with annihilation serves to establish Odysseus in Ithaca. The second mode is subtler. It would seem a denial of Odysseus' name for him to boggle at a little cattle-rustling. That he does so leads some to suppose that his adventures are intended to purge him of the brutalizing effects of the Trojan campaign and bring him home readjusted to civilian life. But the temptation of the cattle of the Sun is more like the temptation of the Lotos than like the Sack of Ismarus. It is a temptation not to crime but to oblivion. To fall for it is the typical weakness of the "innocent" crew, as the proem suggests. Faced with the Planctae, the Reefs of Hard Knocks, they drop their oars. Knowing the mortal danger in eating the Sun's cattle, they do not know it thoroughly enough to forego the immediate satisfaction of eating when they are hungry. Forgetful of homecoming and identity itself, they eat. Of all that band only Odysseus can resist such impulses and hang on interminably, as he does clinging to the fig tree above Charybdis, refusing to drop and be comfortably engulfed.

Odysseus is a master of the delayed response, of the long way round, of the resisted impulse. That is the reason he is able to keep his identity intact. It is courting oblivion to rush blindly into love, as Nausicaa did, and as Penelope, even when reunited with her husband, did not. In Circe's bed, Odysseus would have become just another denatured wolf or lion, if he had not first with a show of hostility made sure of his integrity. As in love, so with eating. Man is a predatory animal; to eat he must kill; but he must know what he is doing. He must not, like the crew and the suitors, take life as a table spread before him, insufficiently aware of the presence of enemies.

He must not even take life as a song, though the episode of the Sirens suggests that this is the most irresistible of impulses. The Phaeacians are certainly not proof against it. Alcinous may think that the meaning of life's pain is that

the gods were responsible for that, weaving catastrophe into the pattern of events to make a song for future generations,[66/67]

but pain must be experienced, not just enjoyed as after-dinner entertainment. Therefore the Phaeacians are victimized by Odysseus' Tale of Woe. Odysseus on the other hand is proof against the Sirens and their singing of "all things that happen on this fruitful earth," just as he is against the Lotos and against Circe. He is steadfast in enduring Teiresias' second mode of pain, the pain of the resisted impulse.

"The steadfast," says a priest in *Murder in the Cathedral*, "can manipulate the greed and lust of others, the feeble is devoured by his own." This leads us from the second mode of pain to the third—introducing the idea of trouble to those insufficiently aware of it. Odysseus in his steadfastness knows the pain of the thirst for life, the danger it leads to, and the trouble involved in successfully gratifying it. He knows it so well ("he saw the cities of many men, and knew their mind"), that he can use this knowledge in manipulating others, for the purpose of getting himself recognized as Trouble. One picture of this is Odysseus in the underworld, sword in hand, controlling the access of the ghosts to the blood. Manipulating the Phaeacians chiefly through their itching ears, he introduces himself to them as Trouble, and wins survival and homecoming. In the second half of the poem, using his lying tales, his wife, and the good things of his house as bait, he maneuvers the upholders and the defilers of his household alike into a position where, bow in hand and arrow on string, like Heracles in the underworld, he can make himself really felt.

For Odysseus to establish his identity at home, manipulation is necessary, manipulation even of those who favor him. It is difficult to get people to accept pain. Even the suitors do not dispute that he was a good king; unfortunately this is not enough to maintain his position in Ithaca. He must get both his pleasant and his hostile aspect recognized at the same time. When they finally are, near the end of the last book, this is signalized by the curious salutation of Dolius, the last to join forces with him: *oule te kai mala chaire,* he says, "hail and rejoice!" But *oule* is an exceedingly rare word, and its auditory suggestions of *oulos* "baneful," and *oulē,* the famous scar, will be felt— something like "Bane and Weal!" For the scar which the boar gave him is in particular the mark of Odysseus as Trouble. Antikleia ("Opposed-to-fame"), in her recognition of her son in the underworld, [67/68] did not seem to understand the scar's full meaning, but it is easy for Eurycleia ("Far-fame") to accept it. After touching the scar as she washed his feet,

joy and pain seized upon Eurycleia at the same time; her eyes filled with tears, and the voice caught in her throat. Touching his chin she said to Odysseus: "Surely you are Odysseus, dear child—and I didn't know my master until I had felt all of him!"

Eurycleia knows both aspects. It is she who has to be restrained from howling in triumph over the dead suitors. Telemachus is not much of a problem either. "I am no god;" Odysseus says, "Why do you think I am an immortal? No, I am your father, for whom you groan and suffer so much pain, accepting the insults of your fellows." Telemachus' difficulty is to determine whether Trouble is a miserable wretch in filthy rags or a very god for splendor. We have met this ambiguity before in the double nature of Heracles.

Penelope's recognition is harder to win. She knows Odysseus' soft garment, and her own hands pinned on him the badge of the dog and fawn; but the predatory side of him she cannot accept. Troy is to her not a great and necessary exploit, but something he merely "went to see," and for this she cannot forgive him. To her Troy is not a source of renown, but "Evil Ilium, not to be named." If Odysseus' manipulation, or his knowledge of the mind of man ever fails, it is with her. In their false-recognition scene, his riddle-name is *Aithōn,* the "blaze" which melts her (19.204-9) but which she cannot face (19.478). In spite of all the help her disguised husband can give her, she reacts to her dream of the eagle, Odysseus, killing her geese, the suitors, not by preparing for his "return," but by deciding, at last, to give him up for good. After the suitors are dead, and Odysseus has had his bath, she still holds out. Even the appeal to her desire as a woman, effective though it was with Kalypso, Nausicaa, and Circe, doesn't work; Odysseus, it appears, will have to sleep alone. In exasperation he asks who moved his bed. In spite of all he has done to make permanent their marriage and the symbol of it, he still cannot tell, he admits, "whether it still stands or whether by now someone has moved it elsewhere, and cut through the trunk of the olive." By this bed and by this exaspera- tion she [68/69] knows him; flinging her arms around his neck, "Odys- seus, don't scold me," she cries, giving him his true name at last. Later, she will accept trouble in more detail. The "immeasurable toil" still to come, none other than the planting of Teiresias' oar, she elects to hear of immediately, though in the first book, after ten years, she could not bear to hear the bard singing of the return from Troy. In the end she takes delight in hearing "all the woes Zeus-sprung Odysseus inflicted on others, and all he himself toiled and suffered." She has accepted the meaning of the name of Odysseus.

Teiresias implied that to win identity one must administer pain, resist all impulses to ignore it, and plant the idea of it in the minds of others. Hence the curious behaviour of the hero in making himself known to Laertes. Checking his own tears and resisting the impulse to "kiss his father and embrace him, and tell him all, how he had come and was back at home," Odysseus instead teases the suffering old man with the pain of the loss of his son. This is the pain which killed Antikleia, but it now serves to make clear to Laertes and Odysseus what they mean to each other.

Laertes knows Odysseus by his scar, but also by some fruit trees, given to Odysseus as a boy, which the old man is still tending for him. There is something obviously fruitful in the pain of this relation- ship between father and son, and the sense of the boar-hunt exploit is there too, especially when later the old man delights to see "son and grandson vying in prowess" in the fight with the suitors' kinsmen. The fruitfulness of trouble has been hinted all along, particularly by the image of the olive. There is the double olive thicket which shelters the hero, naked and alone on Scheria; the green olive stake which puts out Polyphemus' eye; and notably the great olive trunk which makes one corner of Odysseus' bed. The recurrent phrase, *kaka phyteuein* "to plant evils," points to the same fruitfulness. Therefore we can be sure that the life of pain contemplated in the *Odyssey* is fruitful, not sa- distic. The ultimate object is recognition and the sense of one's own existence, not the pain itself. The pain necessary to win recognition may be as slight as the show of anger to Penelope, or as great as the blinding of Polyphemus, but in some degree pain will be necessary. Nothing less than the death of 108 suitors (to say nothing of the faith- less maids), and the readiness to kill the [69/70] suitors' kinsmen, will get Odysseus recognized in Ithaca. Once recognition is achieved, how- ever, pain is pointless. At the very end of the poem, Odysseus "swoop- ing like an eagle" on the fleeing ranks of the suitors' adherents, "might have killed them all." Then, "Zeus-sprung son of Laertes, expedient Odysseus, stop!" Athene cries, ". . . lest Zeus be angry at you." The daughter of Zeus herself, as Circe and others have done before her, now hails Odysseus with the rolling epithets of his full titles. Killing beyond the point of this recognition would anger Zeus, would violate the nature of things. But has Zeus not been angry all along at the hero "who receive so many buffets, once he had sacked the sacred citadel of Troy?" No. The universe is full of hostility, it includes Poseidon, but it is not ultimately hostile. Zeus has been showing Odysseus not anger, but a terrible fondness, to echo Athene's words quoted early in this paper.

It is thus that the *Odyssey* solves the problem of evil, which it raised at line 62 of the first book. "Excessive suffering," says Zeus, or words to that effect, "is due to folly." "So it is," replies Athene; "but what about Odysseus? Why do you odysseus him so, Zeus?" It is a good question; Zeus admits that Odysseus is the wisest of mankind; yet he permits Poseidon to persecute him. It is a good question, and it contains its own answer. In exposing Odysseus to Poseidon, in allowing him to do and suffer, Zeus is odysseusing Odysseus, giving him his identity. In accepting the implications of his name, Trouble, Odysseus establishes his identity in harmony with the nature of things. In the ultimate sense he is "Zeus-sprung," one whose existence is rooted in life itself. [70]

The Epic of Moral Regeneration

GEORGE DE F. LORD

MR. ELIOT'S RECENT ARTICLE, "VERGIL AND THE WESTERN WORLD" (*Sewanee Review*, Winter, 1953), has redefined for us the Christian-like qualities of the *Aeneid* and its hero. Virgil is seen as a sort of prophet, perhaps unconsciously inspired by Judaic thought, who anticipated some of the values of the Christian world. The *pietas* of Aeneas requires his acceptance, at the cost of his personal feelings, of a mission on which a future civilization depends, and this acceptance requires the subjection of his own will with all humility to the will of the gods. Aeneas's mission is everything, its fulfillment ordained by destiny, and yet destiny does not relieve him of moral responsibility for its fulfillment. Thus Virgil fills "a significant, a unique place, at the end of the pre-Christian and at the beginning of the Christian world."

George de F. Lord, "The *Odyssey* and the Western World," *The Sewanee Review*, LXII (Summer 1954), 406–427. Reprinted by permission of the author and the publisher. Copyright by the University of the South, Sewanee, Tennessee.

Mr. Eliot's description of the unique place which Virgil fills in the evolution of Western culture seems to me invaluable for a proper understanding of the *Aeneid*. But the occasional comments that he makes on the *Odyssey* in the course of defining the spiritual qualities of the *Aeneid* give, I think, a wrong impression of Homer's poem. His discussion of Aeneas as "an analogue and foreshadow of Christian humility" is brilliant in itself, but when he tries to show the superiority of Virgil's hero to Homer's heroes he misconceives or underestimates the character of Odysseus and the part it must have played, consciously or not, in the Roman poet's conception of Aeneas. The *Odyssey* presents through the experiences of its hero the birth of personal and social ideals which are remarkably close to those of the Christian tradition and repudiates the old code of the heroic warriors at Troy as resolutely as does the *Aeneid*. In the *Odyssey* we can witness the origin and [406/407] evolution of values which made the Roman ideal possible. Aeneas could not have been without Odysseus, and the drama of Odysseus lies in his struggle out of chaos toward an order which we can still respect. The conflict between Aeneas and Turnus in the final books of the *Aeneid* epitomizes the victory of the new hero, the builder of a civilization, over the old—one might say obsolete—warrior hero with his narrow tribal loyalties, his jealous personal honor, and his fierce passions, who is, whatever his motives, the foe of reason, order and civilization. Virgil, in Mr. W. F. Jackson Knight's words, "made the contrast between right reason and the dark instinct, as of Turnus devil-possessed, secure, and shewed the pitilessness, and the frightful havoc, of mass impulse, knowing it strangely well." (*Roman Vergil*, p. 135) Like Achilles, possessed with *ate*, Turnus fights for glory, while Aeneas fights for a future. Aeneas can only assume the burden of his great mission when he has renounced personal glory and desperate courage, which are the chief virtues of the old warriors of the *Iliad*. His victory over Turnus at the end of the poem is only possible because of his victory over the Turnus in himself at the beginning of the poem.

The *Odyssey* mediates between these two concepts of the hero—the old and the new. Odysseus grows in the course of his experiences from the shrewd "sacker of cities" to the wise restorer of Ithaca. His success at the end of the poem is not accidental, but founded just as surely as Aeneas's on the subjection of his angry or amorous passions to reason, on his recognition and acceptance of his divine mission, and on harmonizing his own will with the divine will. The gods of the *Iliad* may be, as Mr. Eliot claims, "as irresponsible, as much a prey to their passions, as devoid of public spirit and the sense of fair play, as the heroes," but the gods of the *Odyssey* are just and responsible, and the ideal of the poem is "a more civilized world of dignity, reason and order" like that of the *Aeneid*. Odysseus, admittedly, has a less impressive and consequential mission than Aeneas's. He is not destined [407/408] to found a world which history shows is our own. But cannot rocky Ithaca be a type of that world? And cannot Odysseus be thought of as having demonstrated in the restoration of his little country virtues which anticipate Aeneas's as a founding father?

The distinction which Mr. Eliot draws between Aeneas and Odysseus in the following passage in my opinion badly misrepresents the meaning of the *Odyssey*. If Odysseus is the irresponsible and lucky hero he describes, the *Odyssey* is of little interest to us except as an adventure story:

Aeneas is the antithesis, in important respects, of either Achilles or Odysseus. In so far as he is heroic, he is heroic as the original Displaced Person, the fugitive from a ruined city and an obliterated society, of which the few other survivors except his own band languish as slaves of the Greeks. He was not to have, like Ulysses, marvellous and exciting adventures with such occasional erotic episodes as left no canker on the conscience of the wayfarer. He was not to return at last to the remembered hearth-fire, to find an exemplary wife awaiting him, to be reunited to his son, his dog and his servants.

Since Mr. Eliot is only incidentally concerned with the *Odyssey*, and since his comment on Aeneas is so perceptive, the whole matter could well be ignored except for the fact that this misreading of the *Odyssey* is widely held and, I am convinced, blocks the way to one's full understanding and enjoyment of the poem.

Three or four years ago, in the course of studying Chapman's translation of the *Odyssey*, I found a remarkable and apparently little-known book which helped me to understand Chapman's approach while it illuminated the central themes of Homer's poem more fully and convincingly than anything else on the subject I have encountered. Denton J. Snider's *Homer's Odyssey: a Commentary*, published in 1895, is a brilliant demonstration of the spiritual evolution of Odysseus, the moral character of [408/409] his universe, and the pre-eminence of freedom and moral responsibility throughout the poem:

The theme . . . deals with the wise man, who, through his intelligence, was able to take Troy, but who has now another and greater problem—the return out of the grand estrangement caused by the Trojan expedition. Spiritual restoration is the key-note of the *Odyssey*, as it is that of all the great Books of Literature. (pp. 7–8)

Much of what I have to say about the *Odyssey* in the following pages is built upon or developed out of Snider's insights, and I hope that this discussion will send readers on to a unique work of Homeric criticism.

The history of criticism of the *Odyssey* from Hellenic times to the present reveals two principal and unreconciled positions. The allegorical interpreters such as Heraclitus[1], Natalis Comes and Roger Ascham

---

[1] Author of *Allegoriae Homericae*, which apparently belongs to the Age of Augustus. Reprinted in Leipzig (1910) as *Heracliti Quaestiones Homericae*.

were impelled to defend the poem on ethical grounds by representing Odysseus as a *persona* of reason, virtue, and endurance triumphing over enticements to lust, luxury, and greed. The allegorists concentrated on those adventures most susceptible of their sort of interpretation—especially the hero's encounter with Circe or with the Sirens. The fabulous experiences which Odysseus recounts in books nine to twelve were treated as if they were the whole poem, and those episodes in which the hero was least successful in dealing with temptations or obstacles to his return were either neglected or forced quite arbitrarily to reflect the preconceptions of the interpreters. In most of the allegorical accounts one finds a monotonous determination to demonstrate Odysseus' moral perfection on every occasion. Comes' popular compendium of mythology is typical of them all:

Who then is Ulysses, if not Wisdom, which intrepidly passes through every danger unconquered? And who are Ulysses' companions but the passions of our hearts? [409/410]

The allegorists' interest is centered on the *Odyssey* as a moral lesson, and the poem is ignored. They tended to find a simple identification of characters and objects with moral abstractions like wisdom, temperance, lust, and passion. The other school, which has prevailed in the last two hundred years, is "realistic" in its approach and refuses to see any ethical significance at all in Odysseus' career. The realists insist on the primitive nature of Homer's characters. Thomas Blackwell was among the first to propose the historical *apologia*, still current, that although Odysseus was a pirate, piracy was considered respectable in those benighted days: "living by Plunder gave a reputation for Spirit and Bravery." This view supposes that whatever the hero does is endorsed by the poet, just as the allegorical view does. Mr. Eliot's own strictures belong to this tradition, and he would, I suppose, approve of the position taken by Mr. C. S. Lewis:

There is no pretence, indeed no possibility of pretending, that the world, or even Greece, would have been much altered if Odysseus had never got home at all. The poem is an adventure story. As far as greatness of subject goes, it is much closer to *Tom Jones* or *Ivanhoe* than to the *Aeneid* or the *Gierusalemme Liberata*. (*A Preface to Paradise Lost*, p. 26)

In the adventure story what happens to the hero is accidental, and the action is largely external. The interest lies in a series of hair-breadth escapes brought about by the hero's cleverness, stamina, and good luck. The *Odyssey* unquestionably provides this sort of interest, but that is not all.

The conception of the *Odyssey* as an adventure story is, I am convinced, as great an obstacle to understanding it as to see it simply as moral allegory. The first view removes it from serious consideration as one of the world's greatest poems; the second ignores its status as a poem altogether. A third view is required that will recognize the *Odyssey's* great spiritual significance at [410/411] the same time that it recognizes Odysseus as a complex and typically human character. Odysseus' vicissitudes are intimately related to his varying attitudes toward himself, his fellow man, and his gods. Odysseus' "mission" is the greatest known to man—to discover himself and his world and to act effectively in accordance with these discoveries. Such a view as this sees the goal of his return as more than a geographical one and recognizes both the established moral order of the *Odyssey's* universe and the hero's gradual discovery of that order through suffering and error. If the *Odyssey* were as Heraclitus or Comes or Lewis or Eliot represented it, the poem would not have the enduring hold on men's spirits that it has. A morally perfect hero excites no more sympathy than one whose adventures are amoral and therefore accidental and meaningless.

Primary Epic, in Mr. Lewis's terms, is distinguished from Secondary Epic by the absence of "the large national or cosmic subject of super-personal interest." "That kind of greatness," he continues, "arises only when some event can be held to effect a profound and more or less permanent change in the history of the world, as the founding of Rome did, or still more, the fall of man." (*A Preface to Paradise Lost*, p. 28) This distinction as to kinds is undoubtedly a valid one. But the historical consequence of the subject is relatively unimportant if the theme of the epic is typical and universal. Rocky Ithaca may be the type of Rome and Odysseus the prototype of Aeneas. The *Odyssey* has a great design, despite Mr. Lewis, and it cannot be described by "the mere endless up and down, the constant aimless alternations of glory and misery, which make up the terrible phenomenon called a Heroic Age," any more than it can by Mr. Eliot's conception of it as an alternation of marvellous and erotic adventures that leave the hero essentially unchanged.

The chief obstacle to understanding this revolutionary and evolutionary character of the *Odyssey* is the spareness of direct comment or abstract moral statement in the poem. Aeneas's [411/412] destiny is stated in the invocation, and his moral struggles are unmistakably presented in the encounter with Dido and the intervention of the gods, in his foolhardy last-ditch stand at Troy and the admonitory or prophetic visions of Hector and Iulus, and in the similes which compare him and his companions in their rage to ravening wolves and serpents. (See II, 370ff.) The *Odyssey* never explicitly associates the hero's return with his moral and spiritual stature in the way that the *Aeneid* identifies the founding of Rome with Aeneas's *pietas*. Homer, furthermore, externalizes psychological and emotional developments in action. Odysseus is not introspective or reflective in the way that Aeneas is.

The best way I know to illustrate the ideas I have been discussing is to focus on one of the great turning-points in Odysseus' career—his

experiences from the time of leaving Calypso in book five to the beginning of his narrative to the Phaeacians in book nine. This passage introduces the hero after our curiosity about him has been wrought to the
highest pitch in the four books of the Telemachia, and it marks his
escape from the fabulous world in which he has wandered for ten years
since leaving Troy into what we may call the real world. This crisis in
Odysseus' life is announced by a council of the gods in which Zeus
gives orders that the hero is to be released from the island of Calypso
and permitted to sail for home. The divine decision has its counterpart
in Odysseus' own choice. Calypso offers him immortal life with her,
and he rejects the offer in favor of mortal life with Penelope:

Great goddess, do not be angry with me for this. I know myself that wise
Penelope cannot compare with you in beauty or figure, for she is mortal, you
immortal and unaging. Nonetheless, day after day, I long to reach home and
see the day of my return. And if some god strikes me on the wine-dark sea,
I will take it, for I have a heart inured to affliction. In days gone by I have
suffered and toiled greatly in the sea and in war: let this come too. (V, 215–
24) [412/413]

The divine machinery which sets Odysseus free through the
agency of Hermes, as has often been noted, can stand for, or, perhaps
more accurately, is accompanied by, the hero's effective resolution to
accept his human lot and leave Calypso's paradise. For many years he
has longed to depart, yet the intervention of the gods at this moment is
not simply a heavenly rescue party, a Euripidean *deus ex machina*.
The elementary resources needed to build and equip the raft have been
available on Calypso's island all the seven years Odysseus has been
there. What he lacked for a time was the courage to commit himself
once more on the deeps to the strenuous dangers attendant upon such
a journey, a journey which, Zeus specifices, must be made "with guidance neither of mortal men nor of gods."

The voyage to Phaeacia turns out to be the hardest of all. Odysseus' last encounter with the wrath of Poseidon literally beats him to
his knees and drives him once and for all out of the attitude of cocky
self-sufficiency which characterized him earlier. The epithet *polutropos*
—shifty and resourceful—does not carry unqualified approval, especially
when it applies to Odysseus' rugged individualism. The extremities
Odysseus suffers after his raft is wrecked compel him to turn to the
gods for help. The stages by which he is forced to this final resort
dramatize the hero's characteristic reluctance to depend on anyone but
himself. When the sea nymph Ino Leucothea out of pity offers him a
miraculous veil, he suspects that "one of the immortals is once again
weaving a snare for me in bidding me to leave my raft," and determines to cling to the wreckage as long as he can. He still thinks of the
gods' hostility as purely arbitrary. A tremendous wave finally forces
him to use the veil. But when, after two days and nights in the sea, he

comes in sight of the Phaeacian shore, there is nothing but fatal reefs and cliffs beaten by a violent surf. When he tries to cling to rocks he is torn away by the waves and nearly drowned. At last he finds a river-mouth with a shelving beach and makes a spontaneous prayer to the river-god in the [413/414] name of wanderers and suppliants, who are all sacred to Zeus. At this the river's current is calmed, Odysseus wades ashore, sinks down among the reeds and kisses the earth.

From this moment Odysseus encounters only human foes and human temptations. There are no more one-eyed giants or monstrous sea-goddesses or sorceresses who can turn men into pigs. Nor are there any further conflicts with nature—storms, shipwrecks, whirlpools, or threatening starvation. When he falls asleep in the olive-grove by the Phaeacian shore, the wrath of Poseidon is done with Odysseus, and he awakes into a world of purely human values. The change is marked by a striking simile at the very end of book five, when Odysseus sees the grove and feels an impulse of joy and relief:

he lay down in the midst and heaped over him the fallen leaves. And as a man hides a brand beneath the dark embers in an outlying farm, a man who has no neighbors, and so saves the seed of fire that he may not have to kindle it at some other source, so Odysseus covered himself with leaves. And Athene shed sleep on his eyes that it might cover his lids and quickly free him from toilsome weariness. (V, 487–93)

The simile represents the hero's loneliness, exhaustion, and sense of relief as well as his striking capacity for self-preservation in any fatigue or danger. It suggests further than this that here is the essential Odysseus, the very spark of his spirit which no hardships have been able to quench. The realistic detail of the anxious farmer on his lonely farm emphasizes at this stage of the hero's experience the emergence of realistic human adventures.

The phase of supernatural dangers and of the hostility of physical nature which comes between the departure of Odysseus from Troy and his arrival in Phaeacia divides two vastly different human worlds: that of the Trojan war dominated by the heroic code of men and that of family and community life whose values are centered in several extraordinary women—Arete, Nausicaa, [414/415] Penelope. The greatest importance of these women in the *Odyssey* has often been discussed. I need not refer the reader to Samuel Butler's facetious thesis that the *Odyssey* must have been written by a woman or to Bentley's remark that the *Iliad* was written for men and the *Odyssey* for women. It can be shown, I think, that the domestic and social values embodied in or emanating from these women act as a critique of the code of the male warrior just as much as the actions of Turnus or Nisus or Euryalus or of Aeneas on the night that Troy fell reveal Virgil's view of the inadequacy of the heroic code. The behavior of warriors is subjected to a searching and critical scrutiny in the *Odyssey*, although not by much direct comment. Its weaknesses are dramatized in Homer's characteristically subtle fashion. It is extremely significant, I think, that Odysseus enters the world of natural and supernatural disasters after committing an act of violence that becomes, because of the formulaic manner in which it is related, the typical crime of the *Odyssey*. In all his pseudo-autobiographies in the last books of the poem, Odysseus describes his troubles as having originated with a piratical raid against unwary townsmen in which the men were slain, the women and children taken as slaves, and a quantity of plunder carried off. In each case the leader is unable to control his men, who become drunken and careless, and an unexpected counterattack takes its toll of the invaders.

Odysseus' unprovoked attack on the town of Ismarus following his departure from ruined Troy is typical of the acts which cast him out of the world of men, if we except his followers, for ten years. This aggression, which, I am told, Grotius cites as the earliest recorded violation of international justice, is not mitigated in Homer by any mention of the Cicones' alliance with the Trojans. Odysseus relates it in laconic fashion at the beginning of book nine:

From Ilios the wind bore me to the Cicones, to Ismarus. I sacked the city and slew the men, and from the city we took their wives and a store of treasure and divided them among [415/416] us, so that as far as lay in me no man might go defrauded of an equal share. Then I gave orders that we should flee with all speed, but my men, in their folly, did not listen. (IX, 39–44)

Odysseus loses six men from each ship to the counter-attacking Cicones and is then driven into a world of fantastic terrors, which he describes for four books, by a twelve day's storm. He raises land at the Lotus-Eaters', but it is ten years before he sees a human being again, except for his own companions. In his twelve fabulous adventures with monsters, nymphs, demigods, sorceresses, and ghosts he sometimes encounters, as Snider argues, the monstrous personifications of inhuman facets of his own nature, like Polyphemus and the Laestrygonians. In one way or another all these encounters jeopardize his human individuality, or at least that of his followers. His men who eat the lotus lose all memory of home, as he himself does when he hears the Siren's song:

Whosoever in ignorance draws near them and hears the Sirens' voices never returns to have his wife and little children stand at his side rejoicing; but the Sirens beguile him with their clear-toned song as they sit in a meadow, with all about them a great heap of bones of mouldering men, and round the bones the skin shrivelling. (XII, 41–46)

Circe transforms men into pigs who yet retain the same minds they had before. (Is this satirical?) Calypso promises to make him immortal and ageless if he will only live with her forever. But after seven years the delights of this naturalistic paradise have palled to the extent that he is willing to endure any hardship in order to reach home and Penelope. Odysseus' recognition at this point that his innermost identity is inseparably bound up with his home and wife is the key to his escape from the fantastic world, just as his unprovoked attack on society, as represented by Ismarus, opened the door to his entrance into it. [416/417]

The subject of the *Odyssey* is the return of Odysseus to his home and his reunion with his family. Such a subject, as Chapman remarks in his preface, may seem "jejune and fruitless enough." If, however, the hero can return home and rejoin his family only in the course of discovering his proper relation to the gods and to his fellow men, no greater subject could be imagined, for the familiar and common situations in which these discoveries are made are an earnest that the pursuit of *these* heroic ideals is the right and duty of all men and not the privilege of any particular caste.

Mr. L. A. Post, in his recent book *From Homer to Menander*, makes this point in general terms when he speaks of "new resources or a new attitude in himself" which Odysseus must find "before he can win happiness." But I cannot agree with Mr. Post when he says that after many years with Calypso on her island Odysseus "has nothing new to learn. He must merely display his qualities of craft and courage and restraint." It is true that Odysseus behaves with much more self-control in the second half of the poem. The ordeals he undergoes as a beggar appealing to the hospitality of his wife's suitors—the blows and insults he must suffer without answering their violence—require a self-mastery that he has not shown before. Epictetus and Plutarch found in Odysseus aspects of the Stoic. But Homer's interest in his hero extend far beyond the Stoical qualities of endurance and restraint to pursue the dynamic origins of these and other moral virtues in the human spirit.

The chief importance of the Phaeacian experience lies in its dramatizing a new attitude in Odysseus. His emergence from the supernatural world of Lotus Eaters, Cyclopes, Circe, and Calypso has involved, as I have shown, a recognition of the conditions of being human: mortality, limited power and wisdom, and the need for divine assistance. Odysseus' ready acceptance by Alcinous, Arete, and Nausicaa depends on his acceptance of their own social, religious, and political ideal. Phaeacia has all the [417/418] earmarks of an ideal civilization with just enough defects to make the whole picture plausible. The Phaeacians are conspicuously peace-loving. They do not use warfare and migrated long ago from a land beset by the godless Cyclopes to this remote place. The gods, they say, are in the habit of visiting them without disguise. They are charitable to strangers. They excel in the arts of peace—in shipbuilding, sailing, spinning and weaving, and so forth. The queen Arete is the real ruler of the kingdom and settles the disputes of her subjects to the invariable satisfaction of both parties. Odysseus kneels to her for permission to sail for Ithaca and by this action pays tribute to the domestic ideals which Arete stands for. Arete is, perhaps, almost impossibly wise and competent, but Nausicaa stands in the foreground as an extraordinarily real young girl. As Mr. Post says, "It is here that the climax of temptation comes for Odysseus. It is characteristic of Homer to make his good woman more tempting than any bad woman could be."

For Odysseus Nausicaa serves as an enchanting vision of the new ideal, just as fading Helen, with her ornamental distaff and her anodynes, provided Telemachus with a *fin de siècle* vision of the heroic past. Nausicaa appeals to Odysseus by virtue of qualities which make his surrender to her impossible: by her hospitality and charity and courage and deep loyalty to the civilized institutions to which he is now dedicated. In her consuming interest in marriage and in family and household affairs he may well see an image of his own wife. Thus he treats her with unwonted tact and restraint. His manner is a judicious mixture of the gallant and the paternal. With the immortal Circe and Calypso Odysseus had no age, with Nausicaa he is a mature man. Much of the humor in their encounter stems from this discrepancy of ages which attracts them to each other and yet helps to keep them apart. His famous words on their first meeting, when he emerges so delightfully from the underbrush naked and [418/419] holding an olive-branch modestly before him, set the tone of the whole episode:

Show me the city and give me some rag to throw about me. . . . For thyself, may the gods grant thee all thy heart desires—a husband and a home and oneness of heart—great gifts. For nothing is finer than when husband and wife live in one house in one accord, a great grief to their foes and a joy to their friends. But they themselves know this best. (VI, 178–85)

This note is struck again in that exquisite farewell interlude in which Odysseus gently deflects Nausicaa's growing love for him by pretending not to understand her Desdemona-like hints:

Now when the maids had bathed him and rubbed him with oil and had cast a fine cloak and tunic about him, he came from the bath and went to join the men at their wine. Nausicaa, gifted with beauty by the gods, stood by the door-post of the hall and watched Odysseus with wonder and spoke to him with winged words:

"Farewell, stranger, and hereafter even in thine own native land remember me, for to me thou owest thy life."

Then the wily Odysseus answered her:

"Nausicaa, daughter of great-hearted Alcinous, may Zeus, the loud-thundering lord of Hera grant that I reach my home and see the day of my return. Then I will pray to thee as a god all my days, for thou, maiden, hast given me life." (VIII, 454–68)

If Odysseus' rejection of Calypso's offer of immortality was a rejection of a sort of eternal and monotonous existence approximating death, the endless cycle of instinctive gratifications which left the spirit unsatisfied, his rejection of Nausicaa represents, paradoxically enough, his acceptance of a way of life which is more than mere existence. He now sees his own identity bound up with Penelope's. Away from home he is not himself.

I do not think it is doing violence to this crucial phase of the [419/ 420] *Odyssey* to see in the Phaeacian visit a sort of spiritual and ideological revolution in the hero. This involves his reorientation in regard to the dominant values of the poem—the domestic and social values of which I have been speaking. Nor do I think it extravagant to insist that these values which center on the family, on the pre-eminent virtue of hospitality, and on the just administration of the state are shown throughout the poem as superior to what might be loosely designated as the heroic values of the *Iliad*. (In saying this I do not mean to imply that Homer gives unqualified assent to these values in the *Iliad*.) What threatens these domestic values is the old ideal of military glory and honor as man's noblest goal—the individualistic quest for eternal fame in battle. The *Odyssey* never disdains true honor as such, and in the slaughter of the suitors it recognizes that the most extreme punitive measures may sometimes be needed to protect society, but it submits what passes for honor to a searching inspection and shows that heroic deeds are often motivated by greed, accomplished with terror, and indistinguishable from piracy. In this poem Odysseus' career evolves from one set of values toward the other, from the narrow concepts of heroic honor to the broader concepts of the civilized man in a postwar world. Odysseus is not given to introspection, and his change of view is presented in a series of episodes that are emblematic of inner developments. Of these there are three main kinds: (1) a divine visitation; (2) an unexpected emotional response; and (3) a speech in which the hero analyzes his experiences in a way that lets us see implications of which he is only partly aware.

After his first meeting with Nausicaa on the shores of Phaeacia Athene transforms Odysseus, we are told, into a handsome man with hyacinthine locks. He has just bathed in the stream where Nausicaa and her maids have been doing the washing to rinse away "the scurf of the unresting sea." This bath is a spiritual as well as physical cleansing, for [420/421]

Athene the daughter of Zeus made him taller to look upon and mightier, and from his head she made the locks flow like hyacinth flowers. Just as when a smith overlays silver with gold, a cunning workman whom Hephaestus and Athene have taught all manner of craft, and his work is full of grace, even so the goddess shed grace upon his head and shoulders. Then he went apart and sat down on the shore gleaming with beauty and grace . . . (VI, 229–35)

The passage can of course be interpreted to some extent in purely naturalistic and psychological terms: Odysseus looks better after a bath and makes more of an impression on Nausicaa when duly washed and combed than did the uncouth and worn figure who emerged from the underbrush. But the fact that Athene is said to work this transformation is more than a mere *façon de parler*, for this is the first time, chronologically speaking, that she has had anything directly to do with her protégé in more than nine years. This miraculous change occurs at one other critical point in the poem, furthermore, and that is when Odysseus, having accomplished the destruction of the suitors and the purification of his halls, is transfigured before his meeting with Penelope. Both examples mark a rapprochement of the hero and his patroness, and the one under discussion signalizes Odysseus' reunion with all that Athene represents. It is important in this connection that Homer stresses Athene's role as patroness of domestic arts—that Arete and Penelope, for example, are said to be under her peculiar protection: "for Athene had given to them above all others skill in fair handiwork and an understanding heart." (VII, 110–11) It is even more important that the goddess of wisdom, whom the hero offended at Troy, gives at this point a particular mark of her favor.

Secondly, the fact that Homer has chosen Phaeacia as the setting for the hero's narration of what has happened to him in the last decade has more than structural significance. The peace-loving and hospitable Phaeacians who listen to his story serve [421/422] as mute critics of his behavior. On the third day of his stay at Alcinous' court Odysseus asks the singer, Demodocus, to tell of his greatest exploit, the device of the wooden horse. There could be no more impressive build-up to revealing himself as the great "sacker of cities."

"But come now, change thy theme and sing of the building of the wooden horse, which Epeius made with Athene's help, the horse which Odysseus once led up into the citadel as a thing of guile, when he had filled it with the men who sacked Ilios. If thou dost tell me this tale aright I will declare to all mankind that the god has with a willing heart granted thee the gift of divine song."

. . . And he sang how the sons of the Achaeans poured forth from the horse and, leaving their hollow ambush, sacked the city. Of the others he sang how in various ways they wasted the high city, but of Odysseus, how he went like Ares to the house of Deiphobus together with godlike Menelaus. There it was, he said, that Odysseus braved the most terrible fight and in the end conquered by the aid of great-hearted Athene. (VIII, 492–98; 514–20)

Odysseus reacts in a totally unexpected manner to this account of his exploits. His pride in his heroic accomplishments is suddenly transformed into pity for his victims. The moment of self-revelation is presented in a remarkable simile:

And as a woman wails and flings herself about her dead husband who has fallen before his city and his people, seeking to ward off the pitiless day from his city and his children; and as she clings to him shrieking while the enemy behind her strike her back and shoulders with their spears and lead her to captivity to bear toil and woe, while her cheeks are wasted with most pitiful grief, even so did tears of pity fall from Odysseus' eyes. (523–31)

The moment of compassion includes for the first time those heretofore excluded from compassion on the grounds of being [422/423] the "enemy." Until this moment the formalism of war prevented Odysseus from recognizing and feeling the humanity of his foes. Perhaps the effective man of war cannot afford too much imaginative and sympathetic identification with his victims, and must often pay for his effectiveness as a soldier by seeing the enemy as an abstraction or by denying them human status. This is what Odysseus has done up to this moment, and now all the sympathies suppressed or denied flood back upon him. The brutal side of heroic action is suddenly revealed in the question which the simile dramatically presents: does not the warrior's code destroy more than it creates? The question is raised elsewhere in the poem—by the disintegration of post-war Ithacan society under the lawless instincts liberated by the absence of the ruler, by the most sympathetic representation of enslaved or alienated or displaced people like Eumaeus, and by other dramatic incidents, pathetic, like this one, or ironic, like the question Polyphemus addresses to the tiny warriors in his cave: "Are you travelling on business or do you wander at random over the sea like pirates who risk their lives to bring evil to men of other lands?"—to which Odysseus answers proudly that he and his men are the followers of Agamemnon, whose fame is the greatest under heaven because of the city he sacked and the great numbers of people he killed.

The judgments which the *Odyssey* makes on the hero's behavior most often occur in this form. A community or an individual incorporates certain values beside which Odysseus is implicity judged. Peripheral or minor characters are more frequently praised or condemned. Zeus himself expresses loathing for Aegisthus, and his attitude is reflected in the words of right-thinking characters such as Nestor, Telemachus, and Menelaus. Explicit evaluations of this third kind applied to Odysseus are so rare that they carry extraordinary force. An outstanding example is Circe's rebuke when Odysseus has angrily expressed his intention of defending his men against Scylla by force: [423/424]

"Rash man! Is thy heart still set on acts of war and on trouble? Wilt thou not yield even to the immortal gods? She is not mortal but an immortal bane, dreadful, sinister, fierce and not to be fought with. There is no defense; to flee from her is bravest." (XII, 116–20)

It is significant that Odysseus forgets this warning as he threads the straits and arms himself to the teeth without affecting the outcome. Circe's outburst exposes the excessive self-reliance which Odysseus must lose and does lose, as we have seen, before he is saved at Phaeacia from his long battle with the sea.

Even less frequent is the self-critical, introspective speech. In his autobiographical narrative Odysseus does not consciously relate his behavior over the past ten years to any principles, moral or otherwise. We find in his account examples of unregulated pride, brutality, and lust among moments of vision and restraint, and they are defined as such by the religious, social and political idyll of Phaeacia, as well as by the principle of contrast in the individual adventures. Though Odysseus never sums up with a *mea culpa*, he emerges from the telling at harmony with himself and with human, natural, and supernatural elements of his universe. The final stamp of approval on the rehabilitation he has undergone is given in his reunion with Athene in book thirteen. Here he meets his divine protectress undisguised and face-to-face for the first time since the fall of Troy. His words at this moment verge on the analytical, moral judgment:

It is hard, goddess, for a mortal however wise to know thee, for thou changest thy shape at will. But this I know well—that long ago, while we were fighting at Troy, thou wast kind to me. But when we had sacked Priam's towering city, and had gone away in our ships, and a god had scattered the Achaeans, I have never seen thee since, daughter of Zeus, nor marked thee boarding my vessel to ward off sorrow from me. (XIII, 312–19)

One short step further and Odysseus would realize the connection [424/425] between his past acts and the alienation of Athene. We realize it, but Homer prefers the dramatic to the analytical method.

This moment of reunion marks the beginning of Odysseus' role as judge and restorer of Ithaca. The goddess who left him when he sacked her shrine at Troy watches over him throughout the greatest of all his enterprises. Odysseus plays his part through most of the second half of the poem not as a king or a warrior but in the disguise of an abject old beggar. The significance of this disguise is almost inexhaustible. It enables him to test the charity of the suitors, and charity is one of the essential virtues in the world of the *Odyssey*. It suggests the fundamental weakness of all men and their dependence on their brothers. It dramatizes divine immanence in human affairs in accordance with the idea that the gods often take upon themselves the basest and poorest human shapes. It is a further demonstration that human worth is not graded according to rank or position or power. It represents the theme that all men are beggars, outcasts, and wanderers in some sense at one time or another, a theme that is traced through the fugitive Theoclymenus and such displaced persons as Eurycleia and Eumaeus. It is, finally, a test of Odysseus' own inner strength—his patience and self-restraint. As Odysseus experiences the insults and cruelties of some of the suitors and some of his own servants, as he witnesses from the depths of his own experience the blasphemous frivolity of Antinous and Eurymachus, he imposes on himself the hardest task of all for such a passionate and action-loving nature. He holds his peace and leaves the satisfaction of his cause to be determined by the gods. As the beggar who continually appeals to the suitors for alms in the name of Zeus, to whom strangers and refugees are sacred, and in the name of common humanity, which unites men in the experiences of hunger, vicissitude, and humiliation, he displays a courage more difficult for him and more valuable for civilization than he did in the wooden horse. When Ctesippus hits him with the cow's hoof, or Antinous throws a stool at him, he [425/426] stands "firm as a rock . . . shaking his head in silence, and pondering evil in the deep of his heart." In the midst of these provocations to violence he remains just and does all in his power to save some of the better men among the suitors by appeals to their wisdom and sense of justice. Amphinomous has shown him charity, and Odysseus' plea to him is the most explicit statement in the *Odyssey* of a moral theme and at the same time Odysseus' clearest evaluation of his own experience:

Of all things that breathe and move on the face of the earth there is none feebler than man. For he thinks that he will never suffer evil in time to come as long as the gods give him prosperity and his knees are strong; but when the blessed gods decree sorrow for him he bears it reluctantly with an enduring spirit, for our outlook on earth depends on the day to day fortunes which the father of gods and men brings upon us. For I too once prospered among men, but I did many wicked deeds, yielding to my strength and trusting in the power of my father and brothers. Therefore let no man ever be lawless, but let him keep silently whatever gifts the gods give. (XVIII, 130–42)

This shift from power, which is accidental, to the principle of justice, which is in the reach of every man, marks the extraordinary moral revolution which occurs in the *Odyssey* and in the character of its hero. Without this principle the best that life has to offer is "the human and personal tragedy built up against the background of meaningless flux," which C. S. Lewis wrongly finds in the *Odyssey* as well as the *Iliad*. The power and excitement I find in the *Odyssey* stem in large measure from its testimony to the birth of civilization in the emergence of charity and law and order of the flux of passion and aimless brutality.

If one thinks of the *Odyssey* as the rehabilitation of a veteran after a long and terrible war in the course of which the justice of the cause has been betrayed, as is so often the case, by the methods [426/427] of the crusaders; if one sees the hero's long voyage home as an exploration of his identity as man; if one feels that he cannot arrive home in the profoundest sense until he has discovered the metaphysical order of the human community, the deepest significance of this great poem will not, I am convinced, be violated. The historical circumstances of Odysseus' situation are so like ours that his restoration of the waste land within and outside him has the deepest relevance for ourselves. [427]

SUGGESTIONS FOR STUDY

Note: The following topics for discussion and research are intended merely to suggest the kinds of questions that a teacher may raise in class discussion or that a student might choose as subject of an essay.

Homer's Characters

1. Stanford develops Odysseus as an outer-directed man who knows just who and what he is. Assuming this is a valid position, describe the nature of the dramatic conflict of which Odysseus is the center. To what extent is it an external conflict involving a type character running a mythological obstacle course? To what extent, and in what terms, can the character-conflict relationship be seen in a more profound light?

2. Stanford suggests that Odysseus is the archetypal "civilized man" and a representative of humane behavior in a violent world. Moving from Finley's description of the heroic world of Homer, oppose Stanford's humanistic view by arguing that Odysseus is a self-seeking warrior motivated by a highly egoistic sense of his own worth and his own rights. To what extent does the value system dramatized in the epic support this interpretation? To what extent does it not?

3. Can Odysseus be thought of as the "born winner"? How much of his success is a result of his incredible luck and of "who he knows"? How much is due to his skill and his own efforts? Give a fully rounded description of Odysseus' character.

4. Taylor to some extent opposes Stanford's view of Odysseus—he sees the hero beset with an inner conflict. Taylor claims that Odysseus is frequently presented with "the temptation to surrender his individual identity" and that he is involved in a "quest for identity." Justify the application of such a modern psychiatric analysis of character to the hero of a very ancient epic poem.

5. Is a struggle between the rational and the irrational elements of human nature, which Taylor sees as taking place in Odysseus, evident in other characters in the poem?

6. How is Odysseus' style of interaction with women—with Calypso, with Circe, with Nausicaa, with Arete, with Eurykleia, with Athene, with his mother, with Penelope, with the unfaithful serving maids—a significant determinant of his character? Can Odysseus be as easily described as hopping from woman to woman as from island to island?

7. Compare and contrast the characters of Odysseus and Telemachus. Do both undergo comparable internal changes in the course of their journeys? Support the following assertion: Odysseus' story is that of a man in heroic conflict, and Telemachus' story is that of a boy in domestic conflict.

8. What are Telemachus' values? Are they entirely comparable to his father's? How does Telemachus relate to women—to Penelope, to Athene,

to Eurykleia, to the serving girls of his father's house, to Helen, to Nestor's daughter? How does Telemachus relate to men—to his elders, to his contemporaries, to the suitors, to his father, to strangers and servants?

9. Clarke and other critics in this anthology develop the *Telemacheia* as a *Bildungsroman* (a novel of a youth's education to life). Taking into account the arguments concerning the nature of Homeric epic presented by Page, argue that Telemachus' character cannot be described as developing in the manner described by Clarke. Just how different in capacity, will, and intention does Telemachus actually appear to be by the time his father arrives in Ithaca? What, if any, hints do we find that he might have been capable of acting on his own had Odysseus not come home? Discuss Telemachus as a man eternally dependent on one or another parent or friend. At this point, reverse your position and defend Clarke's assertion that the *Telemacheia* is a *Bildungsroman*.

10. Mackail deals with the character of Penelope as if she were a subtly delineated, subtly motivated character in a modern novel. Refer again to Page's analysis of the nature of Homeric epic. How is Mackail's presentation of Penelope actually supported by the *Odyssey*? How is it not? What are Penelope's values? Are they similar to or different from Odysseus' values? Is she a romantic woman? Is she an ideal wife? An ideal mother? An ideal woman? Is she an honest woman? Compare her to Helen, Calypso, Circe, Clytemnestra, Nausicaa, Arete, Eurykleia, and Athene. Is Penelope as much the complete woman as Odysseus is the complete man?

11. Aside from the three main characters, are there many fully rounded characters in the *Odyssey*? If so, how are they developed and presented? Are there any characters that seem to be patterned on some facet of Odysseus' character? If so, do they have a life other than the role they play in complementing and emphasizing Odysseus?

Homer's Universe

1. Discuss the dramatic conflicts of the main characters of the *Odyssey* in terms of the social, economic, and political structures of the poem's world as described by Finley. What does family structure have to do with social structure and power structure in the poem?

2. Consider Taylor's essay in conjunction with those of Finley and Grube. Argue that in the dramatic world of the *Odyssey* a man's sense of "identity" cannot be separated from his possession or lack of power and his "sense of property." What effect does this argument have on your interpretation of Odysseus' character?

3. Can Telemachus in his dealings with the suitors be said to be caught in a power struggle? How do considerations of power and wealth complicate his relationship with his mother?

4. As Grube points out, "it is power that makes the gods divine." What private and public forms does power take in both the divine and human worlds of the poem? What is the relationship between physical and intel-

lectual power in the poem? The *Iliad* has been described as "a poem of force." Can the *Odyssey* be similarly described?

5. How does the relationship of the "thetes" to the "aristoi" (as described by Finley) compare to the relationship of the "aristoi" and the gods? Compare the values and morals of the divine world (as Grube describes them) to the values and morals of the human world of the poem. To what extent are the human and the divine worlds separate in the poem? To what extent do they interpenetrate? Is the *Odyssey* more concerned with the power of the gods or the power of man?

6. Relate Grube's definition of the "heroic code" to the role of Athene in the poem. Compare Grube's view of Athene to Stanford's view of her. What is her dramatic function in the poem?

The *Odyssey:* Epic Style and Epic Form

1. In several of the essays in this anthology, Homer is compared to authors from other cultures and eras: Clarke compares Homer to Faulkner, Hart to Shakespeare, Auerbach to the Old Testament, and Lord to Virgil. Compare these comparisons. Which seems to do the most justice to the *Odyssey?* Do such comparisons elucidate the unique qualities of the epic, or do they tend to reduce the poem to its least common denominators? Can you construct your own comparison of the *Odyssey* to other works of literature— for example, to Dante's *Divine Comedy,* to Tolstoy's *War and Peace,* to James Joyce's *Ulysses,* or to any of the novels of Conrad or Hemingway?

2. Consider the difference between the Homeric *Odyssey* and the modern novel. Do the stylistic features pointed out by Auerbach, and the nature of Homeric oral epic described by Page, preclude a critical analysis of the *Odyssey* based on our techniques of analyzing the novel? If some of the standards we take for granted in considering modern novels are applied to the *Odyssey* (standards of social realism, characterization, style of dialogue and diction, motivation, etc.), the poem could be described as a primitive, unsophisticated novel. What must the twentieth-century reader do to avoid this trap and come to see the *Odyssey* for what it is: one of the world's masterpieces of narrative art?

3. In what ways does the "foreground realism" of the Homeric style (as defined by Auerbach) determine the overall dramatic structure of the *Odyssey?* Does this "scrupulously externalized" style necessarily preclude the possibility of interpreting the poem as an epic of such internalized dramas as "the quest for identity" (Taylor, Lord, etc.)?

4. Apply Auerbach's insights into the structure of the foot-washing scene to the poem as a whole. Where else in the *Odyssey* does Homer interrupt the action at a crisis with a lengthy digression? Can the entire *Telemacheia* be thought of in this light? Can Odysseus' account of his travels to King Alcinous be productively described in these terms?

5. What conclusion can we draw concerning Homeric society from the Homeric style of realism and the points of emphasis of that realism? How

does your answer compare with the picture of Homeric life portrayed in the essays of Finley and Grube?

6. Assuming the validity of Page's argument, what discernible effects do the probable circumstances of the composition of the *Odyssey* have on its style? Its contents? Cite specific examples.

The *Odyssey:* Theme and Structure

1. Jones examines only the introduction of the revenge theme in the *Odyssey*. Show how the theme is developed in the body of the poem and how it becomes fundamental to the total action. That is, revenge is a form of justice; to what extent is the problem of justice, its nature, its absence, and its achievement, an overall concern of the poem?

2. Are problems of justice and revenge factors in parts of the story not directly related to Odysseus' arrival in Ithaca? What other men and what gods are concerned with revenge and justice; and how do their concerns work against Odysseus and his revenge? Describe the *Odyssey* as a tragic story of human and divine justice.

3. Compare Page's general description of the traditional, fixed nature of Homeric epic devices with Jones's specific examination of one of these devices (the "triad"). How does Jones's analysis soften Page's argument? (Also, consider the remarks of Post concerning this matter.) How does such a comparison help the modern reader to establish a critical approach to Homeric narrative? Can you see the principle of triadic structure operating elsewhere in the poem?

4. Jones and D'Arms-Hulley develop different facets of the same theme in the *Odyssey*. Combine the two arguments, develop them more thoroughly, and present an overall description of the guilt-revenge, faithfulness-reward themes of the poem.

5. Within the frame of the occurrence of the *Oresteia* story in the *Odyssey* as described by D'Arms and Hulley, outline the role of love between man and woman in the poem. How many kinds of male-female relationships are active forces in the plot? How are they relevant to the action? How many unfaithful women are referred to or are dramatically presented, and how do their stories provide a dynamic setting for the story of Penelope's faithfulness?

6. Does Jones's suggestion that the *Odyssey* is essentially concerned with revenge tend to reinforce or invalidate the interpretation of the poem as a search for self-identity? Why?

7. A number of the essays in this anthology (Stanford, Grube, D'Arms and Hulley, et al.) discuss the relationships of men and divinity in Homer. Compare several of these essays and discuss the ideas of free will, sin, and guilt in the *Odyssey*. To what extent are the characters responsible for their own fates? To what extent are the gods or other forces responsible? Would you describe the poem as a somber, fatalistic poem?

8. Hart (along with Post) sees comedy in a number of characters and events which other critics take quite seriously, e.g., Helen (Mackail); Telemachus (Clarke); Nausicaa (Lord); Books IX–XII, the story of Odysseus' wanderings (Taylor and almost all other critics); Odysseus' lies and relationship to Athene (Stanford). Taking these things into account, determine to what extent the *Odyssey* is a humane "comedy of manners" (as Post puts it) and to what extent it is a violent tragedy of passion, will, and revenge. In judging the relative proportions of comedy and tragedy in the poem, take the arbitrary and happy (for the hero) ending into careful account.

The *Odyssey:* Three Contemporary Interpretations

1. Lord states that to read the *Odyssey* "as an adventure story" is to remove it "from serious consideration as one of the world's greatest poems." Examine the logic of this assertion. On what artistic and moral assumptions about literature is it based? Balance Lord's view by arguing that *not* to examine the poem as an epic of adventure is to ignore much, even most, of its power and significance.

2. Both Dimock and Lord attempt to present the "larger meaning" of the *Odyssey*. To accomplish this, both to some extent allegorize the story—they try to consider the story in terms of what it "represents." Compare their conclusions. Is it possible to reconcile the views of these two critics? How, in your judgment, would Lord react to Dimock's view that the poem is properly seen as an epic of violence, pain, trouble, and self-assertion? Does this view attract or repel you? Why?

3. Post, unlike Dimock and Lord, does not allegorize the poem or attempt to assign it an abstract meaning. What are the relative merits of these two styles of criticism? Do they complement or cancel one another out?

4. Dimock's essay implies that Homer's epic world is one in which violence and peace, pain and joy are irrevocably and permanently bound together. Lord's essay implies that Homer's epic world is one in which progress from violence to peace, from pain to joy is possible. Which view seems more in line with your reading of the poem?

5. Post, who sees the poem as a comedy, calls Penelope "the emotional center of the epic." Both Dimock and Lord, who take the poem very seriously, see Odysseus as the emotional center. If the poem is centered around a woman (or women), female and domestic value systems must necessarily predominate. Is this so? Describe the epic as a dramatization of several different value systems, sometimes in conflict, sometimes in support of one another; demonstrate your argument by reference to specific events and characters.

6. Assuming that Odysseus is the emotional center of the poem, describe the *Odyssey* as, on the one hand, a story of a journey in the inner world and, on the other hand, a story of a journey in the outer world.

7. Construct a general interpretation of the *Odyssey* as an epic of interlocking and interpenetrating themes: the theme of man alone, of man as a member of a family, of man as a member of a society, of man as a member of a political state, and of man in relationship to the divine mysteries of the universe. Explain how these themes, as they are dramatized, sometimes complement, sometimes complicate, and sometimes conflict with one another. Considering the *Odyssey* from this point of view, can you reconcile the interpretations of Post, Dimock, and Lord?

FURTHER READING: A SELECTED BIBLIOGRAPHY

Note: The following bibliography is for the most part limited to book-length studies generally available in college and university libraries. These books, devoted entirely or in part to the *Odyssey*, were selected with an eye to their usefulness to the non-classicist. Students interested in searching out specialized essays and articles on the *Odyssey* (most of which are to be found in journals devoted to classical studies) should turn to *L'Année Philologique,* described below. Also, many of the books listed below contain useful bibliographical guides.

General Reference

L'Année Philologique. An annual international bibliography of classical and related studies. Clearly organized and thoroughly indexed, this current bibliography is fundamental to research in Homeric subjects. Though it is published in France, the student need not know French in order to make use of it.

Combellack, F. M. "Contemporary Homeric Scholarship, Sound or Fury," *The Classical World,* XLIX (1955), 17–26, 29–44, 45–55. A very useful bibliographical study written in a lucid and witty style. It is a complete survey of all aspects of current Homeric scholarship and criticism, and is a mine of information, direction, and reference for the beginner as well as for the expert.

Lorimer, H. L. *Homer and the Monuments.* London: Macmillan, 1950. A valuable but highly technical presentation of archeological materials relevant to the Homeric poems and their background.

Wace, Alan J. B., and Stubbings, Frank H., eds. *A Companion to Homer.* London: Macmillan; New York: St. Martins Press, 1962. An invaluable, weighty, general reference work concerned with all aspects of Homer, his world, and his poems.

Critical Studies of the *Odyssey*

Bassett, Samuel E. *The Poetry of Homer.* Sather Classical Lectures, Vol. 15. Berkeley: University of California Press, 1938. A general study of Homer's poetic and dramatic style.

Beye, Charles R. *The Iliad, the Odyssey, and the Epic Tradition.* Garden City, New York: Anchor Books, 1966. A general introduction to Homer and the epic genre aimed specifically at nonspecialists.

Bowra, C. M. *Heroic Poetry.* London: Macmillan, 1952. A comprehensive study of the nature of heroic poetry in general.

Butler, Samuel. *The Authoress of the Odyssey.* Chicago: University of Chicago Press, 1967. [With an introduction by David Grene: reprint of the 2nd ed., London, 1922.] A strange, idiosyncratic book which is nevertheless provocative in its insistence on seeing the *Odyssey* as a woman-centered poem.

Campbell, Joseph. "The Night Sea Journey," in *The Masks of God: Occidental Mythology*. New York: The Viking Press, 1964. Pp. 157–177. A thoroughgoing Jungian and mythic critic, Campbell presents the *Odyssey* in terms of archetypal myths.

Carpenter, Rhys. *Folk Tale, Fiction and Saga in the Homeric Epics*. Sather Classical Lectures, Vol. 20. Berkeley and Los Angeles: University of California Press, 1946. Chapters 1–5 are of most relevance to the *Odyssey*. Carpenter attempts to relate the Homeric poems to their ancient source materials. He is, roughly, of the mythic school of criticism.

Clarke, Howard W. *The Art of the Odyssey*. Englewood Cliffs, N.J.: Prentice-Hall, 1967. A useful general study of the *Odyssey* by the author of one of the essays in this anthology. Especially useful as an introduction to the poem for the nonspecialist.

Cook, Albert. *The Classic Line: A Study in Epic Poetry*. Bloomington: Indiana University Press, 1966. A general study of the epic tradition. Chapter 3 contains an interesting interpretation of the *Odyssey* as an epic of experience.

Ehnmark, Erland. *The Idea of God in Homer*. Uppsala: Almqvist and Wiksell, 1935. An analytic presentation of the nature of divinity in the Homeric poems.

Finley, M. I. *The World of Odysseus*. New York: The Viking Press, 1954. A general study of the society reflected in the *Odyssey*. Chapter 3 of this work is reprinted in this anthology.

Greene, Thomas. *The Descent from Heaven: A Study of Epic Continuity*. New Haven and London: Yale University Press, 1963. A general study of the epic genre based on the theme of the divine messenger. One chapter, "Form and Craft in the *Odyssey*," gives insight into this and several other aspects of the *Odyssey*.

Jaeger, Werner. *Paideia: The Ideals of Greek Culture*, Vol. I, trans. Gilbert Highet. Oxford: Blackwell, 1939. A classic study of Greek culture. In chapters 1–3 Jaeger presents the Homeric poems as models of Greek aristocratic ideals and behavior.

Kirk, G. S. *The Songs of Homer*. Cambridge, England: Cambridge University Press, 1962. This general study of the Homeric poems and their background—written for both the specialist and the amateur—is very helpful. Kirk, among other things, is concerned with the oral composition of the poems.

Lord, Albert. *The Singer of Tales*. Harvard Studies in Comparative Literature, No. 24. Cambridge, Mass.: Harvard University Press, 1960. Lord's topic is the technique of oral epic. In Chapter 8 he offers several important observations on the structure of the *Odyssey*.

Michalopoulos, André. *Homer*. Twayne World Authors Series, No. 4. New York: Twayne Publishers, 1966. A general introductory study for the nonspecialist.

Murray, Gilbert. *The Rise of the Greek Epic,* 4th ed. Oxford: The Clarendon Press, 1934. Although somewhat outmoded in approach, this book is still a standard and oft-cited study of the Homeric poems.

Page, Denys L. *The Homeric Odyssey.* Oxford: The Clarendon Press, 1955. A critical examination of the composition and structure of the *Odyssey* from the point of view of those scholars who claim one man could not have written the Homeric poems. Part of Page's Chapter 6 is included in this anthology.

Scott, John Adams. *The Unity of Homer.* Sather Classical Lectures, Vol. 1. Berkeley: University of California Press, 1921. A lucid discussion of the Homeric question (was Homer one or several poets?) from the unitarian point of view.

Snell, Bruno. *The Discovery of the Mind,* trans. T. G. Rosenmeyer. Cambridge, Mass.: Harvard University Press, 1953. Chapters 1, 2, and 8 are especially helpful guides to an understanding of the Homeric idea of divinity and man.

Stanford, W. B. *The Ulysses Theme,* 2nd ed. Oxford: Basil Blackwell and Mott, 1963. Stanford traces the Ulysses theme in Western literature from its beginnings to the twentieth century. Chapter 2 of his study is reprinted in this anthology. Chapters 1 and 3 are also very helpful studies of different aspects of the Homeric hero's nature.

Steiner, George, and Robert Fagles, eds. *Homer.* Englewood Cliffs, N.J.: Prentice-Hall, 1962. An anthology of essays and comments on both the *Odyssey* and the *Iliad.*

Taylor, Charles H., Jr., ed. *Essays on the Odyssey: Selected Modern Criticism.* An anthology of seven essays which approach the *Odyssey* from different points of view. The editor's essay and two others from his volume are reprinted in this anthology.

Trahman, C. R. "Odysseus Lies; *Odyssey,* Books 13–19," *The Phoenix,* VI (1953), 31–43. A subtle analysis of an important motif and structural device in the *Odyssey.*

Webster, T. B. L. *From Mycenae to Homer.* London: Methuen, 1958. This very broad consideration of the Homeric poems, their development and their nature, is perhaps the single most useful recent book on Homer. The beginning student should acquire some background in Homeric scholarship before he tries to digest Webster's complex argument, however.

Whitman, Cedric H. *Homer and the Heroic Tradition.* Cambridge, Mass.: Harvard University Press, 1958. Whitman's book, largely concerned with the *Iliad,* ends with a lengthy discussion of the geometric structure of the narrative of the *Odyssey.*

Woodhouse, W. J. *The Composition of Homer's Odyssey.* Oxford: The Clarendon Press, 1930. A general study of the traditional critical problems raised by professional students of the *Odyssey.*

TRANSLATIONS OF THE *ODYSSEY:*
A SELECTED BIBLIOGRAPHY

This list is divided into two parts: (1) the more important modern translations; (2) the more important translations of previous times. Although the list does not attempt to be exhaustive, the majority of modern translations are included. The editions of the modern translations listed are not necessarily the first editions, but those most generally available. I have briefly commented on these translations, and noted if they are available in paperback editions.

1

Andrew, S. O. Everyman's Library. New York: Dutton, 1953. (Pedestrian pentameter verse.)

Butcher, S. H., and Andrew Lang. Modern Library. New York: Random House. (Late nineteenth-century, imitation King James English, prose translation—widely known, but useful only as a sedative. Paperback.)

Butler, Samuel. New York: Dutton, 1921. (Early twentieth-century prose translation. Readable. Paperback.)

Cook, Albert. New York: Norton, 1967. (Well-done verse translation. Better than any of the prose translations, and can stand up beside Lattimore's verse translation. Paperback.)

Fitzgerald, Robert. Garden City, N.Y.: Doubleday, 1961. (Popular verse translation, but rather too racy and free. Cook and Lattimore are more Homeric. Paperback.)

Lattimore, Richmond. New York: Harper & Row, 1967. (Verse. Lattimore has great skill as a poet and translator, and is generally considered our best translator of Homer. Paperback.)

Murray, A. T. Loeb Classical Library, 2 vols. New York: G. P. Putnam's Sons, 1927. (Heavy prose with facing Greek text. Good index. Useful primarily for reference.)

Palmer, George Herbert. Boston and New York: Houghton Mifflin, 1891. (Adequate prose, as readable as any of the older translations. Paperback.)

Rees, Ennis. New York: Random House, 1961. (Adequate verse translation, but has not been enthusiastically received.)

Rieu, E. V. London: Penguin Books, 1952. (Most popular prose translation, urbane and lucid. Paperback.)

Rouse, W. H. D. New York: Modern Age Books, 1937. (Fairly good modern prose translation. Not as effective as Rieu. Paperback.)

Shaw, T. E. [Lawrence of Arabia]. London: Oxford University Press, 1932. (Quite adequate prose, but translator more interesting than translation. Paperback.)

2

Chapman, George. *The Whole Works of Homer,* c. 1612. (The first complete translation, into English.)

Ogelsby, John. 1656.

Hobbes, Thomas. 1675.

Pope, Alexander, and W. Broome and E. Fenton. 1725–26.

Cowper, William. 1791.

Sotheby, William. 1834.

Bryant, William Cullen. 1871.

Way, Arthur S. 1880.

Mackail, John W. 1903–10.

NAMES IN THE *ODYSSEY*:
PRONUNCIATION GUIDE

Achaeans: a-kē'ans
Acheron: ak'e-ron
Achilles: a-kil'ez
Agamemnon: ag-a-mem'non
Aeaea: ē-ē'a
Aegisthus: ē-jis'thus
Aeolia: ē-ō'li-a
Aeolus: ē'ō-lus, ē-ō'lus
Aetolia: e-tō'li-a
Aias: ā'as
Alcinous: al-sin'ō-us
Alcmene: alk-mē'nē
Alpheus: al-fē'us, al'fē-us
Amphimedon: am-fi'mē-don
Amphinomus: am-fin'ō-mus
Amphithea: am-fi'thē-a
Amphitryon: am-fit'ri-on
Anticlea: an-ti-klē'a
Antilochus: an-til'ō-kus
Antinous: an-tin'ō-us
Antiphates: an-tif'a-tēz
Antiphus: an'ti-fus
Aphrodite: af-rō-dī'tē
Apollo: a-pol'ō
Arcesius: är-ses'i-us
Ares: är'ēz
Arete: a-rē'te
Argives: är'jīvz, -givz
Argos: är'gōs
Argus: är'gus
Ariadne: ar-i-ad'nē
Artemis: är'te-mis
Athene: a-thē'na
Atreus: ā'trē-us, -trös
Autolycus: ô-tol'i-kus
Cadmus: kad'mus
Calypso: ka-lip'sō
Cephallenians: sef-a-lē'ni-uns
Charybdis: ka-rib'dis
Ciconians: si-kō'ni-anz
Cimmerians: si-mir'i-anz, ki-
Circe: sēr'sē
Clytemnestra: klī-tem-nes'tra
Cnossus: nos'us
Cocytus: kō-si'tus

Crete: krēt
Cronos: krō'nus
Ctesippus: te-sip'us
Cyclopes: sī-klō'pēz
Cyprus: sī'prus
Cythera: si-thir'a
Danaans: dan'ānz
Delos: dē'los
Demeter: dē-mē'ter
Demodocus: dē-mod'o-kus
Dionysus: dī-ō-nī'sus
Dodona: dō-dō'na
Dolius: dō'li-us
Dorians: dō'ri-anz
Dulichium: dū-lik'i-um
Elis: ē'lis
Elpenor: el-pē'nôr
Elysian Fields: ē-lizh'an
Erebus: er'ē-bus
Erechtheus: ē-rek'thūs
Erinys: e-rin'is, e-ri'nis
Euboea: ū-bē'a
Eumaeus: ū-mē'us
Eupeithes: ū-pē'thēz
Euryalus: ū-rī'a-lus
Eurybates: ū-rī'ba-tēz
Eurydamas: ū-rid'a-mas
Eurycleia: ū-rī'clē-a
Eurylochus: ū-ril'ō-kus
Eurymachus: ū-rim'a-kus
Eurynome: ū-rin'ō-mē
Gaea: jē'a
Halitherses: hal-i-ther'sēz
Hebe: hē'bē
Helius: hē'li-us
Hellespont: hel'es-pont
Hephaestus: hē-fes'tus
Hera: hēr'a
Heracles: her'a-klēz
Hermes: hėr'mēz
Icarius: ī-kär'i-us
Idomeneus: ī-dom'e-nus
Ilium: il'i-um
Irus: ī'rus
Ithaca: ith'a-ka

Lacedaemonia: las-e-dē-mo'ni-a
Laertes: lā-ėr'tēz
Laestrygones: les-trig'ō-nēz
Laodamas: lā-od'a-mas
Leda: lē'da
Lemnos: lem'nos
Lesbos: lez'bos
Leto: lē'tō
Leucothea: lö-koth'ē-a
Malea: ma-lē'a
Medon: mē'don
Melantheus: mē-lan'thus
Melantho: mē-lan'thō
Menelaus: men-e-lā'us
Mentor: men'tor
Mycenae: mī-sē'nē
Myrmidons: mėr'mi-dons
Nausicaa: nô-sik'ā-a
Neleus: nē'lus
Nestor: nes'tor
Odysseus: ō-dis'us, ō-dis'ē-us
Ogygia: ō-jij'i-a
Olympus: ō-lim'pus
Orestes: ō-res'tez
Ortygia: ôr-tij'i-a
Pallas: pal'as
Peisenor: pī-sē'nôr
Peisistratus: pī-sis'tra-tus
Peleus: pē'lūs, pē'lē-us

Penelope: pē-nēl'ō-pē
Persephone: pėr-sef'ō-nē
Phaeacians: fē-ā'shanz
Phemius: fē'mi-us
Philoetius: fi-lē'shus
Phoenicia: fē-nish'a
Polybus: pol'i-bus
Polycaste: pol-i-kas'tē
Polyphemus: pol-i-fē'mus
Poseidon: po-sī'don
Priam: prī'am
Pylos: pī'lōs
Rhadamanthus: ra-ä-man'thus
Same: sā'mē
Scheria: shir'i-a
Sidon: sī'don
Sirens: sī'renz
Scylla: sil'a
Sparta: spär'ta
Styx: stiks
Teiresias: tī-rē'si-as
Telemachus: tē-lem'a-kus
Themis: thē'mis
Theoclymenus: thē"ō-klī'me-nus
Theseus: thē'sös, thē'sē-us
Tydeus: tī'dūs
Tyndareus: tin-dār'i-us
Zeus: zös